"Who's Afraid Of The Big Bad Witch?" - by - Dr. S. D'Montford

Who's Afraid of the Big Bad Witch

ISBN - 978-1-300-42498-7

Who's Afraid of the Big Bad Witch - Written By Rev. Dr. S. D'Montford - Cover Artwork by Shé D'Montford & Brenden Wills © Copyright Rev, Dr, S. D'Montford, August 2006 Gold Coast Australia. Published by The Happy Medium Publishing Company the publishing arm of Shambhallah Awareness Centre for educational purposes.

All Rights Reserved. The information presented is protected under the Berne Convention for the Protection of Literature and Artistic works, under other international conventions and under national laws on copyright and neighbouring rights. Extracts of the information in this book may be reviewed, but not reproduce without express written permission from the publisher. Reproduction or translation of portions of this publication requires explicit, prior authorization in writing.

Disclaimer: The primary reason for this publication is entertainment and education about Witchcraft and Pagan practices. While Shambhallah Awareness Centre has used all reasonable endeavours to ensure the information in this book is as accurate as possible, it gives no warranty or guarantee that the material, information, or publications made accessible by them are fit for any use whatsoever nor does that excuse you from using your commonsense. Shambhallah Awareness Centre and Rev. Dr S. D'Montford accepts no liability or responsibility for any loss or damage whatsoever suffered as a result of direct or indirect use or application of any material, publication or information obtained from them.

Special Thanks to:- Ken Wills and to all those who blazed the path of understand and tolerance that finally seems achievable in this day and age.

Shambhallah Awareness Centre is a tax exempt Pagan Kirk (Church) and a not for profit organization.

P.O. Box 3541, Helensvale Town Centre. Q. 4212.

http://www.shambhallah.org

The Happy Medium Publishing Company

Who's Afraid Of The Big Bad Witch?

Exposing The Lies About the Craft of the Wise.

*By
Rev. Dr. Shé D'Montford*

"Shall the folly of idiots, and the malice of the scornful, so much prevail that he who seeketh no worldly gain or glory... but only for ... the treasure of heavenly wisdom and knowledge ... be condemned as a Companion of Hellhounds and a Caller and Conjuror of wicked and damned spirits?"

Dr. John Dee in his preface to his work "Mathematicall" - 1584

"It is no great matter to make a goddess into a Witch or a virgin into a harlot; but to achieve the contrary, to give the humiliated dignity, to make the fallen worth coveting, for that either art or character is needed."

J. W. Goethe, - 1832

Table of Contents

"Who's Afraid Of The Big Bad Witch?" - by – Rev. Dr. S. D'Montford

Introduction

Chapter 1
What Is A Witch?

Chapter 2
Are Witches Pagans? What Is A Pagan?

Chapter 3
Are Witches Spiteful and Evil? - Do Witches Hex or Curse Others?

Chapter 3
Are Witches a Lunatic Fringe Group?

Chapter 5
Are Witches Satanists?

Chapter 6
Was Aleister Crowley a Satanist?

Chapter 7
Do Witches Hold Sabbats?

Chapter 8
Do Witches Dance Naked At Their Sabbats?

Chapter 9
Why the Witch Hunts When The Bible Approves of Witches?

Chapter 10
Witch Hunts in Australia

Chapter 11
Isn't the Pentagram the Symbol of the Devil?

Chapter 12
The Witch Legacy - Are There Pagan Foundations To Western Society?

Chapter 13
Do Witches Perform Child Sacrifice?

Conclusion

Appendix: -
About the author and her journey
A Witch Raised In Fear and Pain

Introduction

Witches have more reason to fear the public than the public has to hear them. Misinformation and religious conditioning had resulted in blind fear, hatred and persecution to this day. My personal painful journey is not uncommon. It has not been an entirely blessed one. It was a long and hard road from the terror and the tumult of the first manifestation of my natural psychic abilities to the time when I was able to find my useful place in modern western society as an urban shaman and Witch. My abilities from the start aroused suspicion and harsh judgment. I was subjected to great abuse until I finally found a worthy teacher and my true path. No child should have to go through what I went through. The purpose of starting "Spellcraft Magazine," compiling these facts in this book and sharing my story is to dispel some of the hysteria and spare other gifted individuals a lot of misery.

So lest begin dispelling some illusions and misconceptions.

Chapter 1

What Is A Witch?

Most of us have a preconceived image of a Witch in our minds. Wild women, linked to the unexplained forces of nature, cackling in maniacal, frenzied hysteria. Veiled in myth, reputedly able to turn people into toads, hag like, mad, bad, and dangerous to know. Yet, these images do not seem to fit the group of modern people who are willing to publicly identify themselves as Witches today.

Though many modern media Witches appear to be beautiful, successful, friendly, helpful, and of service to the public, a general survey came up with these descriptors that give modern colloquial identity to the word "Witch":

- "Witch" has come to convey a person bent on nastiness for spites sake.
- Is often used as a substitute for the word "Bitch."
- People fear the word "Witch" as indicating a person who is involved in evil unnatural things and is in league with the Devil

This is a very negative public image. So, what has been responsible for the formation of such dark images in people's minds? Why do these dark images out last the many shining modern examples of Witchery? Is this a reflection of how our society fears wild and empowered women who are linked to the untameable forces of nature? Is it as a result of some dire personal experience? Apparently not. When the survey group was asked, "How many Witches do you know personally?" The unanimous reply was "None!"

So How Do People Form These Very Negative Associations?

Like it or not popular images of what it means to be a Witch come from popular culture. Though we have positive images in the pop culture like 'Samantha' from the 1950s TV series "BeWitched" and the protectors of the innocent on the TV series "Charmed," other enduring images overshadow these.

The most enduring image, in the minds of our survey group, comes from Shakespeare's Macbeth quote below. It was written by command as one of the plays to be given before King James 1st and the King of Denmark, the father of King James's wife, during his visit to England in the summer of 1606. It was a story out of Scottish history, laced with fanciful episodes between Hecate and three Witches (III, 5 and IV, 1). It touched on the ancestry, as well as the personal and political hatred of Witches, of Shakespeare's patron, King James.

"A dark cave.
In the middle, a caldron boiling.
Thunder.
Enter the three Witches

1 WITCH. *Thrice the brinded cat hath mew'd.*
2 WITCH. *Thrice and once, the hedge-pig whin'd.*
3 WITCH. *Harpier cries:—'tis time! 'tis time!*

1 WITCH. *Round about the caldron go;*
  In the poison'd entrails throw.—
  Toad, that under cold stone,
  Days and nights has thirty-one;
  Swelter'd venom sleeping got,
  Boil thou first i' the charmed pot!

ALL. *Double, double toil and trouble;*
  Fire burn, and caldron bubble.

2 WITCH. *Fillet of a fenny snake,*
  In the caldron boil and bake;
  Eye of newt, and toe of frog,
  Wool of bat, and tongue of dog,
  Adder's fork, and blind-worm's sting,
  Lizard's leg, and owlet's wing,—
  For a charm of powerful trouble,
  Like a hell-broth boil and bubble.

ALL. *Double, double toil and trouble;*
  Fire burn, and caldron bubble.

3 WITCH. *Scale of dragon; tooth of wolf;*
  Witches' mummy; maw and gulf
  Of the ravin'd salt-sea shark;
  Root of hemlock digg'd i the dark;
  Liver of blaspheming Jew;
  Gall of goat, and slips of yew
  Sliver'd in the moon's eclipse;
  Nose of Turk, and Tartar's lips;
  Finger of birth-strangled babe
  Ditch-deliver'd by a drab,—
  Make the gruel thick and slab:
  Add thereto a tiger's chaudron,
  For the ingredients of our caldron.

ALL. *Double, double toil and trouble;*
  Fire burn, and caldron bubble

2 WITCH. *Cool it with a baboon's blood,*
  Then the charm is firm and good

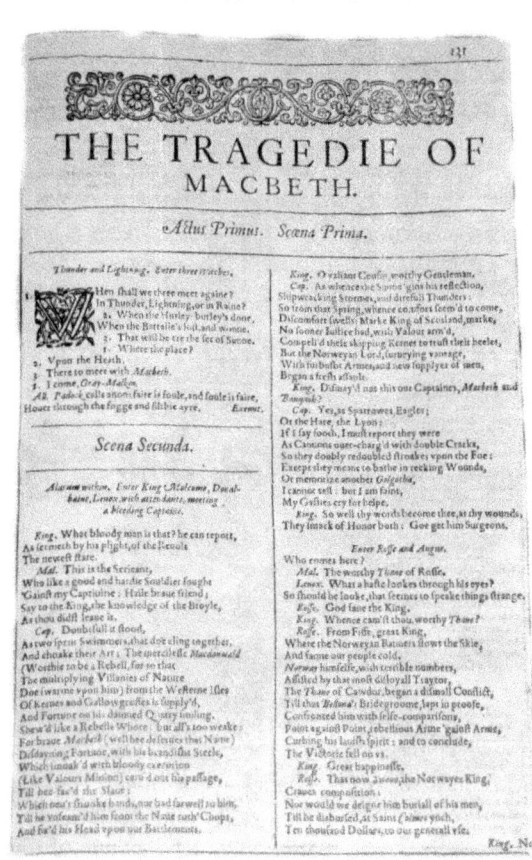

"Who's Afraid Of The Big Bad Witch?" - by - Dr. S. D'Montford

Margaret Hamilton as MGM's Wicked Witch of the West in "The Wizard Of Oz," 1938

Her performance has defined the images of Witches in the minds of a generation, as see with this Family in "Wizard of Oz" themed costumes in the French Quarter of the New Orleans Mardi Gras
Photo used with permission by Infrogmation

The second most enduring image in the minds of our survey group is from a 1939 Hollywood movie.

"I am the Wicked Witch of the West ... and I will get you, my pretty, and your little dog too! Hahahhahahha!."

Margaret Hamilton, whose portrayal became the consummate image of the Wicked Witch, in MGM's "The Wizard of Oz," was not the first choice to play the role. On August 20, 1938, MGM announced that Gale Sondergaard would be cast in the role of the Wicked Witch. The initial intention was to have a glamorous Witch. The first costume sketch for the role was a slinky black dress with sequins and a black sequined hat. As with our survey group, Mervyn LeRoy did not think that the image of a beautiful, sexy Witch would be perceived as wicked and pressured MGM into creating an ugly Witch for this part. Since Gale Sondergaard did not want to play an ugly Witch, the role was offered to Margaret Hamilton on October 10, 1938.

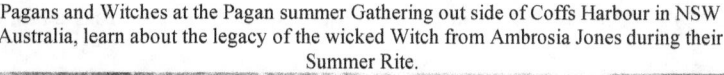

Pagans and Witches at the Pagan summer Gathering out side of Coffs Harbour in NSW Australia, learn about the legacy of the wicked Witch from Ambrosia Jones during their Summer Rite.

Therefore, it would appear that our generation has inherited its prejudices from pervious generations. With egalitarian attitudes and multicultural tolerance becoming fashionable, has anything shifted in this generation's perception of this religious minority?

How Does Our Generation Define 'A Witch' And 'Witchcraft?'

These previous darker images have taken on a perverse validity and been legitimised by academic definition. Here are some contemporary dictionary definitions taken from three different sources: - *Witch -*

Noun

1. *A Pagan*

2. *A female sorcerer or magician.*

3. *A being (usually female) imagined to have special power derived from Satan the devil.*

4. *An ugly evil-looking old woman.*

5. *A fascinatingly attractive, beautiful, charming and young appearing woman.*

6. *In wickedness*

Verb: Witchcraft

7. *To cast a spell over someone or something; put a hex or curse on someone or something.*

These definitions are limited and one-sided. It is surprising to find such limited meaning given to a word that is so controversial in any dictionary.

- Why is this word an exception?
- Does this mean that our society thinks it is acceptable to marginalise this group?
- Is there any truth to any of these definitions?
- How will these accusatory definitions stand up under cross-examination?

You be the judge.

This book will attempt to present the case for those who are often not heard in the media, the Witches themselves. It will ask the unspoken questions that society is too ashamed to openly examine, of accusations of Satanism, nudity, a child sacrifice, as well as asking Witches to answer: -

- What do Witches do?
- How do they define themselves?
- Moreover, how do they explain the unsavoury issues that arise against them in the public eye?

Let us see.

Chapter 2

Are Witches Pagans? What Is A Pagan?

Yes!

All Witches are Pagan but not all Pagans are Witches.

What is Magick?

Though ritual is central to the Pagan community not all Pagans are practitioners of magick. However, the practise of some form of magick is central to all forms of Witchcraft. The closest definition I can give of magick is: - *A ritually practised, scientifically repeatable mystical system of cause and effect, producing change in the natural world according to the practitioners will.* Magick spelled with a 'k' defines this religious-magic as separate from the theatre art of prestidigitation also commonly referred to as magic.

Just as there are many sects with in the major religions, there are also many forms of Witchcraft all having their own names, differing beliefs, diverse origins and individual practises. Whether referring to an African Witchdoctor or a practitioner of the English revivalist 1950's neo-Wicca, all these groups and non-affiliated solitary practitioners can be largely referred to as practitioners of "The Craft of The Wise." When generalising, we will refer to them simply as 'The Craft,' with capital letters.

The Craft Is Not Superstition.

Many famous Craft practitioners have decried dogmatic adherence to superstitious beliefs. Every Craft practitioner knows it is more like learning to cook than holding an irrational belief in the supernatural. It is a practise of things, which, if the method is followed, is always repeatable, though not always explainable. It is called a craft as it will take elements from many things and blend them in to something real and tangible in the physical world. These elements include science, astronomy, astrology, physics, metaphysics, mathematics, hermetics, language, graphology, and geometry. Added to these are a working knowledge of the elements, the principles of energy manipulation, of the spiritual realms, of non-corporal beings, their hierarchy, and their rules. Understanding these things is the beginning of magick and The Craft of the Wise.

Therefore, if all Witches are Pagans then we had best begin by attempting to gain an understanding of what it means to be a Pagan.

What Does It Mean To Be A Pagan?

Pagans often refer to themselves as: "People Of The Earth." However, what does this mean?

Paganism viewed from the outside is like quicksilver – hard to grasp. This is highlighted by the definitions of Pagan in "The Free Online Dictionary" by Farlex: -

1) Pagan - a person who does not acknowledge your God, gentile, heathen (more on this term later), infidel. One who is not a Christian, Muslim, or Jew, especially a worshiper of a polytheistic religion.

2) Non-religious person - One who has no religion, a person who does not manifest devotion to a deity.

3) A paynim - a heathen; a person who is not a Christian, especially a Muslim.

4) Idol worshiper, idolater, idoliser, idolizer - a person who worships idols

5) A hedonist – one who worships pleasure

6) A Neo-Pagan. (http//www.thefreedictionary.com/Pagan)

So again we have six descriptions of what a Pagan could be, but no real defining moments. A closer look at these shows that, though most Pagans think that pleasure is better than suffering, they are usually very religious and spiritual people, who do worship deity, as a personification of nature, represented by images, but they do not worship the images themselves. Many are not Muslim, and some are even Christian. To help us understand what it means to be Pagan it may help to look at the etymology of this fluid word.

Where Does The Word Come From?

The word Pagan comes from the Latin word 'păganus' meaning of the dirt, dirty, yokel or rural. If we look a bit more closely at the Indo/European root PAG of the Latin păganus, we see some other interesting correlations. It can also mean a "CIRCULAR BOUNDARY - staked out on the ground," defining a district, village, country; from which we get the words COMPACT, IMPACT, and IMPINGE, from Latin pangere, to fasten. From the same root comes the words PACE, PAX, PAY, PEACE; APPEASE, PACIFIC, PACIFY, "a binding together by treaty or agreement"; as well as PACT, PATIO, from Latin pacsc, to agree as well as, SPADE, PALE, PALISADE, PEEL, POLE; IMPALE, TRAVAIL, TRAVEL, from Latin for stake fixed in the ground; We also derive the Latin pagina from its meaning, "trellis to which a row of grape vines is fixed." Hence, by metaphor, it also can mean a column of writing, a page; a leaf of a book or a grape vine. From this comes the word PROPAGATE meaning to reproduce and fix in place. Then we also have related words PECTIN, PEGMATITE; AREOPAGUS, MASTOPEXY, from Greek pagnunai, to fasten, coagulate, with the derivative PAGOS meaning large mass or hill. From these we also get the Old English FANG, meaning, plunder, booty, and NEWFANGLED, from Middle English FANGEL, taken, akin to Old High German fangolon, to close, from Germanic fangln, to grasp, all derivatives of Germanic fanhan, to seize; and FAY, from Old English fgan, to fit closely, from Germanic fgjan, TO FIT OR TO JOIN IN A CIRCLE, or FAIRY FOLK! So you can see it was a rather complex and multi-layered term.

Dirty People
Pagans are "People Of The Earth"

The Author, Rev. Dr. S. D'Montford and her partner Ken Wills during a mud earth ritual

It was originally used as in insult, connoting much the same thing as our derogatory term "red-neck," but implying the layers of all of the above. The word appears to have initially been used by legionnaires in Rome as a derogatory term to describe non-combatants or pacifists. The old ways were being used as a reason to escape conscription and as a loophole. A 'religious need' to celebrate the old festivals, could be used as an excuse for soldiers to be absent from particular battles. Therefore it was a non-complementary military term, used to described people who adhered to the old ways of worship when Rome was trying to sophisticate and nationalize its religion into a state controlled organization.

We might say it was first used Pagan to Pagan, so as to speak, to describe those who stuck to the old ways by those who would have been the organised Neo-Pagans of their day. It was much later that it became an exclusively religious slur, when the Christians, who saw themselves as "Soldiers of Christ," began to use it to describe any "non-Jewish" peoples who wished to avoid forced spiritual conscription into Christianity. 'Pagan' began to return to its root meaning in the 4th century, indicating "anyone who worshipped the spirit of a given locality or pagus." It is interesting that the Protestant Reformation actually managed to save many Pagan tales and practices, by saving the language that those tales were recorded in.

So you can see its meaning is much deeper than the simple explanation often given that it was the Greek and Latin word for heathen which means one who attend to the hearth and is covered in soot or dirty. Yet, the term Heathen does lead us to on of the best-preserved allegorical stories about Paganism.

Cinderella

Cinderella is a girl who dwells in the cinders of a hearth fire – a heathen. She is an allegorical representation of all Paganism. The Cinderella story is the metaphorical tale of how noble indigenous practises and magic fell from grace and its proper place as the partner of royalty and was reduced to heathenism - a persecuted place in the ashes. The two ugly, over-decorated, and arrogant stepsisters represent Catholicism and Protestantism in the western version that we are familiar with and in China; it was a critical comment on Buddhism and Confucianism.

How can we draw this conclusion? Lets analyse this story to see its deeper meaning

The themes from the Cinderella story appear in the Pagan folklore of many cultures, China, Vietnam, Italy, Egypt, Australia, and the Algonquin Indians, to name a few. The tale always centres on a kind, but persecuted heroine who suffer at the hands of her stepfamily after the death of her mother. Her father is either absent or neglectful, depending on the version. The heroine has a magical guardian who helps her triumph over her persecutors and receives her fondest wish by the end of the tale. The guardian is sometimes a representative of the heroine's dead mother. Most of the tales include an awakening sparked by a shoe that causes the heroine to be recognized for her true worth. In the Chinese version, written in the middle of the ninth century A.D., the heroine of the Chinese tale is Yeh-she. A magical fish is Yeh-she's helper who uses a golden shoe to identify Yeh-she to the prince who wants to marry her.

The version that we are most familiar with was retold and written down by Charles Perrault in 1697 and translated into English in 1729 as "The Tales of Mother Goose." These were a collection of Pagan folk tales remade into witty stories purged of coarseness suitable for a salon audience.

"Who's Afraid Of The Big Bad Witch?" - by - Dr. S. D'Montford

Who Was Charles Perrault And Why Did He Write About Pagan Themes?

In 1663, Perrault was appointed as a secretary under the finance minister to King Louis XIV. He was a major participant in "The Quarrel of the Ancients and the Moderns," which pitted supporters of the literature of Antiquity, the "Ancients," against supporters of the literature from that century, the "Moderns." "The Quarrel of the Ancients and Moderns" was a cover, for deeper opposed views. The very idea of Progress was under attack on the one side, and Authority on the other. This led to critical reassessment of the products of Antiquity that would eventually bring Bible Scripture itself under the magnifying glass. His strong and lightly veiled criticisms cost him his post as secretary after he had served in that position for 32-years in 1695, at the age of 67. In retaliation for his abrupt dismissal, he published "The Tales of Mother Goose," under the name of his 17-year-old son. Despite this Charles Perrault became widely known and founded a new literary genre, "The Fairy Tale," in which he held that wonder, magic, decency, noble actions and commonsense were superior to the pontificating of science, the moral plays of the church and the political proPaganda of the state.

To do this, he returned to the simple indigenous Pagan fables of Europe with added contemporary social commentary. "The Tales of Mother Goose" is recognised as an attack on authority in the form of literary criticism with analogues on the rise of religious censure-ship, scientific inquiry and on systems of politics. Mother Goose was a representation of the Earth Goddess and dressed as a Witch. The Witch-hunts had finished in France at this time, yet here was a representation of the things the church and state had fought against retuning from afar riding on the goose's back. They were powerless to stop her. From his version of Cinderella in this book, we received the fairy godmother, the symbol of spiritual realm looking after its young practitioners, the pumpkin carriage, the main status symbol at the time humbled to the level of cow fodder, the animal servants, the value of humble loyalty over highly paid assistance and experts and the glass slippers, the beautiful but fragile way of the ancient traditions.

Leonardo DaVinci's "Lady With An Ermine." This is one of his famous Pagan puns. The lady pictured is Celia Galliani, the mistress of the Duke of Milan. Her name is derived from the word "Galen" meaning pure or ermine. She encouraged her lover to oppose the Borgia's Popes and encourage freethinking, which was considered Paganism at the time. DaVinci was thus implying that to be Pagan was to be pure, as does the Cinderella myth.

Some scholars think Perrault confused "vair" the French word for "ermine or fur," with "verre" the French word for "glass." If this is the case then a further pun against the aristocracy and the church is intended as ermine fur is what edged royal and papal robes. The "Hermine," as it is called in French and German is associated, because of the similarity on the sound of the words, with the god Hermes and thus Hermetic Magick and Neo-Platonist philosophy. The ermine was a symbol of purity as legend said that in order to catch one you only had to chase it towards the mud. It would allow itself to be captured rather that allow itself to be dirtied. In this popular myth we see another Pagan pun. The people of the earth, forced into meniality, refusing to allow themselves to be morally and spiritually sullied. For this same reason, the court of Milan, that Leonardo DaVinci originally served, adopted the ermine as its symbol, because it refused to be sullied by the despotic rule of the papal Borgia's.

The Grimm Brothers' German version, known as "Aschenputtel," or "Ash Girl," does not have a fairy godmother. It was more Druidic in its metaphors. The heroine plants a sacred tree on her mother's grave from which all of the magical help appears in the form of a white dove and gifts. At the end, the step-sisters' eyes are pecked by birds from the tree to punish them for their cruelty. Perrault's version is considerably daintier than the Grimm Brothers version but no less Pagan or magickal. There was also a slightly subversive bite and underlying, dry criticism of the aristocracy in Perrault's other stories in this book. For instance, the subtext of "Puss-in-Boots" is that the right clothes and a fine castle can make a "Marquis of Carabas" out of a miller's son. The fun of Perrault is the contrast between the mock-heroic folktale context and fashionable life.

Perrault concludes "Cinderella" with thinly veiled heathen or Pagan morals. Below are his conclusions: -

"Moral: Beauty in a woman is a rare treasure that will always be admired. Graciousness, however, is priceless and of even greater value. This is what Cinderella's godmother gave to her when she taught her to behave like a queen. Young women, in the winning of a heart, graciousness is more important than a beautiful hairdo. It is a true gift of the fairies. Without it, nothing is possible; with it, one can do anything.

Another moral: Without doubt, it is a great advantage to have intelligence, courage, good breeding, and common sense. These, and similar talents come only from heaven, and it is good to have them. However, even these may fail to bring you success, without the blessing of a fairy godfather or a fairy godmother."

What We Can Conclude From Perrault's "Cinderella"?

What can we conclude from Perrault's tale about the forgotten beautiful heathen, one who is covered in ashes or cinders from the hearth – a Paganus?

In this metaphorical tale of *"... a daughter, of unparalleled goodness and sweetness of temper, which she took from her mother, who was the best creature in the world."* Is replaced by *"...the proudest and most haughty woman that was ever seen..."* The allegory here is that royalty looses its power to these things *"... for his new wife (*The Church*) governed him entirely."*

In order to gain power, the Church dealt in double crossing and intrigues. It destroyed the practise of paratge. "Paratge" meant something more than honour, courtesy, chivalry, or gentility, though our concepts of honour, courtesy, chivalry, and gentility all owe something to the concept of "paratge." It praised high ideals, promoting a spirit of equality based on common virtue and deprecating discrimination based on blood or wealth. Paratge is an old Pagan concept of honour that includes a sense of balance with nature and the karma of "The Three fold Law of Return" and empathy. It was intrinsic to early Pagan beliefs and unfortunately; it seems to somehow be lost in the modern Pagan practise. Indigenous Pagan practitioners appealed against the inquisitions on the grounds of paratge. Raymond VI, Count of Toulouse railed at Pope Innocent III *"...the Church at Rome and the preachers are covering paratge with shame."* The French church and state launched the first inquisitions against practitioners of this Pagan concept and all but eradicated it. Our story says that they *"... could not bear the good qualities of this pretty girl, and the less because they made her own daughters appear the more odious. She is given "... the meanest work of the house.... When she had done her work, she used to go to the chimney corner, and sit down there in the cinders and ashes, ...However, Cinderella, notwithstanding her coarse apparel, was a hundred times more beautiful than her sisters, although they were always dressed very richly."* In this metaphor, we see that the priestesses who served the royalty are forsaken for the status symbols that church and state offer them.

Yet, a window of opportunity is opened for Cinderella to return to her former status and better, by a creature, that is a combination of The Goddess of the Fairy and the spirit of the deceased mothers from the past. Enough of an illusion is created for the son of the King, the next generation of government, to look long enough to see past the outer trappings of success, status and power to see the deep inner beauty and nobility of this ash dwelling heathen. However, at the stroke of midnight, fearing the worst, the Paganus cinder dweller has to flee before they all discover who she truly is. This leaves a longing and creates a search for truth that lasts until the fragile ground that she stands on, the glass slipper, is revealed. Eventually she bravely stands up for herself, on her transparent position, and is revealed in her full glory for all that she was in the past and will be in the future. The new generation of government rejects all of the status and hypocrisy and rushes to commit to something *"...no less good than beautiful..."* a future full of magic, wonder, humility, and noble values.

So to be a Pagan, a Heathen, a dweller in the ashes is to be a creature *"...of unparalleled goodness ... the best creature in the world."* We are keepers of something, though it is currently demised and outwardly appears to be coarse, that is *"... a hundred times more beautiful than her sisters, although they were always dressed very richly."* Perrault's tale is a sartorial warning to the church and state that Pagans are biding their time, getting on with the meaner tasks in life. Till one day indigenous Pagan practises will be given their chance to return to their former place permanently, not temporally, standing up shakily on flimsy glass, no longer covered in ashes, but magically transfigured, irresistible and invaluable.

The author and her partner help raise money for the Randwick's Prince of Wales Children's Hospital's cancer wing, by participating in The Sydney Body Art Push Bike Ride. The over 400 rainbow painted ritualists find many willing financial sponsors for their ride through the streets of Sydney in the worlds largest sky-clad Pagan inspired ritual in order to raise money to give to the larger community

Chapter 3

Are Witches Spiteful and Evil? - Do Witches Hex or Curse Others?

"Do what you will and harm ye none..." is the golden rule for Witches. Though this form of the phrase is taken from the "Wiccan Rede," most sects of Witchcraft carry a form of it as a central code. In other words, the working of the magical will is the same as the first principle of the Hippocratic oath for doctors: - "Do No Harm." They are encouraged to ponder all of the possible repercussions of the desired outcome before they perform the magickal act. Witches take this very seriously. It is the guiding principle in all forms of The Craft and has serious consequences for the Witch who breaks it.

Rede of the Wiccae

"Being known as the counsel of the Wise Ones:

Bide with in the Laws ye must In Perfect Love and Perfect Trust.

Live an' let live - Fairly take an' fairly give....

Soft of eye an' light of touch - Speak little, listen much....

When ye have need, Hearken not to others greed.

With the fool no season spend Or be counted as his friend.

Merry meet an' merry part - Bright the cheeks an' warm the heart.

Mind the Threefold Law ye should - Three times bad an' three times good....

True in love ever be Unless thy lover's false to thee.

Eight words ye Wiccan Rede fulfill - An' it harm none, Do what ye will."

Gerald Gardiner 1950

It is reflective of the golden rule in every other religion where it is only a suggestion without consequences:

Christianity: *"So in everything, do to others, what you would have them do to you, for this sums up the law and the prophets"*
-- New Testament: MT 7:12 NIV

Baha'i: *Lay not on any soul a load that you would not wish to be laid upon you, and desire not for anyone the things you would not desire for yourself.*
-- Baha'u'llah Gleanings

Buddhism: *Treat not others in ways that yourself would find hurtful.*
-- Udana-Varga 5.18

Confucianism: *One word which sums up the basis for all good conduct...loving-kindness. Do not do to others what you would not want done to yourself.*
-- Confucius Analects 15:23

Are Witches Spiteful and Evil? - Do Witches Hex or Curse Others?

Hinduism: *This is the sum of duty: do not do to others what would cause pain if done to you.*
-- Mahabharata 5:1517

Islam: *Not one of you truly believes until you wish for others what you wish for yourself.*
-- The Prophet Mohammed, Hadith

Judaism: *What is hateful to you do not do to your neighbour. This is the whole torah; all the rest is commentary.*
-- Hillel, Talmud, Shabbat 31a

Native American Spirituality: *We are as much alive as we keep the earth alive.*
-- Chief Dan George

Jainism: *One should treat all creatures in the world as one would like to be treated.*
-- Mahavira, Sutravitanga

Sikhism: *I am no stranger to no one; and no one is a stranger to me. Indeed, I am a friend to all.*
-- Guru Granth Sahib, pg.1299

Taoism: *Regard your neighbour's gain as your own gain, and your neighbour's loss as your own loss.*
-- T'ai Shang Kan Ying P'ien, 213-218

Unitarianism: *We affirm and promote respect for the interdependent of all existence of which we are a part.*
-- Unitarian principle

Zoroastrianism: *Do not unto others what is injurious to yourself.*
-- Shayast-na-Shayast 13.29

As Witchcraft, or as it is also termed, Pagan indigenous magical practise, is recognised as being the oldest form of spiritual belief on the planet, pre-dating all of these organised religions, it is likely that all of these maxims have evolved out of this first rule of The Craft of the Wise.

Three Fold Law of Return

Also known as "The Rule of Three." Breaking this first principle of The Craft has serious and direct repercussions. Any mature craft practitioner will not attempt to perform anything negative as they have learnt that the universe is run on Newtonian laws. This grand patriarch of physics was also an alchemist who studied Magick and the hidden meanings in mythology and their connection with the realm of matter. When he was accused of Witchcraft, he wrote many religious tristis in order to save himself. He wrote more works on these subjects than he did on science. Therefore, it should be no surprise that he was able to scientifically prove one of Witchcraft's basic laws. *"For every action there is an equal and opposite reaction and cost."* In physics class, we learnt that 'opposite' is not defined as bad verses good. However, following Newton's principles we can clearly see that the energy one gives out one gets back. For instance, if you push against a wall, the wall is pushing back with an equal amount of force, if it was not, the wall would fall over. Therefore, what is 'equal' and 'opposite' is not always obvious.

Sir Isaac Newton

Before Newton, Witches called this "The Law of Three."

There are many variations of the Law Of Return:

"Ever Mind The Rule Of Three
Three Times Your Acts Return To Thee"

"This Lesson Well, Thou Must Learn
Thou Will Gets What Thee Dost Earn
Mind the Threefold Law you should,
Three times bad and three times good"

"Ensure that your actions are honourable,
for all that you do shall return to you, threefold, good or bane."

These last two quotes are from Wiccan classic texts called "The Book of Shadows." These statements mean if Witches do good acts good comes back to them, and if they were ever silly enough to attempt anything bad, they would only do it once, because it will come back to bite the Witch in question so fast and so hard, it will make their head spin. Harm tends to beget harm, and it is true that one good turn deserves another. People remember another's charity and are more likely to aid them in return. It is more than a moral code. This is considered the basic law of Witchcraft and as Newton expressed it, an unbreakable universal principal. 'Good' in the above quotes could be substituted with 'in harmony with nature,' while 'bane' is not evil, it is just working contrary to natural law. The triquetra symbol pictured here is the representation of these laws. As such, it was used by the Celts as a protective amulet.

Witches see that all actions need to be balanced. Imbalance can have chaotic results. Using the metaphor of getting what you earn, the cash box will soon be empty if one does not occasionally put money into it as well as take it out. The more baneful a request, the more resistant the world will be to your intended magickal will. For instance, a ritual asking for good health by a person who cares for him or herself physically is a straightforward thing for the forces of nature to work with and grant. However, a smoker with emphysema asking for healthy lungs whilst still smoking is going to take considerably greater effort by the physical and spiritual participants in the ritual.

Yet, we understand that the world does not work as simplistically as these quotes make it sound. Donating to charity will not mean that the Witch will be reaping huge financial rewards. It is more akin to The Four Green Laws of Ecology:

- Everything is connected to everything else.
- Everything must go somewhere.
- Nature knows best.
- There is no such thing as a free lunch.

When Magick is performed, a Witch often asks for assistance from spirit or invokes the Gods for a favour. Therefore, there is cost involved, and this cost is dependent upon the nature of the magick being worked, the spirits being worked with, and the amount of energy out-put required in order to achieve your desired results. There is a World War II story, about how the English Witches delayed the German advance into their country long enough for Britain to have its new air defence ready for the famous Battle of Britain. They did this by invoking storms and the forces of nature to assist them. Unfortunately, the Witches put out so much energy in defence of their country that several of them lost their lives.

Protection From The Negative

People really begin to relax their attitude towards the craft when they realise that protecting themselves from any negative act is simple. This little spell can hurry the process of the "Threefold Law of Return" along. With this spell anything negative becomes like a boomerang, it wont even land it will just go straight back to where it came from.

- Find a quiet place.
- Sit still with your eyes closed,
- Focus and visualise breathing out through every pore of your skin whilst you say the following at least three times: -

"Thy curses and thy sorcery,

"Who's Afraid Of The Big Bad Witch?" - by - Dr. S. D'Montford

Have not the power to injure me,

Take thy curses on to thee,

And thy invoke the Law of Three."

Are Witches Bitches?

"What a horrible Witch of a woman!"

Any one can have a bad day or be a little snappy but is it correct to use the word Witch as a substitute for the word bitch?

Witches come in two genders. A male Witch is simply called a Witch not a warlock. The word warlock is an old Scottish term for a war traitor or an oath breaker.

However, women who are Witches are often very strong minded and independent. These very traits often result in derogatory terms being slung at them by people who feel threatened or challenged by this.

Historically as a group, Witches have stood up for their beliefs. Yet, they are individualistic and think for themselves. They protect those they love. They are often innovators like Newton, and many other famous people we will discuss in this book, who spoke their mind and did things their own way. Witches have often stood up to injustice and will not allow themselves or others to be down trodden. They use their talents to benefit others. Yet, when they need time and space to themselves they have the wisdom to take it and the commonsense to ask for energy and support when they need and deserve it. Witches are often multi-skilled and talented. They are individuals that rise to the challenge of seemingly impossible tasks and triumph. They speak what is in their hearts and try to lead a noble life reflective of the qualities of their deities. They are often outspoken and determined and defiantly refuse to play the victim or martyr roles, though they have been martyred for these very things. If these things make someone a bitch, then it cannot be a bad thing.

Therefore using the word Witch as a substitute for bitch is an insult to Witches and what they stand for.

Chapter 4

Are Witches a Lunatic Fringe Group?

NO!

As previously stated, Witchcraft, or as it is also termed, Pagan indigenous magical practise, is recognised as being the oldest form of spiritual belief on the planet, pre-dating all organised religions. It is the largest, oldest, and most common belief system in the world. Did you know that...

- More people in Hungry, Russia, and the Ukraine declare themselves as Witches, than Orthodox.
- Most of Asia, India, and Japan practise some form of spell work.
- Statisticians forget to count Africa. I have been there it is amazing. Everyone practises Pagan beliefs to some extent, even the whites.

The official number of people just in the Neo-Pagan movement worldwide is 1,000,000 approximately, according to the religious statistics gatherers at www.Adherenst.com, and fall under the category of "Other" religions. However, Witches and Pagans are not limited to the Neo-Pagan movement. There are many "old" Pagan movements around the world. If we include African Traditional Indigenous practitioners and their Witch-doctors as well as the traditional Asian/Chinese figures from the above pie graph, we can see that practitioners of The Craft of The Wise are closer to a minimum 17% of the total world population making them the 3rd largest religious group. If you add to this, members from other religions that also practise the craft the figure would be much larger. Many followers of Islam, Hinduism, and Buddhism also perform some indigenous form of The Craft. Many people in Europe practise the craft of the wise whilst also participating in some form of orthodox Christianity. Thinking about this shows that we are a major, but very quiet slice of the pie.

Hex Returns and Russian Witches

It seems that the Russian, Romanian and Hungarian governments now want a slice of this pie as going to see a Witch in those countries is thought of as a legitimate form of therapy. Is the state about to crack down on its legitimised traditional and corporate Witchcraft practitioners? Far from it!

"Who's Afraid Of The Big Bad Witch?" - by - Dr. S. D'Montford

Witches are viewed with national pride because of their impressive results, the amount of income they generate and for boosting tourism. Companies consult them, and Witches even had a stand at a recent export trade fair.

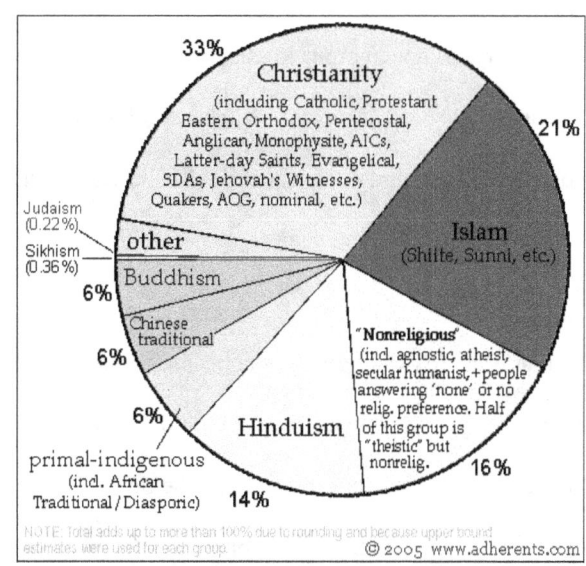

However, the government now wants its cut. *"If they sell something, whether it's a potion or a curse, they need to pay tax. They need to be made to follow the same laws as everyone else."* said Andrei Chiliman, the mayor of Bucharest's First District, and the first official to risk the Witches' wrath by ordering a census. He is stirring up a cauldron of trouble for Witches whose tax-free spells he says: *"...are costing the treasury millions of dollars a year whilst providing them with a black-market income and a relatively luxurious lifestyle."* Across these countries, tax officials are gathering details of over 4000 professional Witches so their incomes can be assessed. Yet on an average they only see seven clients a day and charge about $A15 a session which only gives them a slightly below average wage and keeps them away from needing government assistance for poverty. Could this be the start of a taxman's Witch-hunt? Monica Petrescu of Bucharest Press said on August 28, 2006 that, *"...the Witches are infuriated by the census..."* Maria Campina, 57, the self-proclaimed White Magic Queen and leader of the Romanian Witches, said: *"Why should we pay taxes when we don't get anything from the state? We already do a lot for our country. Whenever there is an important Christian celebration, we perform a ritual to protect the country from natural disasters . . . That has to be worth more than any tax income."*

Bon Po Do It In A Circle
Tibetan Bon-Po performs a ritual in a circle with in a grove of trees.
Pagan tradition is reflected in many religions.

"Russians know that happiness comes through relationships...," says, Dr Oleg Korolyenko, a local psychologist. "...We don't have marriage guidance, but we do have Witches.," reports Julie Butler in "Marie Clare." Because of the way dissenters were treated within the communist Soviet system with Psychiatrists having dissidents locked away in mental institutions, Russians and Romanian's still do not trust any form of psychotherapy. So if their husband strays or their lover will not commit, Russian women do not see a therapist, they visit a Witch and buy a good old-fashioned love spell. A typical Witchcraft clinic in a Moscow office block, has a garish interior that looks more like a empty nightclub with walls illustrated with classical art prints, and the words "Magick" and "Merlin" in pink flashing neon.

Despite orthodox Christianity, the people of these countries still take their national indigenous religion, of Witchcraft, very seriously. They see no dichotomy between going to church in the morning and to consult the local Witch in the afternoon. Even the Soviet Union's ban on all religions did not squash the passion for the paranormal. In fact, just the opposite has happened. It has grown into what is now a multi-billion-rouble industry. Magicians and hypnotists appear on television and can become stars. Institutes of parapsychology and hypnotism are only taken to be credible if their walls are covered with certificates from Witchcraft schools. In Italy, you can tune in for your Sunday morning service with the local telly evangelist or the local magician. There are endless endorsements from respected professional people of Witches miraculously curing illnesses or returning straying partners.

A Major World Religion In Most of the World

The world is not just the United Stated the United Kingdom and Australia. If we include the majority of the world, we can see that Witchcraft is a major world religion. It has always been. As a major world religion in this book we will spell both Witch and Pagan, and their derivatives, with a capital letter, as you would for Catholic or Hindu.

Prejudice and proPaganda do not allow people to see these facts clearly.
Devaluing these belief systems begins with simple things like spelling them with lowercase characters. This is part of the proPaganda. Additionally, if you do see clearly, we can discern who was the original target of proPaganda. By deconstructing the word it becomes obvious.

pro-PAGAN-da.

Chapter 5

Are Witches Satanists?

NO!

Witches DO NOT believe in The Devil, Satan or Hell.

These are seen by Witches as unnatural. The Devil, Satan, and Hell are largely much later Christian inventions. Though Witchcraft is inclusive and will readily accept teachings from other religions, it does not adopt the harmful dogma of any other religion. The aim of Witchcraft is to seek a personal relationship with the forces of nature not with a fictitious devil. Witches do not worship evil or un-natural things? Witches are connected to nature in a personal relationship. Many are herbalists and use traditional healing methods. They see nature as sacred and many are activists campaigning to protect the planet.

Satanism Is A Form Of Christianity And Has Nothing To Do With Witchcraft.

People who practise Satanism are just practising inverted Christianity. Before the fall of the last French King, "Black Masses" became popular in Europe. The intent of these was to blaspheme, rebel against the Catholic Church, and perform the reverse of what the despotic state church instructed. They were however still performing Christian rites in reverse.

Anton La Vey, who wrote the Satanic Bible for rebellious university students, knew how to put on a show. He was a circus performer who was sickened by the hypocrisy of the Christian churches. Therefore, in 1968 he shaved his head and announced the formation of the Church of Satan. To lampoon the church he put on the clerical collar. Nevertheless, his inclusion of the glued on red plastic horns, a plastic toy store pitchfork, a goaty beard, and narrowed eyes gave him the necessary demonic look. He was making money, having lots of weird sex, and giving people a show. He stated in his Satanic Bible that if people were foolish enough to believe the show they deserved to be taken advantage of. However, Le Vey was very good at selling his entertainment to the press. People want to believe the misinformation as it makes for a good story like the images opposite. The truth is often too boring to sell the papers.

Neither The Church of Satan nor Black Masses have anything to do with Witchcraft. Some people who practise Satanism say that they do, however, people who do these things are just acting out scenarios from bad 1970's movies and do not understand the craft at all.

1960s And 70s Pulp Fiction About The Craft Is Still Quoted As Fact Today

If They Don't Worship The Christian God and They Don't Worship The Devil, Who Is Left? Who Do They Worship?

Witches and Pagans have more options than that! The concept of an evil demi-urge is relatively recent, gaining popularity in the Middle East only about 1000 years BC. Paganism has existed much longer and in every country of world before that. The concept of a good god verses a bad god did not begin to spread around the globe until the event of Christian proselytising about 300 AD.

The Light Verses The Dark

Witches do not see things as entering in to a struggle of polar opposites. Rather they see things as existing in perfect balance. If energy gets pushed too far in one direction or the other things become unbalanced and then disturbances will occur and nature will take drastic action to right itself. As the pendulum swings out it must return to the other direction passing through all points in the arc. Fore every action there is an equal and opposite reaction. Witches do not have any deity that is wholly evil or wholly good. They see nature as being a balance of these forces. Light is not seen as better than dark, there cannot be a 24-hour period without both. Life on this planet would cease without both. The earth would fry if it was daylight all the time and freeze if it was dark continually. Life depends on balance not polarity though things are portrayed as pairs in Witchcraft: -

- Male & Female
- Sun & Moon
- Life & Death
- Goddess & God

They are seen as being balanced; not struggling.

Witches do not see things as having to be one thing or another. They allow for the full spectrum of personality in their deity as well as humans. As such when a Witch or a Pagan communes with a deity they are communing with a particular aspect of that personality. They get to know it like a friend. Then as a friend, the deity is willing to add its energy to the individual's will in order to accomplish a specific goal. As with friends if an individual is moving house they can ask their friends for assistance and they will usually get it. However, if the individual was to expect that the friend would do it all for them and they could sit back and do nothing, the friend would feel they are getting used and would refuse any further assistance. A relationship with deity works in much the same way. Contrary to popular fiction and some Christianised grimoire, deity, and spirit cannot be ordered it can only be requested.

The only demand that spirit will without fail obey is the demand to leave. As with any personality deity and spirit will not enter where it is not invited and will not remain where it is not welcome.

There are endless books on Pagan deity and the various ancient and modern pantheons. Suffice to say, deities are the personification of things in nature: -

- Goddess = Mother Earth - Moon - nurturing
- God = Fertility - Sun - regeneration
- Elements =
    - Earth
    - Air
    - Fire &
    - Water

Witches vary widely on what they believe deity is. Some feel that deity is a manifestation of the individual, while others feel that deity exists outside of the individual and is part of the 'primal cause' of the individual. Some Witches believe both! Like light is both a wave and a particle, they feel that deity exists both inside and outside the individual, which it is both part of the creation of the individual and created by the individual. Holding two apparently conflicting opinions at the same time is not seen as irrational, rather it is simply seen as a scientific fact of nature that quantum mechanics is only beginning to try to explain. Witches know that deity exists, often viewing ritual as a scientifically repeatable method for proving deity's existence.

There are eight basic levels of existence that are accessible: -

Nothingness

1) **Thought** - a concept that exists in space and time with out weight mass or position.

2) **Emotion** – a concept that is given tangible energy that may be connected to a place and time.

3) **Shade** – an emotion that becomes more tangible and may have mass or position.

4) **Ghost** – a shade that can make its presence felt in the physical world.

5) **Spirit** – a pre-existing energy that is incorporeal and part of nature that is often linked as part of a physical manifestation i.e. place, physical creature, mineral or rock, or element.

6) **Egregore** – any of the above that has been given so much energy by creatures from the physical world that it begins to exists with its own personality and can interact as an individual with other individuals.

7) **Deity** – any of the above that can gather and lend its own energy.

8) **Human** – the final physical manifestation of all of the above.

Does this mean that deity creates us or that we create deity or both? "What deity is," is a question that physicists and philosophers will continue to debate.

The Source Document For The Black Mass, Was The Church's Own "The Malleus Maleficarum"

Satanists are performing the Catholic Church doctrines as set down in the "The Malleus Maleficarum" in 1486-87. This is NOT Witchcraft. "The Malleus Maleficarum" or "The Hammer for Witches" was a tristie drawn up by Heinrich Institor and Jacob Sprenger, systematising "The Church's Doctrine of Witchcraft," that bore no resemblance to the surviving Pagan practices of Europe that it was designed to wipe out. It confused Witchcraft with Jewish religious practise. It made outrageous claims like the Witches

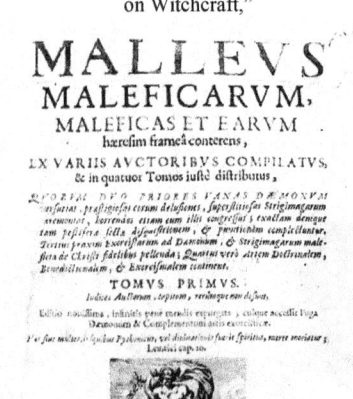

The frontis page for "The Malleus Maleficarum" or "The Hammer for Witches" that remains the Catholic Church's doctrine on Witchcraft,"

Sabbat was an opportunity for Witches to gather and kiss Satan the Devil on the bottom. It was one of the best proPaganda documents in history laying down a regular form of trial, and a course of examination. It was equal in its effectiveness to the later proPaganda pamphlets and slander campaigns of Hitler against the Jews. In fact, it was more effective, as many people still erroneously believe these things about Witches. Pope Innocent VIII issued the celebrated bull Summis Desiderantes in 1484, directing inquisitors and others to *"..put to death all practitioners of Witchcraft as heretics.."* This meant death to all those who participated in any religious practice that was different to that of the Catholic Church on the legal excuse of Witchcraft. This opened the way for the Witch hunts to begin. Dr. Sprenger computes that as many as nine million persons have suffered death for Witchcraft since the Papal Bull of Innocent. As late as 1705 two women were executed at Northampton, England for Witchcraft.

How To Identify A Witch

According to the Malleus, a Witch could be identified in four ways.

1) Witches were believed to meet with the devil; perform the unholy kiss, i.e. kiss the devil on the bottom; to get naked, drink, dance and to boast about their evil deeds. The Witches Sabbats were traditionally held on Friday evenings in churchyards, at crossroads or other out of the way places.

2) A Witch renounced her baptism. This meant she was commonly known by a name other than the one, which she received at her baptism. This is why a pet name is called a nickname, "Old Nick" being a euphemism for the devil.

A 15th century wood block cut of a fictional Witches Sabbat as described in "The Malleus Maleficarum"

3) A Witch received the devil's mark, which was not painful or did not bleed when pricked with a needle. It was taken as conclusive proof that a Witch had renounced her Christian baptism. Any wart crusty, cancerous growth, or piece of thick skin sufficed as proof.

4) Lastly, a Witch performed malefic i.e. evil deeds by supernatural means. Witches were accused of causing destruction of crops, cows to stop giving milk and making people ill.

Any of these was enough for you to be brought on trial, all of the accused possessions were sold to pay for the trail and then they were tortured until they confessed to justify the process and executed.

Confessions

The prosecutors required confessions before they could execute a Witch. Many of the Witch suspects have left confessions behind. Though many under torture willing admitted to all four of the Malleus's accusations to relieve their suffering, many refused. Confessions were not freely obtained from most Witch suspects who wished to keep their good name in tact. It was common to use what we would now call torture to get confessions of guilt from the accused. Methods of torture could be sadistically violent and sometimes performed in public, however other less gross method were often effectively employed. Thumbscrew, branks, or scold's bridle, a device for depressing the tongue and keeping suspects quiet are common implements. There were also a number of more subtle tortures used, such as waking and light deprivation. In "waking" or sleep deprivation, Witch suspects were deliberately kept from sleeping. Local guards took turns to stay in the torture chambers with the suspects. If they fell asleep, it was the job of the guards to march them up and down the prison to keep them from sleeping. After a number of nights without rest people would do anything to be allowed to sleep. Light deprivation can have much the same effect. This process continued until they made a confession. These methods also can also cause hallucinations during which babbling gibberish was recorded as confessions. In those cases, the smallest thing was played up to be a confession. A meeting with a man in black was claimed their inquisitors to be the devil. Simply preparing a roast goose could be twisted into preparing a meal for the devil. Few of them confess to anything supernatural.

Imprisonment, Torture and Execution

The Witch suspects were often held for 6 months in appalling conditions. They were deprived of sleep, warmth, and light. They were prodded all over their bodies with long thin pins to discover their Witch's mark. Professional Witch prodders were hired for this job. Witch trails were a very profitable industry. One John Kincaid from Tranent in Scotland, hired to conduct the proddings in Forfar, the final large-scale Witch-hunt in Europe, was presented with an honorary burgess-ship as a reward for his work. Once a confession was obtained, a trial could be held. Trials were swift, perfunctory affairs with a guilty verdict inevitable. The convicted Witch was lucky if she was merely banished. The less fortunate ones were executed by burning at the stake hanging or the more merciful method of strangulation and then having the lifeless body burnt in a barrel of tar.

After becoming aware of these inhuman atrocities sanctioned by one religion against another and performed upon millions of innocent victims, whom do you feel really are the servants of evil?

Chapter 6

Was Aleister Crowley a Satanist?

No!

Crowley didn't describe himself as a Satanist.

The popular press continues to demonise Crowley. After his death, when they were safe from a liable suit, they dubbed him, "The Wickedest Man In The World." Not only does he fall woefully short of that description, quite to the contrary, his words and his actions whilst alive show a person who was truly altruistic, heroic, and self-sacrificing to his cause of the liberation of mankind. Crowley's whose stated life purpose was a rebellion against such Christian judgemental labels, would have been appalled at the gullibility of those who believed he was. He sort to teach people to be strong, to think for themselves, and to experience things before they cast judgment upon it, to push themselves to their limits so that each individual knows where their own limits are. His highest hope was that all people would one day pursue their own dreams without letting them be crushed by societies moreeés. He saw the artificial concept of sin as the biggest control mechanism in society.

Raised in the stifling literalism of the Protestant Christian Brethren sect he rebelled against their controlling, hypocritical, sanctimonious, superior attitude based on what he felt was an incomplete belief system. He sought to break down these negative stereotypes by embodying them and *"free human kind from all restriction and repression."* In order to achieve this, he ironically imposed rigorous and extreme regimes upon himself and his acolytes. He hoped that by dressing himself up in ridiculous labels he could expose societies controlling fraud of The Emperor's New Clothes with his own nakedness. Eventually, after his death, he did.

Early Life

Born, Edward Alexander Crowley in Leamington Spa, Warwickshire, England on October 12, 1875. He never legally changed his name to Aleister. Crowley explains his adoption of the pseudonym "Aleister" this way: *"For many years I had loathed being called Alick, partly because of the unpleasant sound and sight of the word, partly because it was the name by which my mother called me. Edward did not seem to suit me and the diminutives Ted or Ned were even less appropriate. Alexander was too long and Sandy suggested tow hair and freckles. I had read in some book or other that the most favourable name for becoming famous was one consisting of a dactyl followed by a spondee, as at the end of a hexameter: like*

32

"Who's Afraid Of The Big Bad Witch?" - by -

A young Crowley studied English literature at Cambridge in 1895

"Jeremy Taylor." Aleister Crowley fulfilled these conditions and Aleister is the Gaelic form of Alexander. To adopt it would satisfy my romantic ideals. The atrocious spelling A-L-E-I-S-T-E-R was suggested as the correct form by Cousin Gregor, who ought to have known better. In any case, A-L-A-I-S-D-A-I-R makes a very bad dactyl. For these reasons I saddled myself with my present nom-de-guerre—I can't say that I feel sure that I facilitated the process of becoming famous. I should doubtless have done so, whatever name I had chosen."

Here follows a partial list of other pseudonyms that Crowley used. Some of them have been used as a parody by other authors too. You may be familiar as names of these names as characters from books and movies about magick. For instance, Leo Vincey was the hero/victim of the magickal drama in the later Rider Haggard novels "She," and Sgt. Pepper was use as a title for the Beatles most successful album:

* Abhavananda
* Alex C. Crowley
* Alice Wesley Torr
* Alys Cusack
* Ananda Vigga
* Ankh-af-na-Khonsu
* Arthur Grimble
* Baphomet as the X° in O.T.O.
* Barbey De Rochechouart
* C. S. Hiller
* Christeos Luciftias
* Comte De Fenix
* Cor Scorpionis
* Count Vladimir Svareff
* Cyril Gustance
* Dost Achiha Khan
* Edward Storer
* Elaine Carr
* Ethel Ramsay
* Fra. H. I. Edinburgh
* Francis Bendick
* G.H.S. Pinsent
* George Archibald Bishop
* George Raffalovich
* Gerard Aumont
* H. D. Carr
* Herr Hermann Rudolph Von Alastor
* Hilda Norfolk
* J. Turner
* James Grahame
* John Roberts
* Katharine S. Prichard
* Khaled Khan
* Ko Hsuan
* Ko Yuen
* Lavinia King
* Lemuel S. Innocent
* Leo Vincey
* Lord Boleskine
* Mahatma Guru Sri Paramahansa Shivaji
* Mahatma Sri Paramananda Guru Swamiji
* Major Lutiy
* Maria Lavroff
* Mark Wells
* Martial Nay
* Mary Smith
* Michael Fairfax
* O Dhammaloyu
* Ol Sonuf Vaoresaji ("I reign over ye")—Adeptus Major
* Oliver Haddo
* Ou Mh (O.M.—" No, definitely no! or Not Yet!")—Adeptus Exemptus
* Parzival —Adeptus Minor
* Percy Flage
* Percy W. Newlands
* Perdurabo ("I will endure til the end")—Neophyte
* Rev. C. Verey
* Reverend P. D. Carey
* S. J. Mills
* Sgt Pepper
* Sheamus O'Brien
* St. Maurice E. Kulm
* Ta Dhuibh
* The Beast 666
* Thomas Wentworth

Was Aleister Crowley a Satanist?

* To Mega Therion ("The Great Beast")—Magus

* Vi Veri Vniversum Vivus Vici (V.V.V.V.V.—"By the force of truth, I, while living, have conquered the Universe")—Magister Templi

Crowley was close to his father, Edward Crowley; a wealthy retired brewer and owner of Crowley Ale, who was a very unorthodox lay preacher of the Plymouth Brethren sect. Crowley believed his father to be the 'best of men' and when he died cruelly, slowly strangled by tongue cancer, it caused him to question the reality of a Christian God. He had conflict with his mother Emily Bertha Bishop, when, after his father's death, she sent him to live with his maternal uncle, Tom Bishop, who, by all accounts, abused young Alexander.

After his father's death, he became increasingly rebellious. He attended Cambridge in 1895, where he studied English literature. Here he encountered another form of social mind control, academia. As a rebellion against the hallowed halls of 'great' literature, he thumbed his nose at this institution by publishing a surprisingly successful collection of technically bad, tacky, and tasteless pornographic poetry that lampooned and parodied the classics. By having it released under a pseudonym in continental Europe, he could not be expelled nor prosecuted for obscenity.

Chess Master

Crowley learned to play chess at the age of six. He edited a chess column for the local newspaper and joined the university chess club at Cambridge. He beat the president of the Cambridge University Chess Team in his first year. He practiced two hours a day with the aim of becoming the world chess champion. However, when attending a chess conference in Berlin in 1897, he suddenly gave up his chess aspirations. He describes it this way: *"My one serious worldly ambition had been to become the champion of the world at chess...But I had hardly entered the room where the masters were playing when I was seized with what may justly be described as a mystical experience. I seemed to be looking on at the tournament from outside myself. I saw the masters—one, shabby, snuffy and blear-eyed; another, in badly fitting would-be respectable shoddy; a third, a mere parody of humanity, and so on for the rest. These were the people to whose ranks I was seeking admission. "There, but for the grace of God, goes Aleister Crowley," I exclaimed to myself with disgust, and there and then I registered a vow never to play another serious game of chess. I perceived with praeternatural lucidity that I had not alighted on this planet with the object of playing chess.*

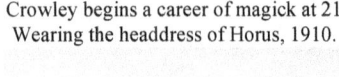
Crowley begins a career of magick at 21 Wearing the headdress of Horus, 1910.

"Who's Afraid Of The Big Bad Witch?" - by - Dr. S. D'Montford

Introduction to Magick

Crowley was introduced to several magical orders whilst at Cambridge. He eventually gained access to the prestigious Golden Dawn sect, which included several former Cambridge English graduates such as Brahms Stoker and W.B Yeats. Crowley progressed though the ranks with unprecedented speed. Nevertheless, he became very disillusioned with the Golden Dawn's policy of teaching false mysteries to the lesser ranks and keeping the true mysteries only for the upper ranks. He accused them of "playing with magick." He saw this restriction of accurate knowledge as another form of social control. Crowley believed the purpose of magick was to be empowered and free from social control and this freedom was the right of any brave enough to step out of the herd. He attempted an unsuccessful take over to reverse this decision. After such initial high expectations, he left the order in disgust.

At 21 Crowley inherited a large trust fund that freed him from any financial worries. He left Cambridge and put the Golden Dawn behind him to pursue his own studies of magick. In 1900 he travelled to Mexico for a mountaineering expedition and whilst there he was initiated as a 33° Mason. In 1902, he travelled to Ceylon to begin the practice of yoga in with Allan Bennett, an associate from the Golden Dawn.

Regalia required to perform the Abramelin operation. Crirca 1911

The House at Loch Ness

In order for him to begin his magick properly he decided to establish contact with an entity that would serve as an intermediately for him with other spirit entities. In classical magical texts this is referred to as "Gaining knowledge and conversation with your holy guardian angel," or "your Genius." In 1903, he purchased an isolated property, Boleskine House at Loch Ness in Scotland that was suitable for performing an extreme ritual process that would allow him to achieve this objective. Crowley explains why he needed to purchase such a specific house: *The aspirant must have a house secure from observation and interference. In this house, there must be an oratory with a window to the East, and a door to the North opening upon a terrace, at the end of which must be a lodge. He must have a Robe, Crown, Wand, Altar, Incense, Anointing Oil, and a Silver Lamen. The terrace and lodge must be strewn with fine sand. He withdraws himself gradually from human intercourse to devote himself more and more to prayer for the space of months. He must then occupy two months in almost continuous prayer, speaking as little as possible to anybody. At the end of this period he invokes a being described as the Holy*

Guardian Angel, who appears to him (or to a child employed by him), and who will write in dew upon the Lamen, which is placed upon the Altar. The Oratory is filled with Divine Perfume not of the aspirant's kindling.

What Is The 'Holy Guardian Angel,' 'Genius' or 'Higher Self'?

Some describe it as the highest spiritual part of ones self. However, many traditions specifically describe it as the personal spiritual companion that is always with us and therefore we are never alone. Middle eastern tradition called this the Genii and many fairy stories are made about it such as the genii in Aladdin's lamp. It is from this word 'Genii' that we get our English word 'genius'. This shows that it is also responsible for moments of great inspiration and intelligence that transcends or goes beyond. When we have communion with our Holy Guardian Angel, it can guide us in the direction we choose. It can also be asked to act as an intermediary with other spirits and Gods on our behalf. Crowley says: *"After a period of communion with the Angel, he summons the Four Great Princes of the Spirit World, and forces them to swear obedience. On the following day, he calls forward and subdues the Eight Sub-Princes; and the day after that, the many Spirits serving these. These inferior Spirits, of whom four act as familiar spirits, then operate a collection of talismans for various purposes. Such is a brief account of the Operation described in the book."*

It never judges the individual. It will never refuse any of its individual's requests that are within its power to grant. It always allows the individual to be his or her own value. Indeed no great spiritual progress is made with out it. For those serious about advancing along the spiritual path, the mystic union with your Holy Guardian Angel must be achieved.

In eastern traditions the Holy Guardian Angel is colloquially called a 'Genii' or Nãgas in Sanskrit and Yaksha/ Yakshinîs in Tibetan, and is often represented as a large snake or elephant in a protective posture. These spirits are often depicted as riding on a human's shoulders. In fact the Hindu overlord of all the genii' name is 'Kubera', which literally means "riding on a man." This is the equivalent of Augoeides of Iamblichus, the Atman of Hinduism, and the Daemon of the Gnostics.

Shakespeare's play "The Tempest", is a medieval depiction of a Greek hermetic Magician named Prospero, highlighting his relationship with his Genii and the active assistance it renders to help right an injustice and to make things work out for the best for him and his family. It is one of the few of Shakespeare's plays in which no one dies. This play is presented in an accurate fashion with minimal Christian censorship. This free style of writing about one's genii, when compared with the contemporary work of "Dr. Faustus" by

Marlow, which was heavily steeped in the Christian fear proPaganda of the time, could have only been penned whilst Shakespeare felt secure under the protection and patronage of Queen Elizabeth 1st. She was the most powerful and successful English monarch, who was an actively practising hermetic Magician herself under the tutelage of the likes of John Dee and Sir Francis Bacon. Given this fact, it is interesting to note how Elizabeth 1st miraculously came through many hazards and obstacles in her ascension to the throne paralleling those of Prospero in the play. What is also interesting is the amazing secession of the English Empire from the Roman Catholic Church, during her successful reign. The Holy Roman Catholic Church had a vice like grip on the world of her time, to choose to step away from it and actively oppose it was thought to be suicide. However, not only did she survive, she thrived taking the then weak and waning British Empire along with her. It should not escape your attention that the name 'Prospero' means 'one who prospers', given the rise and rise of this amazing single lady in the height of historical chauvinism, who was a bastard child with a very tenuous claim to the throne. Her example is very heartening to any, like Crowley, that seek to fully empower themselves so as to no longer be oppressed by arbitrary moral systems and seemingly insurmountable odds.

The Abramelin Operation

The Abramelin is an austere method set out, in the 1300s by a Chaldean/Jewish mage of that name, in order to attain knowledge and conversation of your Holy Guardian Angel or H.G.A. *"...each man will procure for himself those which be of his nature and genius and fit for that wherein thou wouldest employ them. ... And in all cases thou shalt avail thyself of the power and command of thy Holy Angel."*

It is a 6-month process of purification, isolation, recitations, sleep, and food deprivation and other strict disciplines, designed to bring about an altered state of consciousness. Naturally, under these circumstances, some level of psychosis can occur, there for it is seldom performed. Indeed many modern practitioners who have performed this operation are often left with some form of neurosis. However, the author of the text, a Cabbalist called "Abraham the Son of Simon" felt it was safe enough, if performed properly, for both of his sons to perform when they became "of age." He felt this method was a precious "holy treasure," that could be learnt by anyone, even if they were not a "natural master," of the arts. Though this book is often touted as demonic, anyone who has ever read it can see that quite clearly the opposite is true. It is almost biblical in its reverence for the divine as is evidenced by its opening statements. *"The Book Of HOLY MAGIC, Which God Gave Unto Moses, Aaron, David, Solomon, And Other Saints, Patriarchs And Prophets; Which Teacheth The True Divine Wisdom."* It is a device to invoke angels using "God's Holy Name" and the prefaces and the footnotes by the translator, S.L. MacGregor Mathers shows that it has been used by Catholic Popes.

People who have performed this operation, at first think that the results that they achieve are mere hallucinations, apart from one thing. Fine river sand is placed on the entranceway to the consecrated room in which the meditations and magickal workings are done. It is raked over by the mage upon entrance to the room. Footprints appear in the sand, as proof that what has happened is more than illusionary.

Crowley himself felt that any other magical operation was, in a sense, evil. He explains: *"As was said at the opening of the second chapter, the Single Supreme Ritual is the attainment of the Knowledge and Conversation of the Holy Guardian Angel. It is the raising of the complete man in a vertical straight line... Any other operation is black magic...If the magician needs to perform any other operation than this; it is only lawful in so far as it is a necessary preliminary to That One Work.* He then softens his position. *There are, however many shades of grey. It is not every magician who is well armed with theory. Perhaps one such may invoke Jupiter, with the wish to heal others of their physical ills. This sort of thing is harmless... It is not evil in itself... Until the Great Work has been performed, it is presumptuous for the magician to pretend to understand the universe, and dictate its policy."*

Contrary to his public image Crowley did not endorse any magick that is self-serving or results-oriented; He regarded these things as impure.

There are much easier ways that are just as effective, which do not damage one's mental health, to contact your personal H.G.A. However, Crowley being the man he was, had to do things the hardest possible way to prove to himself he could. Crowley successfully contacted his H.G.A. who revealed that his name was Aiwass from Egypt. However, Crowley did not complete the exercise as McGregor Mathers of the Golden Dawn sent him an urgent request for his assistance with an internal matter in the order. Crowley never returned to complete this extremely difficult process.

Rose Kelly

Working with the H.G.A. is often linked with meeting your soul mate and not long after breaking off the Abramelin operation, Crowley met Edith Rose Kelly. She was without a doubt the most influential person in Crowley's life. Rose was from a wealthy family and was the sister of the painter Sir Gerald Kelly, one of Crowley's best friends. Rose was a year older than Crowley, an independently wealthy widow and beautiful. Since having come out into society, she had gained a reputation as an exceptionally accurate trance channel and parlour medium. It was love at first sight. Theirs was an intense spiritual as well as a physical relationship and it is rumoured that they were married the day after their first introduction. It was a whirlwind romance and they decided to go to Egypt, the home of Aleister's H.G.A. for their honeymoon.

The union of a naturally gifted psychic with a talented magician has a long history of success from the time of Moses and Aaron through to Calligastro and his child clairvoyants during the French revolution, and of cause the legendary Dr. John Dee with Edward Kelly, Rose's forefather. Rose and Aleister's choice of Egypt for their honeymoon was no mere whim. They were there to see what their combined talents could reveal. Ambitious as always, and in keeping with his taste for middle eastern magick, they decided that the first thing they wanted to do was to perform a Goetic ritual in the King's chamber of the great pyramid invoking "The Bornless One" or God himself. The Goetia is a grimoire of magickal angelic invocations attributed to King Solomon. This resulted in Rose entering a trance and repeating, *"They are waiting for you."* When Crowley asked her who it was who was waiting for him. Rose replied "Horus" and the others. Horus is the Jesus figure in ancient Egypt, born of a virgin and the champion of all goodness. When Rose came to her senses, she confessed that she didn't know who Horus was but that she could Identify his

The beautiful and wealthy Edith "Rose" Kelly was a gifted medium of some renown

image at the museum. The next day they March 21 1904 attended the Boulaq Museum in Cairo; Rose did recognize an image of the god, on a painted stèle bearing the catalogue number 666. Indeed the last verse on the reverse side of the stèle translates to give a message that could be applied to the H.G.A. *"O Unique One, who shines as the moon, ...O deliverer of those who are in the sunshine, open for him the spirit world. Indeed Osiris... shall go forth by day to do that which he wills upon the earth and among the living."*

Crowley had, for reasons previously mentioned, chosen to own the name "Beast 666" in one of his magical orders. Therefore, Crowley took the discovery of this stèle 666 to be a personal sign.

DOES THE NUMBER 666 HAVE ANYTHING TO DO WITH WITCHCRAFT?

NO!

In the King James Version of the Bible, Revelation 13:18 reads:

"Let him that hath understanding count the number of the beast: for it is the number of a man; and his number is Six hundred threescore and six."

Please note that it does not connect the number to Witches nor Satan. It is the number of a man.

Many Bible translations have footnotes saying the number translated from the original Greek could be 616. Absolute confirmation of this was found in ancient fragments of papyrus from Revelation discovered on a rubbish dump in 1999 by the Egypt Exploration Society, dated from about 300 A.D. '616 is clearly visible to the naked eye, in the third line, being *"chi, iota, sigma."* not 666.' explains David Parker, Prof. of New Testament Textual Criticism and Palaeography at the University of Birmingham in England.

"This is an example of gematria, where numbers are based on the numerical values of letters in people's names," says Parker *"Early Christians would use numbers to hide the identity of people who they were attacking: 616 refers to the Emperor Caligula."* He wanted to erect his own statue in the temple at Jerusalem. That would be congruent with Mark 13:14 *".. the abomination standing in the holy place, let the reader use discernment."* The number 666 may have been inserted into later translations as it represents the name Nero, the ancient Roman emperor known for persecuting Christians.

Crowley taught ancient gematria to his students and was well aware of the fact that this number and this passage in Revelation correctly signified Nero, the Roman Emperor most famous for trying to stamp out Christianity. Crowley saw himself as trying to release humankind from the tyranny of hypocritical Christian morals. Crowley adopted the name "Beast 666" as he felt that his life's purpose was to free people from the chains of an outdated, arbitrary and judgmental set of rules that stopped them being all that they could be and living their dreams.

Rose Channels the Book of the Law

Eighteen days after finding the Stèle 666, often referred to as The Stèle of Revealing, just as described in The Book of Abramelin, Crowley began to receive messages dictated by an unearthly voice, identifying itself as Aiwass, through his trance channel bride Rose. Many people do not realise that Rose was so involved. Even though The Book of Abramelin and Crowley's writings state that:

*...At the end of this period he invokes a being described as the Holy Guardian Angel, who appears to him **or to a child employed by him, and who will write** in dew upon the Lamen, which is placed upon the Altar.*

Crowley thought of Rose as a wilful child and indeed, she was already carrying their first child. Crowley's writings make it unclear as to how much involvement she had in the process even though Rose clearly stated when asked that she channelled for an hour each day whilst her husband wrote down the text of The Book Of The Law. It was dictated in Cairo between noon and 1 P.M. on three successive days, April 8th, 9th, and 10th in the year of 1904. Crowley gave this work a Masonic name: "Liber Al Veg Legis" meaning "The Book of the Law." It has influenced all modern magical writings. This book has been described as irreverent by many as it reprises Crowley's distaste for all controlling organizations that prevent people from achieving great things by prescribing arbitrary moral codes and crippling guilt. It was to supersede the current moral laws for the next aeon or 2000 years. To Crowley's mind the first set of laws were given on stone tablets and were smashed which the Decalogue or the Ten Commandments, the harsh laws, replaced. Two thousand years later, as human kind was able to cope with less stringent guidelines, the Christian Laws softened and replaced them. It appeared that 2000 years later this new law book was to again soften and replace those laws with one simple rule. *"Do what thou wilt shall be the whole of the law. Love is the law, love under will."*

Upon return to England Crowley put the manuscript away in the attic and did not revisit it for five years. About four months later, in July 1904 Rose gave birth to a beautiful little girl who Crowley referred to as his "Magical Child." He named her Nuit Ma Ahathoor Hecate Sappho Jezebel Lilith Crowley.

Was Aleister Crowley a Satanist?

Mountain Climbing in Tibet

Crowley began climbing as a teenager and in 1891 became a local hero for climbing the perilous chalk cliffs at Beachy Head, Sussex in England. Crowley became an accomplished mountain climber in his own time, and is still highly regarded in mountaineering literature, although silly rumours based on his reputation, rather than the facts reported in the popular press are often mentioned. His mentor in the world of climbing was Oscar Eckenstein, a highly skilled climber, who was also a student of Eastern philosophy, in which Crowley was keenly interested.

Crowley in the Himalayas

In 1902, Crowley attempted Chogo Ri or K2, the second tallest peak in the world. On that climb, the expedition achieved a yet unbroken record of the greatest number of days spent on a glacier. Being 65 days on the Baltoro. He also had the record for the greatest pace uphill over 16,000 feet. Being 4,000 feet in 1 hour 23 minutes on Iztaccihuatl in Mexico in 1900.

Eckenstein left - Crowley right

In 1905 Crowley, received permission to proceed and partial funding from Sir Francis Younghusband, British magistrate for the area, who had lead the successful British invasion of Tibet in 1901 and a prominent member of the British Secret Service. Therefore, this permission and funding, that lead to the attempt on the world third highest mountain, Mt. Kanchenjunga in the strategic eastern Himalayas, really came from the British Secret Service, no doubt on the promise of some return of information to them. Crowley openly stated that he had worked for the British secret service several times in his life. Crowley fit the Secret Service profile perfectly. He was a highly intelligent Cambridge drop out, who was charismatic, had travelled widely, spoke several languages, bisexual, and was not chained by moral censure. The British Secret Service also has a history of working with magicians since the time of it's establishment by Queen Elisabeth 1st. It is incomprehensible that so many people have difficulty in believing his claim.

Before Everest's true height was established in the mid-1800s, Kanchenjunga was thought to be the world's highest mountain. It was unconquered and the dream of every professional climber in that day. It was also inaccessible due to political unrest between Russia and England. Many climbers still consider Kanchenjunga to be the most difficult ascent in the world. Scaling it involves a much longer approach hike, the mountain is prone to bad weather, and normally takes more than three months to tackle. Climbing Mount Everest normally takes two months. To this day only 195 people have climbed Mount Kanchenjunga, according to the Nepal Mountaineering Association.

Crowley was well aware of all of its dangers and was elected to lead the band of six climbers and their 136 coolies and Sherpas for this reason. There was a rebellion against Crowley on the trip for two reasons. Firstly, he beat one of the Sherpas for stealing, who consequently left the troupe. This increased everyone's load and was not appreciated. Crowley pointed out that theft could become life threatening in extremes but this was forgotten under the weight of the heavier packs. Secondly, when they had reached 25,000ft, the five other members wanted to take a more direct route than Crowley had planned. Crowley understanding the danger they were leaving themselves open to, refused to go with them. Dr. Guillarmod took charge. Crowley decided to take the majority of the Sherpas and most of the supplies, go around the longer safer way, and meet up with them if they survived. They did not. Halfway through their short cut they realised they had made a bad decision and began descending again too late. An avalanche swept them away. Crowley witnessed this from the safe route he had chosen but was powerless to help them. Four of the other climbers died. It took three days for he, the other survivors, and the remaining Sherpas to dig out the bodies. Despite claims to the contrary, there is not much that Crowley could have done. He reported these events upon his return and never climbed again. Kanchenjunga remained unconquered for a further fifty years when in 1955, British climbers George Band and Joe Brown reached the summit using the route that Crowley plotted out in 1905.

Crowley the loving Father to his magickal child

Further Asian Travels

Another dispute that Crowley had gotten himself into with the Golden Dawn, was his desire that the order should explore the unbroken, still working, and still used, far eastern magical traditions more deeply. So, taking their 2-year-old magickal child with them, Rose and Aleister decided to mount another magickal discovery tour to Asia, where Crowley had spent time working for the British Secret Service under the cover of mountain climbing. He had a friend, Allan Bennett who was studying Hinduism and Buddhism and ancient sacred languages there. They travelled to Vietnam and Shanghai with plans to go to Sri Lanka and Burma.

To Crowley's frustration, the formerly pampered upper class Rose proved to be a poor mother under the riggers of travel, without the usual assistance of an English nanny. Far from the hygiene of the British health care system, the child contracted typhoid and died. Crowley blamed Rose for this and could not bear to look at her any more. He abandoned her in Shanghai. Disillusioned with everything, Crowley sort comfort with Allan Bennett who was studying yoga in Burma.

Allan Bennett

Yoga, originated in the Indus Valley over 5000 years ago but is now firmly established as a tradition here in the West largely because of the work of the founders of the western magickal traditions. They brought Yoga to Western consciousness in the late 1800s almost half a century before the arrival of the popular Yoga gurus in the 20th century.

Allan Bennett is arguably the foremost of these. Crowley leaned heavily on him, when he published "Eight Lectures on Yoga," in 1939. Aleister Crowley was three years his junior and he looked up to and admired Bennett all his life. Both were pioneers in bringing the mysticism of the orient to Westerners. Both men were associated with the Golden Dawn and Bennett was adopted by Macgregor Mathers, a founding member. They parted ways in 1900, on bad terms because of Mathers' antagonism toward "orientalism" and Bennett's attempts to introduce this into the occident tradition. Bennett went to a monastery in Ceylon, now Sri Lanka, where he studied Magadhi, an ancient Indo-Aryan language in which many Hindu and Buddhist texts are written, and became a pupil of Sri Parananda, who taught him Hatha Yoga, as well as Pranayama. Crowley sought out his friend in Sri Lanka and Burma to further his Yoga studies which began years previously with Eckenstein. Crowley's time with Bennett was the catalyst to his returning to his spiritual work, which resulted in a powerful samadhi experience for him on the China/Burma border in 1905.

Drugs

Allan Bennett, Crowley's mentor, was said to have "instructed Crowley in the magical use of drugs," especially opium to ease his grief after the death of his daughter, whilst in Asia. However, Crowley states that he first developed a drug addiction after his doctor prescribed heroin for his asthma and bronchitis. Crowley also experimented with psychedelic substances whilst in Paris during the 1920s and it was there that he was first introduced to the cactus peyote. In October of 1930, Crowley dined with Aldous Huxley in Berlin, and it is said that he introduced Huxley to peyote on that occasion. In 1922, he wrote a novel entitled, "Diary of a Drug Fiend," which presented a hope of rehabilitation by means of Magickal techniques and the exercise of True Will. However, the doctors continued to prescribe heroin for his chest infections until his death.

Crowley's Wives and Children.

After the death of her child in Asia, Rose went back to England, recovered from her grief and loss and continued on with her life as a medium until she died at 58 years of age. Crowley and Rose had one more child in 1906 Lola Zara Crowley, and did not divorce until 1909 when Rose wished to remarry to a Mr. Goymley. Contrary to popular opinion Rose and Crowley remained amicable after their divorce until Rose's death in 1938.

Crowley had five children in total, three of which are still alive, by four different women, only one of which was one of his two wives.

- He had Nuit Ma Ahathoor Hecate Sappho Jezebel Lilith (July 1904-Spring 1906) and Lola Zaza (b.1906) to Rose Crowley
- Anne Léa "Poupée" (Feb. 1920-Oct. 14, 1920) a sickly child who tragically only lived a few months to Leah Hirsig
- Astarte Lulu Panthea (b. 1920) was borne to Ninette Shumway
- Finally, his only son Aleister Ataturk (b.1938) was born late in his life to Patricia "Deidre" MacAlpine, who was not connected to his magical work in any way.

His second wife was Maria Teresa deMiramar did not bear him any children. They were married in 1929. They never were divorced, although by 1930 their marriage had collapsed, largely due to Maria's worsening mental condition.

The Victor Neuberg Effect

Eventually Crowley began to return his interest to "Liber Legis," explaining his own lack of interest in it this way: *"I have fought this Book and fled it; I have defiled it and I have suffered for its sake."*

In 1907, Crowley founded the Order he called the A∴A∴ meaning "Argentum Astrum" or "Silver Star." One of his first initiates was a young poet named Victor Neuberg. In 1909 just after he had divorce Rose, Crowley went into the Sahara Desert with Neuberg who was his lover and acolyte. In the near sensory depravation of the desert, they performed an Enochian working combined with a sex-magick act, to access the energy of "Choronzon" or '333,' supposedly the Dweller in the Cabbalistic Abyss, believed to be the last great obstacle between the adept and enlightenment. Thelemites believe this entity's function is to destroy the ego. There is some conflict around this story as Crowley was notoriously inaccurate with spelling. It is not clear if he may have meant 'Coronzon' as described by John Dee and Edward Kelly in their Enochian workings or 'One of The Forgotten Ones' who is invoked atop the

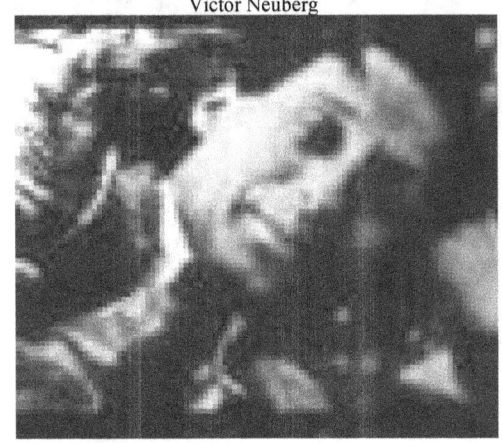
Victor Neuberg

Pillars of the Abyss, traditionally called "She," which may have resulted in the adaptation of the Spanish word 'Corazón' meaning 'Heart' or "Empty Heart." Crowley describes himself being seized with an emptiness and feeling an overwhelming need to be the female passive receptive partner in a sex magick act in the ritual. To top off this confusion, Neuberg claimed that none of this was true that they simply invoked the spirit of an Egyptian workman.

Sex Magick

However, the results of this exercise were immediate and far-reaching. Among other things, Crowley realised that sex could be a sacrament. That it was holy and empowering. Sex magick became seen as a powerful fast track method of achieving your will. Sex magick is the use of the altered states of consciousness, passion and energy of any sex act, solo or partnered, as focus for the desired for effects in the physical world. This was inspired by Paschal Beverly Randolph, who wrote of using the "nuptive moment" or orgasm as the time to make a "prayer" for events to occur. It resulted in a series of rituals described in the book "The Vision and the Voice." As well as a set of homosexual rituals called "The Paris Workings."

Crowley explains how significant this event was for him understanding "Liber Legis" this way in his work "Magick": (Crowley), *to whom this revelation was made with so many signs and wonders, was himself unconvinced. He struggled against it for years. Not until the completion of His own initiation at the end of 1909 did he understand how perfectly he was bound to carry out this work. Again and again He turned away from it, took it up for a few days or hours, then laid it aside. He even attempted to destroy its value, to nullify the result.* Yet, after his acceptance of Liber Legis, Crowley tirelessly laboured for the rest of his life to promulgate it.

In 1913, Crowley was initiated into Ordo Templi Orientis by Theodor Reuss. The following year Crowley was advanced to the X° and became head of O.T.O. in Great Britain and Ireland. That same year, while on a trip to Moscow, he wrote the Gnostic Mass.

The Abbey of Thelema

In the 1920's, Crowley began calling his belief system "Thelema" meaning "Will." Many would be surprised to find that the concepts of "Thelema" and "Do What Thou Will" did not arrive from Crowley or his "Liber Legis." Yet, in 1920 along with Leah Hirsig, Crowley founded "The Abbey of Thelema" in Cefalú, Sicily, an experimental commune based on the principles of Thelema as described in the works of Rabelais. The inscription on the gate to The Abbey of Thelema was taken from his works:

Grace, honour, praise, delight,
   Here sojourn day and night.
      Sound bodies lined

With a good mind,
Do here pursue with might
Grace, honour, praise, and delight

François Rabelais, a professor of Medicine and a monk at Fontenay-le-Comte of the Franciscan order, wrote a series of popular fictional books in 1532 that were condemned as heretical by the academics at the Sorbonne and banned by the Roman Catholic Church. They tell the satirical and amusing tale of two giants, a father named Gargantua and his son Pantagruel. In the stories, the giant Gargantua builds The Abbey of Thelema has a swimming pool, a house cleaner service, and no clocks in sight, as Gargantua feels God would want his servants to enjoy themselves. Harmless fun is poked at humourless and austere monastic institutions and their outdated morals and mode of dress. Belying the humour was a very real concept of the utopian ideal society:

Was Aleister Crowley a Satanist?

All their life was spent not in laws, statutes, or rules, but according to their own free will and pleasure. They rose out of their beds when they thought good; they did eat, drink, labour, sleep, when they had a mind to it and were disposed for it. None did awake them, none did offer to constrain them to eat, drink, nor to do any other thing; for so had Gargantua established it. In all their rule and strictest tie of their order there was but this one clause to be observed, "DO WHAT THOU WILT;" because men that are free, well-born, well-bred, and conversant in honest companies, have naturally an instinct and spur that prompteth them unto virtuous actions, and withdraws them from vice, which is called honour. Those same men, when by base subjection and constraint they are brought under and kept down, turn aside from that noble disposition by which they formerly were inclined to virtue, to shake off and break that bond of servitude wherein they are so tyrannously enslaved; for it is agreeable with the nature of man to long after things forbidden and to desire what is denied us.

For teaching these things, the press labelled him evil and a heretic just like Rabelais. In 400 years, not much had changed.

Yet, some discipline was needed, as it was magical school. The general programme included daily Salutes to the Sun, a study of Crowley's writings, regular yogic and ritual practices that were to be recorded, as well as general domestic labour. The object was for students to devote themselves to the 'Great Work' of discovering and manifesting their 'True Wills.' Crowley's methods for breaking down this social conditioning of those enrolled at The Abby were extreme. He pioneered a method that was so effective, that both the British Secret Service and C.I.A. later adopted it as their deconditioning method. In it, Crowley would administer drugs to a willing participant who had the method fully explained to them. They were then closed in a room with graphic and scary Pompeii style images and Thelemic slogans painted on the walls. It resulted in the release of their fear and repression. Some of Timothy Leary's later LSD Experiments were based on Crowley's work at The Abby.

In 1923, after one of the acolytes at The Abbey died from a chest infection, a hysterical woman built it up in the press to have resulted from a supposed animal sacrifice. He was expelled from Italy by order of Mussolini due to pressure from the press.

In 1926, Crowley visited Gurdjieff, who firmly repudiated Crowley.

In 1935, Crowley lost a libel suit he brought against the artist Nina Hamnett for calling him a black magician in her 1932 book, "Laughing Torso." The main witness for the defence was the same hysterical woman who had libelled him in the Italian newspapers. Nina Hamnett had fought against a libel charge by using libel. For some reason the courts allowed this libellous testimony. Crowley had lost his personal fortune to the costs of the court system and was bankrupt. Members of his various magickal orders contributed funds towards his upkeep and personal welfare.

Crowley the Spy

During the WW1, Crowley wrote demeaning and antagonistic letters to the Germans in the American press. The British press, not understanding the workings of disinformation and derision, denounced him as a traitor in the popular press.

During World War II, Crowley lead rituals on the English cliffs, as did Queen Elisabeth 1st over 400 years earlier, designed to invoke bad weather to keep the Germans out of England until they could assemble their new air force for the famous Battle of Britain. Some of the magicians associated with this ritual died due to the amount of energy and effort they put into using magick to protect their country.

Crowley In Her Majesty's Service

British Secret Service agent Ian Fleming, the man who wrote the James Bond stories, was amongst those who proposed a disinformation plot in which Crowley supplied Nazi official Rudolf Hess with faked horoscopes and false information about an alleged pro-German circle in Britain, via an MI5 agent. Keen to collect this information Hess flew to Scotland himself, crashing his plane on the moors near Eaglesham, and was captured.

Fleming then suggested Crowley as an interrogator, using his methods of social deprogramming developed at The Abbey of Thelema, to determine the influence of astrology on other Nazi leaders. Fleming also suggested that Britain could use Crowley as a carrier for Enochian code through Europe the way Queen Elizabeth 1st had done with John Dee. Even after all, of this service to his country he was again labelled a traitor in the popular press.

Retirement and Death

In 1945, at the end of the war, he retired to Netherwood, a boarding house for old people in Hastings, England. On December 1, 1947, at the age of 71, and with his nine-year-old son Ataturk by his bed, Aleister Crowley died. His ashes were scattered on the property of Karl Germer, Crowley's successor to the OTO.

Sympathy For The Devil

Yet, with in 10 years of his death, the spirit of Crowley was set to rise again. He understood that a belief system has a used by date and that the era of sin and guilt was on the way out and that a new era of liberation was on the way in. Less than twenty years after his death he became an icon to the freedom seeking generation of the 60's.

In the 1950s, Kenneth Anger produced a series of counter culture films loosely based on the myth of Crowley. In the 60s, The Rolling Stones wrote a song about him and Rosaleen Norton and their modern day media Witch hunts called "Sympathy For the Devil." The Beatles featured him on their "Sergeant Pepper's Lonely Hearts Club Band," album cover. Using one of Crowley's pseudonyms, they implied in the title track's lyrics that Crowley had influenced all of the lives of all of the people featured on the cover. *"It was twenty years ago today, that Sergeant Pepper taught this band to play."* Led Zeppelin and Black Sabbath iconised him in their work. Jimmy Page eventually bought Boleskine House. Robert Anton Wilson and Timothy Leary wrote about his hallucinogenic experiences. To the free love generation of the 60's Crowley's work embodied the desire for free uncensored expression and the need for social rebellion to break with the past.

Crowley became a legend. The stories, both negative and positive have become bigger than the man. However, it must never be forgotten that Crowley was only human, flawed and frail, sickly, and persecuted, yet he achieved so much in his life. He could be as repellent as he was magnetic. He deliberately antagonised those who were slandering him and gave them more ammunition in the false hope that they would embarrass themselves by creating ridiculous stories that no one would believe. Yet, just as in the story of The Emperor's New Clothes, the fools not wishing to appear foolish would only see him that way. He sort the best in human nature and forgot to allow for the worst of its stupidity. He was childish, he was arrogant, and he was often rude to his supporters and admirers. Still, he was a man with a vision for the future. Crowley is mythic, but there are aspects of this myth that are very positive. His appetite for life, his resilience, he was determine to challenge himself and the world around him. He was a warrior, not afraid to challenge anything, spirit or human and because of these things, at great cost to himself, he achieved his goal of changing the way that society looks at itself and others forever.

He was far from a perfect man but he was an alchemist who performed The Great Work of liberating the human mind from its self-imposed slavery and thus magically enabling the world to change.

Chapter 7

Do Witches Hold Sabbats?

YES!

The word "Sabbat" was not used by Witches before the advent of "The Malleus Maleficarum," it was placed in there as a bastardisation of the Hebrew word "Sabbath." Ironically, "Sabbat" became a term that was given arbitrarily to the eight main Pagan solar celebrations. Lunar celebrations are called Esbats. There are 13 of these each year. Buildings where Witches held meetings were described in the Malleus as synagogues. Jewish people and practitioners of The Craft were lumped in together as heretics with several other groups and it became a bit of a blur. Nevertheless, the quick and easy name to describe these eight main yearly festivals has stuck.

Witches do not think of one day as more holy than the next. Once your awareness opens up you cannot live in a world where spirituality is only something for Sundays. Every moment and everything is sacred.

The cycle of the Sabbats is commonly referred to as the Wheel of the Year. It is our small wheel in the greater cycle of things. The small cog in the larger machine of the universe. All things are cyclical; this life is cyclical in order to fit in with the arrangement of the universe.

What are the Sabbats?

Sabbats are the markers of this earthly cycle.

The word "Sabbat" comes from the same root word as the Hebrew word "Sabbath," meaning a period of rest. However, this word is originally Babylonian, designating the quarter days of the lunar cycle. That is the full, new, first and last quarters, which occur about every seven days. It slipped into the Hebrew language to denote their day of rest and prayer, which occurred every seventh day. Sabbat became a term that was given arbitrarily to the Pagan holidays, that is Witchcraft's "Holy Days," during the inquisitions.

Witches Kept Complex Almanacs

In order to understand these festivals you must remember that they are not man-made. It is not a calendar anniversary of dates that have any historical import, nor are they randomly chosen social institutions, such as Labour Day or Father's Day. The calendar that we currently use, The Gregorian Calendar, has only been used for the last 420 years. The Catholic Church instituted it in 1582. It is clumsy and not terribly accurate and does not fit in with the days, seasons and the cycles. It has had to be readjusted several times since its inception. The most famous of which is the addition of the arbitrary leap year. More on this later. The wheel of the year is much older. In fact, these eight Sabbats existed long before humanity did, as they have always been a basic part of how this planet works. These holidays simply mark the turning points in the cycles of nature. Our planet spins on its axis that is tilted to its orbit around the sun. So once a year this creates a twenty-four hour period with a night that is the longest night of the year, and the shortest day. This is the winter solstice whilst in the opposite hemisphere; we have its opposite, the longest day of the year, and the shortest night, the summer solstice. These are the two "solstices." Six months later, or half way around the wheel of the year we have the opposite situation. Half way in between this, we have a balancing point, two more days that are equally important. Each spring and autumn there comes a day when the hours between sunrise and sunset and sunset and sunrise are exactly equal. They are called the "equinoxes."

The Biological Clock That Makes Us All Tick?

No matter how sheltered our lives are from nature, nor how urbanized we become, all of our lives are governed by a built in biological clock. Its ticking is there in all life forms, animal, mineral and vegetable. Its rhythm may get sluggish due to environment, or lack there of, and lifestyle. Yet, the fact that it exists cannot be argued. Its ticking is metered by solar and lunar revolutions as seasons and cycles. The more primitive the life form, the more obvious the effect of these annual seasonal changes.

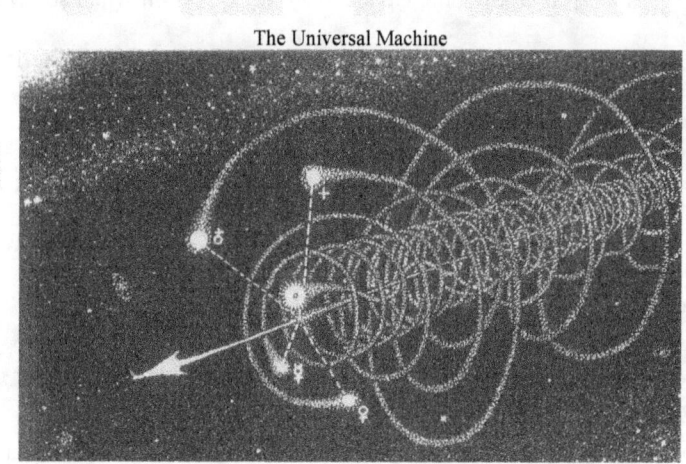
The Universal Machine

The biological clock is most evident in the cycles of reproduction of the species. Agrarian cultures, of which Witches were the spiritual consultants, depended upon these cycles for their lives. Those of us who have everyday dealings with gardens, animals, and insects and those of us in primary industries today, are more attuned to these than urbanites locked into an artificial daily office routine. Nevertheless, wherever we live and work, we are affected by these cycles. By a Witch becoming conscious of these cycles and hooking the cogs of their personal cycles in to this vast universal machine, they are better able to accomplish their magickal will using the momentum of these huge forces.

Is The Effect On Humans Of Celestial Cycles Only Minor Or Imagined Superstition?

The 2007 Anglers Almanac cites the following studies. In 1792 it was observed and documented that the brain of head surgery patients would "swell and swage according to the tides" under the silver plate covering the operation orifice. U.S. police statistics have revealed a correlation between the lunar cycle and violence, with peaks occurring during the ☽ new and ○ full moon phases. For thousands of years, people whose lives have been dependent on fish as their staple diet have observed the link of behavioural and reproduction cycles of marine life directly with the cycles of the moon. This does not just apply to fish. The work of Jane Hardwick-Collins has pointed out that the mysterious surprise "second ovulation" cycle of women, which mucks up the rhythm method of contraception, occurs only when the phase of the moon is the same as the phase that occurred on the woman's birth date! In European coastal areas, human birth has often been linked with high tides and death to low tides. The nurseries are full at high tide and the morgues are full at low tide. Hence, the old expression when someone is dying naturally of old age, "He's going out with the tide." In the Western Pacific, some races believe the opposite that people die on an incoming tide, but that birth occurs on the outgoing tide. Research in 1973 suggested that lunar effects on the timing of human births could be explained in cultures without electricity, "Where the moon provides the principle night time illumination." The moon certainly affects reef fish spawning, which occurs on the outer edge of the reef on the ebb of the highest of the spring tides. The highest spring tides occur at or just after the ● New Moon and the ○ Full Moon. In winter, the higher of the two daily high tides will occur at night, the cycle reverses with the seasons. American biologist Frank Brown observed that oysters which normally open their shells at high tide, shipped from the coast to a laboratory more than 1000 km inland, and stored in a body of water without tides changed their daily rhythm to coincide with the moon's upper and lower transits, the equivalent of local "high water," in only 14 days! In another study, a colony of single celled alga, Hantzchia virgata, which in its natural environment recedes beneath the sand during periods of high water to escape foraging fish, then re-emerges after the tide abates, was transferred to a marine laboratory. In the laboratory, the alga continued to hide and emerge in concert with the moon's daily passage.

It is not the tides that trigger the behaviour so much as the moon itself, or rather the phase of the lunar cycle, in conjunction with the sun and the stars, which in turn affects the tides. Just like the tides, all living things, and the water they contain, are sensitive to subtle influences created by magnetic forces, electrical radiation, gravitational fields, barometric pressure, and even cosmic rays. An eleven-year study of potatoes showed their daily rhythm of metabolism occurs according to sidereal time or the position of the stars overhead.

Effect Of The Moon On Bodies of Water

As the moon is much closer to the earth than the sun is, its gravitational pull is much greater than the sun's. Generally, the earth's water pulls toward the moon, not the sun. However, when the sun, moon and earth become aligned, the combined gravitational pull on the water of our planet is at its greatest, creating spring tides i.e. the highest high tides and the lowest low tides. These occur twice in a lunar month, when the moon passes between the earth and the sun (●New Moon) and when the moon is on the other side, putting the earth between it and the sun (O Full Moon). When the moon is at 90° to the line between the sun and the earth, the gravitational effect on our planets water is at its lowest, resulting in neap tides i.e. the lowest high tides and the highest low tides. These also occur twice in a lunar month, during the ◐ First and ◑ Last Quarters. The lunar effect, and not the tides themselves, is believed to be a major controlling factor in the biological behavioural patterns of life on earth.

Apparent Southern and Northern Hemisphere Moon Reversal

In the southern hemisphere, more things are reversed than just the seasons. In The Southern Witches Almanac, we have to reverse the seasonal Sabbats from north to south. That is why we swap the standard symbols for the ◐ First Quarter and the ◑ Last Quarter in this almanac. The standard symbols depicting the First and Last Quarters of the moon, are based on how observers in the northern hemisphere see the moon, thus they are not appropriate for this almanac. "The Southern Witches Almanac" uses the symbols that are correct to how most people in the southern hemisphere see the moon. For example, someone Tokyo looking up into the sky at a first quarter moon would face south and see the moon lit on the right side looking something like this ☽ which is the standard symbol for the first quarter. However, someone in Australia would face north to see the moon, which would appear to be lit on its left side it would look like this ☽. Therefore, the symbol of the horned moon ☽ ○ ☾ applies to the northern hemisphere only. In the southern hemisphere, the moon's horns turn inward giving our symbol a wide pregnant look. ☾ ○ ☽

Northern and Southern Inclination

However, the position of the moon can depend on the observer's latitude north or south of the equator, and the moon's extent of declination north or south of the celestial equator at the time. Not everyone in the southern hemisphere will see the first or last quarters the same way. Sometimes the crescent appears to lie on her back or front. This is because when the moon revolves around the earth, its orbit sends it north and south of the equator. When it is north of the Equator, it is in its northern declination the moon appears to lay on her back, points up ᨆ. When it is south of the Equator, it is in its southern declination and the crescent of the moon will appear with its points down ᨅ. Someone looking at the moon from northern

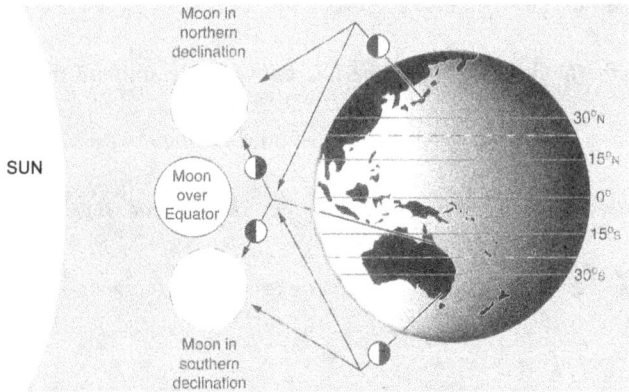

Australia when it is in its northern declination, will see the same shaped moon as someone in southern Australia, although much higher in the sky. When the moon is in its southern declination, the Australian observer will see it as the Tokyo observer sees it, but much higher in the sky and visa versa.

Major And Minor – As Above, So Below

Major times are when the moon is near its upper or lower transits. Moon Above is when the moon is above the observer's head. Moon Below is when the moon is on the other side of the earth quite literally beneath the observer's feet. Minor times occur when the moon is roughly halfway between its upper and lower transits. Add six hours to the start of a major time to find the approximate start of the following minor time. When sited major times are shown with a capital "M" and minor times with a lowercase "m."

The Moon, The Tides, The Sun, And The Stars

The earth is affected by three major types of time, lunar, solar and sidereal i.e. the revolution of the earth and sun in relation to the stars. Solar time manifests itself annually through the seasons and the eight Sabbats. Lunar time manifests itself monthly through the moon phases, esbats, and daily behavioural patterns. The effects of sidereal time on earth are less obvious but contribute to the rhythm, mood, and power of life. Daily oceanic and human tides are governed by the Lunar Day. Certain phenomena occur with precise regularity during the Lunar Cycle. To grasp the significance of this, you need to understand the relationship between Lunar Time and Solar Time.

Solar Time is based on: -

The rotation of the earth around its axis = 23 hours 56 minutes and 4 seconds = 1 day.

1) By running our day to our watches and other artificial timepieces, we loose 3 min 56 sec per day and we wonder why we have a feeling that we are running out of time. Allowing for the tilt on the axis to bring us back to the same position of the sun takes exactly 24 hours but does not allow for the natural movement of the day through the seasons, so we muck up our biological clock further by introducing daylight savings.

2) The orbit around the sun = 365 days 6 hours 9 minutes and 11 seconds = one year.

3) You can see from this why our leap years do not really fit either. This artificially forcing of time into neat non-varying increments is the basis of our Gregorian calendar system. This is very messy and needs to be more plastic, no matter which way you look at it. Given this, and the greater influence of the moon on our reproductive and agricultural cycles we can see why our wise ancestors opted for lunar calendars.

4) Luna Time is based on: -

5) A Lunar Day = 24 hours and 50 minutes measured in solar time. = One complete rotation of the moon around the earth. This is also called a Tidal Day and explains why the tides always occur an average 50 minutes later each day. Though the moon rises in the east and sets in the west, the moon's orbital motion is toward the east. Each day, the moon moves another 12

degrees toward the east on the sky's dome. From this view, the moon appears to move clockwise – widdershins - as it revolves from west to east around the earth.

6) A Lunar Month = 29 days 12 hours 44 minutes and 2.8 seconds, measured in solar time. = One complete revolution of the moon around the earth in the same way that the earth travels around the sun. The phases of the moon occur in a lunar month.

1) The Eight Phases Of The Moon, which occur in a lunar month, as seen from the southern hemisphere
2) New Moon;
3) Crescent Moon waxing (horns point away from the sun); Widdershins or Clockwise.
4) First Quarter;
5) Gibbous Moon waxing;
6) Full Moon;
7) Gibbous Moon waning;
8) Last Quarter;
9) Crescent Moon waning (horns point toward the sun). I.e. Deosial –

10) A Lunar Cycle = a little more than 18 solar years or 235 lunar months = One complete rotation of the phases of the moon until they recur on the same Gregorian calendar days as they did during the previous cycle. Often called a Saros or the cycle used to measure eclipses. That is why similar eclipses will occur every 18 years. There are 19 eclipses in a Saros, which means if there is a full moon on your birthday this year, there will be another one in 19 years time. There is 18.618 years in the moons node cycle or the place where the slightly elliptical orbits of the sun and the moon cross.

The Other Five Main Influences

These are the ancient, great and godlike influences on us of five other celestial bodies them being: -

1. ☿ **Mercury** – Travelling rapidly through the sky, often appearing to quickly change direction and to travel backward (i.e. going retrograde). He was attributed with affecting creatures of the earth in the areas of: Travel, Speed, Communication, Commerce, Healing, Intelligence, Trickery, and Magically manifesting your will swiftly.

2. ♀ **Venus** – Bright and attractive in the morning and evening skies, whose orbital patterns in relation to the earth form such a beautiful dance in the sky. She was attributed to affecting the earth with: Beauty, Love, Growth, Desire, All things pertaining to the feminine, Marriage and Materialism

3. ♂ **Mars** – Appearing red, strong at times in the evening sky with harsh transits behind the sun, and long retrogrades where he appears to travel in the opposite direction to everything else. He was attributed to affecting the earth with: Strength, Healing, Protection, Dynamic energy, Invincibility, Conflict, and all things pertaining to the masculine.

4. ♃ **Jupiter** – The larger of the two giants, appearing in our skies to be the conductor of the harmony of the spheres from which all of the other planets run to do his bidding. Large but distant in the night sky he was attributed to affecting the earth with: Magnanimousness, A sense of humour, Wealth, All things pertaining to a father and nobility.

5. ♄ **Saturn** – One of the two giants of our system, slow moving through the night sky, taking seven years to return to the same spot in the dome of the night sky and 20 years to form a perfect hexagram pattern with his son Jupiter often referred to as the Golden Clock. He is the farthest planet visible with the naked eye and appearing to be chained by his rings through a telescope. He was attributed to affecting the earth with; Time, Endings, Cycles, Repeating patterns, Judgment, Imprisonment, Wisdom, Age, and All things pertaining to a grandfather.

Witches Almanacs carefully chart the cycles of these seven celestial bodies in relation to the earth, each other and the ancient festivals. An almanac present their alignments, occlusions, retrogrades and eclipses and give them a general meaning of their combined energies available for the Witches use at that time. This helps them to plan your rituals, festivals, and spell work for the most auspicious times that will make the correct energies available to assist them in accomplishing their magickal will. They may then overlay this framework on the background of the constellations of the Zodiac.

Zodiac Constellations

The ancient star clusters we know as the twelve constellations of the Zodiac, continuously rotated through the night skies behind the dramas played out by our solar system. Two thousand five hundred years ago, when our common zodiacal system was first devised, it was noted that the appearance of certain constellations overhead occurred during significant times of the year, i.e. ♈Aires during the lambing season of the northern hemisphere and ♌Leo when the lions would come closer to the towns - and hence were given their names. Their influence on the earth has been noted and charted. These became the velvety star spangled tablecloths on which the planets in our solar system served up their banquet to us.

Their influence is as follows: -

- ♒**Aquarius:** Idealism, Humanitarianism, Innovation, Groups, and Organizations.

- ♓ **Pisces:** Mystical, Airy, Dreamy, Contemplative, and Musical

- ♈**Aires:** Potent, Fiery, Pioneering. Active. Impulsive, and Challenging

- ♉**Taurus**: Comfort, Pleasure, Building, Creating, and Material Possessions

- ♊**Gemini:** Dichotomy, Investigating, Inquiring, Communicating, Artistic, and Indecisive.

- ♋**Cancer:** Introspective, Patriotic, Community, and Home

- ♌**Leo:** Ego, Loyalty, Sunny, Leadership, Achievements, and Showmanship

- ♍ **Virgo:** Order, Organization, Critical, Efficiency, and Analytical.

- ♎**Libra:** Balance, Justice, Partnerships, Peacekeeper, and Middle Ground.

- ♏**Scorpio:** Secrets, Mysteries, Power, Death & birth, and Revenge.

- ♐**Sagittarius:** Adventure, Travel, Philosophy, Sports, and Risk Taking

- ♑**Capricorn:** End of the Cycle, Keeper of ancient wisdom, Business, Organizer, Achieving, Status, Family

This zodiacal wheel of the year sets the mood or the flavour of the Witch's spell work. The planets will move through these constellations at their own pace. The moon, however, moves into a new zodiacal constellation every 3 days. The moon will always be ○ Full in the constellation that is opposite it on the wheel, to the sign that the sun is in and will always be New in the same sign that the sun is in. E.g. ☉Sun in ♍ Virgo = ○ Full Moon in ♓ Pisces and ● New Moon in ♍ Virgo. These can vary according to whether the zodiac wheel you use has been calculated on Heliocentric being the position of the stars as they were when the zodiac was used in ancient Greece 2500 years ago, or Sidereal the position of the stars overhead

The Wheel Of the Year

The cycle of the Sabbats is commonly referred to as the Wheel of the Year. It is our small wheel in the greater cycle of things. All things are cyclical; this life is cyclical in order to fit in with the arrangement of the universe. The wheel is thus split into two halves (or four quarters) for summer/autumn and winter/spring. The two halves are ruled by a Light God when the days are getting longer and a Dark God when the nights are getting longer. The wheel is then divided at the cross quarters. The two equinoxes and two solstices are the minor Sabbats, and the cross-quarter days are the major Sabbats. These bisect the quarters falling at the exact midpoint of each. With these in place, a diagram of the cycle of the year begins to look like an eight-spoked wheel, thus "Wheel of the Year." This eight-spoked symbol is a sacred symbol in several religions. Books often list arbitrary dates for the major Sabbats, but there exist astronomical methods for putting the cross-quarter days more precisely in-between the minor Sabbats. (or you can just check with your local observatory) When calculating dates remember the rather inaccurate Christen calendar that we use today was not used by our ancient members of The Craft. They used the great almanac over head.

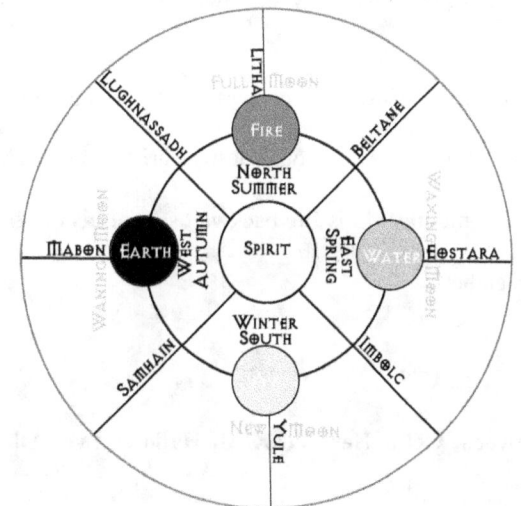

The cross quarters were regarded as more important than the solstices or equinoxes because this is the mystical point of change, the crossroad. The seasons change on the old calendars at this point. It is the time when things have the most potential according to the I-Ching. It has swung out as far as it can. Things on this day become not really one thing or another. The season will change on that day. The angelic guardians of the season change post, so as to speak, and things can slip through. For example, it is not really summer any more and it not yet autumn and this is true for each day of the true change of season. This is the point of magick! The vale between the worlds becomes the thinnest and interaction with other dimensions is most likely.

It is interesting to note that in most agrarian societies their days start at sundown on the previous day so that this point of change would happen in the middle of the allocated day. Many of the festivals will be given over a 2 day period i.e. the summer solstice occurs between the 22-23 of December where as, if the day starts at sundown, you get the full solstice in one calendar day rather than splitting it up by beginning and ending at an arbitrary midnight. Therefore, Beltane in the southern hemisphere should actually be from the sundown on the night of October 31 through to sundown on November 1. This festival is flipped for the northern hemisphere due to our opposing seasons and becomes Halloween or Samhain.

These Sabbats are solar festivals, and so their mythology illustrates the life cycle of the God principle in nature, which we associate with the sun. As we have also stated the 52 Luna phases are also Sabbats. The 13 Luna cycles illustrate the life cycle of the Goddess principle in nature.

There are 8 Solar Sabbats and 13 Luna Esbats, or full moon celebrations, a year. Eight is to thirteen gives us the phi ratio of 6.18, of which the pentagram is the visual representation. While the Esbats are generally reserved for magickal workings, the eight Solar Sabbats are celebrated in most agrarian cultures as harvest and planting festivals. They take their names and some of their purposes from a variety of Pagan cultures.

It is ironic that Christians converted and retained many of the Pagan festivals into Christian ones. Yule became Christmas even though Jesus Christ could not have been born in a mid winters eve. If you count the years and months of his life backwards from his death, it comes closer to the start of October than the end of December.

THE SABBATS

Halloween, Celtic New Year, All Hallows Eve, All Saints Day, Samhain (sow'en) –means "The End of Summer"–

Major Sabbat: - The Change from Autumn to Winter.Is approx May 1st - 15 degrees of Taurus in the Southern Hemisphere or approx November 1st - 15 degrees of Scorpio in the northern hemisphere.

Mythology: The Day of the Dead and Divination. The Goddess mourns her marriage for the duration of winter to the Dark God. She arrives upon the earth with her fairy minions from the under world and the veil between the worlds stands open for them for the night. The Dark God takes up the ruler ship of winter, leading the underworld minions of the fairy realms on a Wild Hunt upon the earth.

This is the most magical night of the year. Exactly opposite Beltane on the wheel of the year. It is Beltane's dark twin. Samhain is The Craft's New Year and the Feast of the Dead. Death is necessary for rebirth. It is a time to honour loved ones who have passed on, by setting a place for them at the evening meal. It is also a time to commune with other worldly beings. Yet, the New Year then as today is celebrated with chaotic noisy festivities bringing on a symbolic end of the world and a birth of a new. The trick or treating is an echo of this and of The Wild Hunt.

Yule, Midwinter

Minor Sabbats: - Winter Solstice – Is approx 22 June in the Southern hemisphere and the December 23 in the northern Hemisphere.

Mythology: The death of the God of light - On the 23rd day of December the sun does not even crest the horizon in Ireland. It is a day with out sunlight. The longest night. The Yule log is burnt in our darkest hour, representing the God Lug laying down his life in the battle to maintain warmth and life for us. On this day, the wise God Lug, does battle with the darkness on its home territory, and dies on the 23rd, 'The No Name Day', the day with out sun. Then late on the 24th the sun/son raises and is reborn again and on the next day, 25th is the celebration of this The Christians adopted this as Christ-mass or Christ's Birth… The tree is decorated as a symbol that the body that was burnt in hell is now raised in immortal glory. Gifts of food are given as a reflection of the gift he gave for us. By imitating this generosity, others will remember us forever, for our great love of humanity. Sound familiar. This is Yuletide. 'Tis the season to be jolly. The Sun is reborn, it is generous to all, and we are its children. We can reflect it's light, the shining human spirit, into the darkest hopeless hearts from the 23rd to the 25th and indeed through out all of the rest of the year. Evergreens, holly, ivy, and mistletoe are symbolic of immortality and resurrection as they are still living and green in the dead of winter.

Imbolc (im'molc or im'bolc) means, "in the belly of the mother," or **Oimelc means** "milk of ewes," for it is also **Lambing Season, Candelmas,** and **Saint Brigit's Day**

Major Sabbat: The Beginning of Spring – 2nd August or 15 degrees of Leo in the Southern Hemisphere, or February 2nd or 15 degrees of Aquarius in the Northern Hemisphere

Mythology: Imbolc is the beginning of spring. Sacred fires are lit to help warm and wake the earth. Historically, Imbolc was an Irish Holy Day dedicated to Brigit or Bride, goddess of creativity, smithing, and healing especially midwifery. Since she symbolized the fire of birth, the glow of good health, the fire of the forge, and burning poetic inspiration she came to personify the new warmth and life of spring. The Roman Church adopted this symbolism as Candlemas, the day to bless all the church candles the newly blessed candles are used to bless the throats of parishioners, keeping them from colds, and sore throats. Maidens dressed in white are adorned with crowns of blessed candles.

Eostre (Eestr'a) – **Ostra, Easter, Lady's Day**,

Minor Sabbat: Full moon closest to the Vernal equinox around 22nd September in the Southern Hemisphere or around the March 22nd in the Northern Hemisphere.

Mythology: The earth has recovered from winter and is in full bloom. Eggs and bunnies symbolise this abundant and fertile state. It was essentially a fertility ritual to ensure the success of the crops and the flock. It dates back to Assyrian times when it was sacred to Ishtar, later Teutonic lunar Goddess Eostre the Goddess of sex and death and Isis, who was the first Immaculate Conception. Many ancient legends recount a Goddess returning from an underworld spontaneously pregnant without the need of her mate at this time of the year. The Incas celebrated this festival to their goddess with a harelip. It was the best time for a woman to give birth to ensure the child's survival through a harsh winter. Eostara is nine months before Yule, the festival of rebirth birth. The gift of an egg dyed red at this time ensured that your wealth would continue to grow.

Beltaine, Beltane, Bealtaine, Bealtuinn, meaning "Bel-fire" or "the fire of the Celtic God of Light, Bel, Beli, or Belinus or the Middle Eastern God "Baal" May **Day, Cetsamhain** literally "opposite Samhain," **Walpurgisnacht** and **Roodmas**

Major Sabbat: The Beginning of summer. Approx November 1st, 15 degrees of Scorpio in the Southern Hemisphere or 15 degrees of Taurus, or around May 1st in the Northern Hemisphere.

Mythology: Beltane is principally a time of unashamed human sexuality and joy. Weddings are frequently held on or around Beltane. Beltane, the start of summer, is the most important Sabbat after Samhain. Its primary focus is not a fertility celebration; rather it is a celebration of joy and life. Named for the Celtic fire god Bel, the Light God takes over ruler ship from the Dark God. The lighting of fires celebrates his restoration. These fires have healing properties, and sky-clad Craft practitioners jump through the flames.

Other Beltane customs include: Morris dances, Maypoles, beating the boundaries around your property and repairing fences and boundary markers, young girls bathing their faces in the dew of May day morning to get beauty and retain youth, milkmaids processions with chimney sweeps and other costumes, archery tournaments, sword dances, feasting, music, and drinking. Then of course, there are the greenwood marriages of couples that will spend the entire night making love in the forest until they greet the new May sunrise. They will return with garlands of flowers to decorate their homes.

Midsummer, Litha means "the opposite of Yule," **Night of the Verbena** (Vervain)

Minor Sabbat: Also known as Summer solstice – approx. Dec 23rd in the Southern Hemisphere and approx. June 22nd in the Northern Hemisphere.

Mythology: Litha is another fire festival with large bonfires lit after sundown to provide light to the revellers and for warding off mischievous fairy folk. Midsummer's eve represented the apex of the God's life. Variously called the Oak King, Jack in the Green or Pan with a lower torso of a satyr and cloven hooves and horns he was the archetypal Wild Man of the wood, the King of the fairies. Following their King on a romp through the countryside made this night second only to Halloween for its importance to the Wee Folk, who especially enjoyed playing tricks on a fine summer's night. If you wished to see fairy folk, this is the best night to do it. You only had to rub fern seed onto your eyelids at the stroke of midnight. Carrying a bit of rue in your pocket, or wearing your jacket inside out, can protect you from spiteful fairies. If you can't do that and you must travel on midsummer's eve you must stay on the old strait ley lines, till you get to your destination other wise you may be lead astray by the fairy folk and get lost forever.

On this Midsummer's Eve when the faerie folk were so active, it was a time to strengthen the magickal boundary of the city. This was called "Setting the Watch." To do this the streets were lined with lanterns, and people carried lanterns on poles as they wandered from one bonfire to another accompanied by Morris dancers, and people dressed as a unicorn, a dragon, and six hobbyhorse riders.

Other things to do on Midsummer's Eve included decking the front door with birch, fennel, St. John's wort, orpin, and white lilies. These five plants are thought to have special magical properties on this night. However, some accounts say it is rue, roses, St. John's wort, vervain, and trefoil. St. John's wort is picked and used by young women to use it in divining a future lover. Staying up throughout the shortest night is popular especially in various spooky places. If keeping watch in the centre of a circle of standing stones did not result in either death or madness then you can gain the inspiration to become a great poet or bard.

The two symbols of this Holy Day are the spear, the symbol of the Sun God in his glory, and the cauldron, the symbol of the Goddess in her bounty. Swapping the words of the great rite for "As the spear is to the male, so the cauldron is to the female."

Lughnasadh (loo'na sah or loog' nsah) **Lammas, First Harvest Festival, Loaf-mass, First fruits, Tailltean**.

Major Sabbat: – the start of Autumn approx. February 2nd or 15 degrees of Aquarius in the Southern Hemisphere or 15 degrees of Leo, or approximately August 1st in the Northern Hemisphere

Mythology: Aging God

Lughnasadh is and was the time of the first harvest, when the first fruits harvested were given as a token of thanks to the gods. The Christian Church also assumed this, as this was the day on which loaves of bread were baked from the first grain harvest and left on the altars as offerings. It is a time of sacrifice and thanksgiving for the sacrifices that allow us to continue. It is also a feast to commemorate the funeral games of the Irish Sun God Lugh, hosted to commemorate the death of his foster mother, Taillte. That is why the Lughnasadh celebrations in Ireland are often called the Tailltean. One feature of the festival is the "Tailltean marriages," a marriage that lasted for only a year and a day or until next Lammas. At that time, the couple could decide to discontinue the arrangement by standing back to back and walking away from one another, thus bringing the Tailltean marriage to a formal close. Lammastide was also the traditional time of year for craft festivals. A ceremonial highlight of such festivals was The Catherine Wheel. A wagon wheel was taken to the top of a hill, covered with tar, set on fire, and ceremoniously rolled down the hill. Symbolizing the end of summer, the flaming disk representing the Sun disappearing into the valley behind the hills

Mabon, Harvest Home, Second harvest, Michaelmas

Minor Sabbat: Autumnal equinox - approx. the March 22nd in the Southern Hemisphere and approx. September 22nd in the Northern Hemisphere

Mythology: This is the day of the year when the God of Light is defeated by his twin and alter ego, the God of Darkness. The autumnal equinox is the only day of the whole year when Light is vulnerable and it is possible to defeat him. This is the sacrifice of the spirit of vegetation, John Barleycorn, occurring one quarter of the year after Midsummer. Often this corn spirit was believed to reside in the last sheaf of grain harvested, which was dressed in good clothes, addressed by name, and then woven into a wicker-like man form. This effigy was then cut and carried from the field, and usually burned, amidst much rejoicing. This annual mock sacrifice of a large wickerwork figure, representing the vegetation spirit, may have been the origin of the misconception that Druids made human sacrifices. The Spirit of the Barley, Whiskey, is also readily consumed during this festival.

Mabon is the name give to the festival in modern times. It is the name of a Celtic god who was imprisoned only to return at a later date. The name does not appear to have been historically attributed to any festival.

These Sabbats are more than an excuse for a whole bunch of unruly Pagans to get together and to have a piss up. The Sabbats should be studied by the serious Craft student. They come to know this flow and its feel it colours its warmth's and its nuances. This cycle will be reflected in every life cycle, and every thing in every life on the planet.

Most indigenous cultures teach a form of it. To the North American Indians, the Wheel of the Year becomes The Medicine Wheel. They still use its practical application to heal and sort out life's problems. For example, an illness will follow its personal Wheel. Fever flares and things can become very chaotic for the organism. We could say this illness is in its Litha/Midsummer mode. If the illness is very bad, the sick individual will hallucinate just as the people saw fairy folk at Litha. Nevertheless, a student of The Craft will know that it has reached it peak. The healer can then help move the illness through its life cycle more quickly by doing things to aid the onset of its next season, Lammas, the first harvest, by feeding the ill person with very fresh good quality food.

Another situation in which this cyclical understanding of life can be used was expressed by a North American Indian friend of mine, Richard Little-Feather. He told me this amusing story: *"My neighbour stormed into my place very hot under the collar, in his midsummer (Litha) mode saying, "Your fence is falling over onto my yard." Therefore, I moved him quickly to the cross-quarter (Lammas) by offering him a cuppa and giving him a bite to eat, whilst we discussed it. Then I moved him to the cooler autumnal equinox (Mabon) mode by gently reminding him that we were equal in this as we shared the declining fence. He thought about this for a while and he cooled right down and stopped talking to me altogether. He had moved very quickly to his 'Day of the Dead' (Samhain) season. So, I thought if he is going to move through all of these seasons so quickly then I would assist him to keep moving quickly so that we could get a quick resolution of the problem. To do this, I assured him that he wasn't all alone and then I offered to help him. Reminding him, as we do each other at midwinter that we were neighbours and we must look out for each other's welfare. He left and nothing was said or done for a while. The cycle slowed right down. He was going through a long midwinter mode on this. Therefore, I stuck my head over the fence about a week later and decide to move him to the next cross-quarter mode of 'The Return of the Light.' (Imbolc) I literally said to him, " Any light at the end of the tunnel regarding this old fence?" which started a discussion of our finances and we began to plan to fix the fence and gave it a starting date and that will be this little problem's day of rebirth (Eostra). Well probably have a BBQ to celebrate when it is fixed to take it right through to the final cross-quarter (Beltane) and completely finished this messy little cycle."*

This can be applied to all interpersonal relationships, like mothers communicating with their teenage children and loving relationships. It is as equally applicable to helping restore illness to health, finances, and work situations.

By studying and gaining an understanding of these cycles and how they affect and can be applied to their daily life, Witches are utilising a slice of knowledge essential to our well being, which has been forgotten in recent times.

Chapter 8

Do Witches Dance Naked At Their Sabbats?

YES! Occasionally

This is called a "Skyclad" working. It literally means "Clad In The Sky" and therefore there is nothing acting as a blockage between you and nature or between you and spirit. Thus, it enables one to better raise and direct magickal energy. This is a legitimate custom that pre-dates modern attitudes towards the human body.

It is a sacred state. Many Witches see the naked female body as representing the Goddess, and the naked male body as representing the God. It is a reminder that The Sacred exists in all of us. Many Pagans do not accept the standard Western moral taboos regarding the naked human body. They regard these taboos as unhealthy and unnatural. It removes blockages to ego and rank and station. All are equal. There are no social distinctions when clothing is laid aside. All are as we come into this world and leave it. It makes an empowering and positive affirmation that there is nothing shameful about the human form and that we are not slaves to sin and guilt. It says that we are the other people and not the race of the people that are afflicted with inherent and unhealthy personal shame. You do not have to have a good body to feel comfortable participating in a Skyclad ritual. The idea of conforming to some impossible ideal of physical beauty is a form of cultural imprinting. Witches are aware of this and consciously reject it.

Other than holding hands in the circle, people rarely touch each other in a skyclad ritual. Hands are kept to oneself, unless clearly and unambiguously invited. If anyone breaches trust and respect in a skyclad ritual they are asked to leave and are never allowed to attend another.

Skyclad workings are not orgies. Skyclad rituals are no more sexual in nature than clothed rituals. Being skyclad during ritual does not ever imply a sexual invitation or expectation. No sex is involved unless the stated specific purpose of the ritual is as a sexmagick ritual. It is recommended that only experienced ritualists participate in sexmagick. It is considered to be an advanced form of magick that is usually only practised by couples or in small closed rituals. Skyclad rituals are very respectful. In closed covens, working skyclad can foster feelings of trust and equality. People do look at each other. They are not

Alexander and Maxine Saunders coven became famous for getting their clothes off and being media friendly

A young Janet Farrar at her Alexandrian initiation

blindfolded or have their eyes closed. However, there should never be anything sleazy about it. It is up to the individual if they feel uncomfortable in this regard to put their clothes back on or quietly leave the circle. It is acceptable to put clothes back on for any reason what so ever at any time, if the individual feels cold or emotionally uncomfortable or simply changes their mind. It is expected that the individual will do this quietly and without a fuss so as to not disturb other participants. Issues can and should be discussed later. A good example of a skyclad ritual was filmed by the National Geographic in the "Taboo" series entitled "Nudity" of my Sydney coven performing an Esbat.

Being skyclad in any ritual is optional. It is the individual's and the group's choice whether or not to work this way. No stigma is attached to those who choose not to disrobe during skyclad rituals or change their minds and put their clothes back on. Not all groups or covens work skyclad. Most do. Some Pagan festivals are 'clothing optional' this means the individual can be dressed, undressed, wear body ochre, paint themselves, wear masks etc. At clothing-optional events, there may be times when clothing is compulsory. For example, naked people may not be permitted in kitchens for health and safety reasons. Most large organised festivals have a dress code written into their 'Code of Conduct' issued to attendees. Skyclad rituals occur in different contexts: small groups in private homes, large public Pagan festivals, in same-sex groups, mixed groups, and family-based covens. Pagans are very protective of children. No ethical group or teacher will let an under 18-year-old participate in a sky-clad ritual. As the Pagan Awareness Network or P.A.N. points out: *"This is for the protection of the child as well as the group. Witches get enough bad press as it is, and nobody wants to face hysterical accusations of paedophilia or ritual abuse."* If a person is under 18, and really believes in working skyclad, there is nothing stopping them from practicing skyclad as a solitary with their parents permission, in the privacy of they own room with their door locked and the curtains drawn.

The following points are some that are outlined in a pamphlet created by the Pagan Awareness Network to educate newcomers about this facet of Pagan practices that some may find confronting:

Skyclad Law

- It is illegal for anyone to touch you in an inappropriate manner without your prior consent. This is true irrespective of whether you are at a clothed or a skyclad ritual.
- Laws exist in each state of Australia concerning public decency. It is illegal to be naked in a public place. A public place is any place you might reasonably expect to be seen by a member of the public. This can include private property. A back yard with high fences is unlikely to be regarded as a public place, but the front garden in view of the street is a different matter.
- Privacy is the key to any successful skyclad ritual.

Skyclad Etiquette

- Never make remarks about another person's physical appearance.
- Never take photos of people without their prior consent. This includes anyone in the background.
- What happens in the circle stays there. Do not discuss ritual occurrences with someone who was not there. Do not discuss what other people did at a ritual, unless it somehow affects you i.e. if you felt unsafe, have issues, and now want impartial advice.
- Never laugh at another naked. That is a big no-no in Pagan circles. It is considered a gross breach of etiquette to laugh or make deprecating remarks about another, as this debases the sacred context and group trust.
- Involuntary erections do not raise any eyebrows. Pagans know that there is nothing shameful or embarrassing about something as natural as human sexuality. As long as it is not occurring in a way, that is threatening or offensive. If any individual feels awkward or confronted by the situation, including the person with the erection, they have the option to leave.

For more information contact http:www.Paganawareness.net.au

Chapter 9

Why the Witch Hunts When The Bible Approves of Witches?

Does The Bible Prohibit Witchcraft?

NO!

The word "Witch" only occurs once in the Bible in Exodus 22:18 in most English translations: -

"Though shalt not preserve a Witch alive."

In Deut. 18:10, the masculine form of the word, is interpreted as *"Enchanter."*

These are interpretations of the words mekhashshepheh, the feminine form of the word, and mekhashshepheth, the masculine form of the word, which is more correctly translated as: -

"A POISONER" or "ONE WHO POISONS."

Witchcraft Approved of in the Bible

There are many examples of positive Witchcraft that is approved of in the bible. Here follow some of the most famous: -

- The so called 'Witch of Endor' in 1 Samuel chapter 28, was viewed favourably in the Bible as she spoke to the deceased prophet Elisha and delivered a message from God to King Saul.

- In the book of Tobias, in the Catholic Cannon, the angel of God teaches Tobias to cast spells using a fish's liver.

- Moses as the son of Pharaoh's daughter, and next inline for the throne of Egypt, studied high Pharaohnic magick, which he used to defeat Janees and Jambrees the Egyptian royal court's magick-practising priests and students of a lesser form of magick.

- Indeed it is thought provoking that the word "Ihowa," meaning "shaman" in the Alti-mountain ranges where Moses spent his 40-year exile, is very phonetically close to the biblical Aramaic word "YHVH" translated into English as "Jehovah." This implies that Moses may have used a combination of his Pharaohnic Magick training and indigenous shamanistic techniques (said to be an early form of the Cabbala) for his successful magickal battles in Egypt.

"Who's Afraid Of The Big Bad Witch?" - by

The Witch of Endor

- The Three Magi or magick-practising priests from the Far East were approved of in the New Testament for using their skills to identify the Messiah and for giving him expensive prophetic gifts signifying his life's path.

- Jesus himself did not disapprove of Witchcraft, magic or its associated skills otherwise he could not have performed any of his miracles. He was often accused of idolatry, necromancy and of being a magician. For example, in John 18:30, Pilate is "… answered and said unto him, "If he were not a magician we would not have delivered him up unto thee."" The term here used is "kakon poiwn" a technical term for dark magician! Yet this word some how becomes "malefactor" in the King James Version. It is translated into Latin by Theodotion and Tertullian as "malethicus," or magician! Also in Mark 3:22; Matthew 19:34; 12:24 he accepted the term and never denied it. In Luke 11:15 it says, "He casts out demons by means of foreign Gods." This was actually true as he uses an invocation to Eros, "Iao Adenoi" the Greek god of love, to exorcise a demon! He never spoke against magick nor Witchcraft.

Dr. M. D. Magee makes some very interesting points about Jesus the Magickan: -

Stories of magickians in ancient magical writings, many predating the first centaury, also fit the gospel accounts:

- Anointing or baptizing to signify special selection
- Being made a magickian by the descent of spirit
- Being declared a God
- Experiencing mystical phenomena in the wilderness
- Exorcism and miraculous cures
- Teaching with authority and no apparent formal education
- Calling followers, who joined him as if enchanted
- A wandering and holy man with dedicated faithful followers
- Becoming so famous as a miracle worker, that other magicians use their name
- Neglect of pedantic, man-made, laws that impose hardship rather than enlightenment, freedom or justice
- Associating with all walks of life, even low-life

- Initiation of followers into their own mystical variations.
- Twelve selected and given the powers including the authority to exorcise spirits
- Being seen transfigured in a vision, with supernatural beings, by several people.

It is only logical that when a person does the things that a magician does, using magical techniques, and has magical experiences, he may certainly be thought of as a magician. Jesus' enemies and some of his friends believed him to be a mage. There are over twenty instances of Jesus participating in what was accepted magickal practise at the time in the synoptic (Ordinary) gospels. These include: -

- The magi visiting the infant Jesus. This shows that other magickians are willing to do him homage as a great mage.
- The miracles in Mark were presented in a magical style
- The disciples attend as the magickian's apprentices.
- Mark 3:22-27; Matthew 10:25; John 7:20; 8:48, 52; 10:20; Mark 6:14 all imply that Jesus is possessed by the deceased John the Baptist, and is therefore practising necromancy, of which he was openly accused of several times.
- The story of the descent of the spirit as a dove accompanied by the disembodied voice at Jesus' baptism are common to other accounts of magickians contemporary with and preceding Jesus.
- The Eucharist as a God-eating ritual was common magickal practise, with its earliest forms in Egypt.

Some other supporting texts of Jesus being a Witch or a magician are: -

- The Quran 5:113 says that Jesus' miraculous healings, the raising of the dead and his making living birds from clay are called sorcery.
- The Hayat of al-Damiri calls Jesus an "enchanter, son of an enchantress."
- Mandæan texts call him a magickian, emanating from the planet Mercury, ruled over by the angel of all Magicians.
- Apocryphal works explain some of the puzzles of the gospels by stating that Jesus was a powerful magickian.
- In the Acts of Pilate, Pilate's wife has dreamt of Jesus as a sorcerer: "Did we not tell you he was a sorcerer? Behold! He has sent a dream to your wife."
- The East Indians in Acts of Thomas admire Thomas as a magickian.
- Paul is accused by the Greeks of being a sorcerer for persuading betrothed women to refuse to marry.

It should be duly noted that Jesus performed and instigated many magickal rituals. Christians are fond of saying, that Jesus works his miracles only by his own word, this is manifestly untrue in fact it is a lie. Here are some examples: -

- He made the clay for the blind man's eyes. Egyptians considered there was power in spittle. In Egyptian myth, Thoth healed Horus's blind eye with spit. Jesus simply copied this miracle. This miracle was widely known by the time that Vespasian became emperor as Vespasian had performedd this miracle several times himself. Jesus uses spit spells three times, once in John 9:6 and twice in Mark 7:33 and 8:23.
- He ritually fasted
- He instigated the ritual meal
- He told his disciples to use words of power including his name and ritual prayers

All just the same as rituals performed by other magicians contemporary to and preceding him.

Acts of the Apostles Chapters 8 and 13, indicate obvious similarities exist between the apostles and magicians and that the apostles' power equates with the feats performed by several magicians in antiquity. Acts does not deny that neither magick works nor does it state that it is evil, but says that it is a wrong system of ideas. Acts seeks to show that the Christian worldview is better and right. The distinction is arbitrary. It depends only, on which Gods are preferred. The only difference exists in the framework of understanding and the validity with which it is viewed. Believe that your magick is worked only through acceptable Gods and it is good. If it is worked through unacceptable gods, then it is obviously not. Yet, the phenomena of magick and religion are the same. The prominence of angels in Matthew, Luke, and Acts testifies to a belief in magic and its pre-biblical Persian Zoroastrian origins. Angelic names had magic power. The invocation of angels to this day is practised as a form of magick. The Persians call them yazatas, and they stand for the cosmic forces of the universe. In the gospel of Luke the word, "Ophthe" is used to describe a different supernatural entity appearing as a vision. In Luke 2:10, a heavenly host of angels appear at Jesus birth. Only one angel appears at his death and resurrection in the Garden of Gethsemane when Jesus is expecting the whole host to appear again. There is no clear distinction between Jesus and other eastern magicians. In magic, humans possess power. In religion, powers are reserved for superior beings.

According to Christianity, God works miracles and demons work magic. Yet, to the onlooker, the results seem the same. Christians violently exorcise demons and kill other humans using the miraculous name of Jesus and the mystical sign of the cross. Von Harnack writes: that "Christianity has become a religion of magick, with its centre of gravity in the sacramental mysteries."

Dr. M.D. Magee sums it up this way: "Though Christians think they can see a distinction between good and bad magick, no one else can. Christians have simply been conditioned to believe that their heroes do good magick and others do evil magick, and even the abominable history of Christianity cannot persuade them otherwise. They are certainly in the grip of a powerful magic, but the question is whether it is what they think." http://www.askwhy.co.uk/christianity/0618Magic.php

Moses, Daniel, Elisha, Elijah and all of the prophets of the bible all used one form or another of the Witches arts including but not limited to: -

- Prophesying the future
- Dream Interpretation,
- Fore-telling Events,
- Divination with the Urium & Thurim
- Miraculous magical events etc.

Though the skills of Witchcraft are referred to positively in the Bible, as these are practised by all the Biblical prophets including Jesus and the Levite priest class, some translations misinterpret several words that indicate a FORIGN PREISTLY CLASS practising these things as the word 'Witch' in 1 Sam. 15:23; 2 Kings 9:22; 2 Chr. 33:6; Micah 5:12; Nahum 3:4; Gal. 5:20. In the popular sense of the word, no mention is made either of Witches or of Witchcraft in Bible scripture, as the word did not exist until much later.

King James the 6th of Scotland is King James the 1st of England

When was the Word "Witch" First used?

The word "Witch" was first used in popular English literature in 1380. It was derived from the Indo-European word 'weik' that refers to religio-magic despite what many people, including renowned Witches, would have us believe. King James Version of the Bible erroneously adopts this word in the late 1600s for translation of one instance of the word mekhashshepheh, meaning poisoner. Witch is not found in any earlier translations

How Did Such a Gross Mistranslation Happen?

Witch hysteria was stirred up in Scotland by King James 6th, yes the guy responsible for the popular English translation of the Bible, whilst trying to eradicate conspiracies against his reign. He was the one who had the word "poisoner" changed in his new biblical translation to the word "Witch," to justify his use of old laws for political expediency. This word has continued to be mistranslated in subsequent English translations resulting in continued prejudice and mistreatment of others to this day.

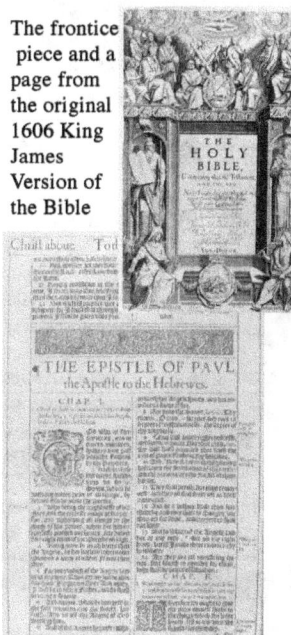

The frontice piece and a page from the original 1606 King James Version of the Bible

Several things contributed to this deliberate mistranslation. With the creation of the new Church of Scotland, laws were passed in 1563 that made it illegal to either be a Witch or to consult a Witch, in an attempt to stamp out indigenous Pagan practices. Scotland being rebellious, insular, and proud of its own traditions, largely ignored this parliamentary act. Indeed the Scottish have a long tradition of ignoring parliamentary acts. This law was not acted upon for twenty-six years and almost forgotten, until 1589, when King James used it for political reasons. This Act of Parliament was not abandoned in Scotland until 1736.

With Elisabeth 1[st,] old, childless, and near death, he was the only serious candidate for accession to the

Queen Elizabeth 1st on her coronation day at 25 years of age

crown of England. Elizabeth was the woman who had executed his mother; additionally she was the daughter of Anne Boleyn, later executed for Witchcraft herself, the woman who had been used to eliminate his grandmother from the throne of England. In James' mind a Witch was responsible for both his mother's and his grandmother's demise. He had a grudge against Elisabeth who was called "The Witch Queen" of England. James found a way to turn the favour and prestige afforded The Craft under Elisabeth's reign against it, and furthered his own political career at the same time.

Queen Elizabeth 1st The Witch Queen. The Golden Age of The Craft

Queen Elizabeth Alexandra Tudor, that is, Queen Elizabeth the 1st of England is infamous in history for being "The Witch Queen of England." How did she earn such a title?

She was the Daughter of Anne Boleyn and King Henry 8th. Henry had Anne Boleyn executed on the grounds of Witchcraft in an attempt to side step political unrest because of an illegal divorce and Catholic revolts. Elizabeth's life was in jeopardy from that time on. She grew up a cautious and quiet child, very aware of how tenuous her life was. Wealth, beauty, power, and privilege made her the target of the jealous, of plots of well-wishers, and the schemes of those that sort to over throw her whole royal family. She learned to remain aloof and apart, she signed nothing, and avoided those who might be seen as rebels. She studied mathematics, science, languages, politics, espionage, and economics. Out of an urgency to acquire the skills that would give her a life saving edge, she shunned the arts that most young ladies of the court studied. Later she became an avid patron of the arts because of this. Her only frivolous indulgence was dancing. She loved the passionate and vigorous Volta, also known as 'The Witches Dance' where the male partner places his hand between the female partner's legs to lift her high into the air. It was later to become her court dance. It was so named because in the mind of the public at that time, Witchcraft was associated with liberal sexual attitudes where the female was sexually aggressive.

2nd Wife of Henry 8th, Anne Boleyn, mother to Queen Eliszabeth, pictured here at 14 years of age, and cousin to Henry's 5th wife Catherine Howard also executed for witchcraft, shared her name with the white handled witches knife, and may have been the matriarch of a family of witches

Boleyn Crest

Witch Filled Family

Elizabeth's matriarchal line was also under constant attack, often for Witchcraft. Apart from Anne Boleyn's very Witchy name, (A boline, correctly pronounced the same way, being the white handled Witch's knife used to harvest herbs.) there appears to have been some truth to Robert Cochran's assertions that her whole family practised a royal form of The Craft of the Wise. King Henry had affairs with two other women of her family. Anne's sister Mary, who had been the lover of two of the French kings, as well as Elizabeth's cousin Catherine Howard who was also executed on the grounds of Witchcraft and treason. The song "Green Sleeves," referencing Anne as a woman skilled in the art of herbal healing, was written by

King Henry 8th. In this atmosphere, it is likely that Elizabeth was also taught some of The Craft by her mother, aunties, and cousins at court.

Close to the time of her father's death, she was 4th in line for the throne. No one considered her too be a real prospect. She was legally illegitimate and socially disgraced. There had been rumours of an illegitimate pregnancy to her much older ambitious mentor Thomas Seymour, who was later executed for marrying king Henry's widow and plotting against Elizabeth's half-brother Edward 1st. Though Elizabeth denied the affair and pregnancy as nothing more than rumours, her ill father and her beloved brother shunned her because of this public scandal. Elizabeth, who was very close to both, became totally isolated. It is interesting that she withdrew into seclusion for a year. It has never been historically clarified if a child was born or aborted or if indeed, she was ever pregnant. She continued her studies under Rodger Aschog who realised her potential and trained her to be queen. Even so, Elizabeth took a very hands-on approach to the running of her rural estate. She made the property become self-sufficient, supplying all the needs of her household, all of her staff and field hands. There was enough produce from her rural estate for sumptuous entertaining and excess to trade for delicacies. Quite an accomplishment for a young woman in her teens in that era. She was loved by her staff and field hands. Her frugality and understanding of the cycles of agriculture was later to aid her to turn England from the brink of bankruptcy to the wealthiest nation in the world during her reign.

Consequences of An Inquisition Inclusive Reign

When her father died. The succession passed to the king's only son, Elizabeth's younger half-brother Edward, who was terminally ill. Edward willed succession to his best friend, Lady Jane Grey, whose radical reforms saw her quickly removed from the throne after only thirteen days. Royal succession then passed back to Catholic Mary Tudor, Henry's oldest child by his first wife. As one of Mary's first acts she invited the Roman Inquisition into England to burn three hundred heretics, mostly Protestants, at the stake in the Marian Persecutions. Though previously protected by Pope Alexander 4th, Pope Innocent the 8th declared Witchcraft to be heresy in 1484 and also subject to inquisitors. The high number of executions carried out, and the ensuing Catholic/Protestant civil and cold war during a reign that lasted only five years, resulted in that queen being tagged "Bloody Mary" in the pages of history. This internal strife left the country destitute.

Elizabeth was not on the list. Yet, with her quiet composure, she appeared to have a vision that, if she did nothing, and avoided the intrigues, one day she would sit on the throne of England and must be ready for this when the opportunity presented itself. Her self-stated life motto "Video et taceo" was very similar to the Witch's motto: "To see, to know, to dare, to will and keep silent." Elizabeth loved irony and rhetoric in Latin, a mark of a great orator and statesman for her time. On her coat of arms is the Latin motto often quoted by Rosaleen Norton in defence during her own Witch trials in the 1950's and 1970's in Australia: "Honi Soit Qui Mal y Pense" meaning "Evil is to him who thinks evil."

If not for this code of conduct, Elizabeth would have lost her life. She came very close to death for a third time whilst 'Bloody Mary' was on the throne. As Mary became ill and it became obvious that the Protestant Elizabeth was the next successor, the Catholics implicated her in a plot against Mary. Elizabeth was arrested and imprisoned in the tower of London for two months. Yet, Mary loved her half-sister as they had been close childhood friends, and wished to be reconciled before her death, so no evidence was manufactured against Elizabeth. Elizabeth was returned to her estate under house arrest until Mary's death in 1558 when Elizabeth was twenty-five years of age. From the time of King Henry the 8th's death to Elizabeth 1st succession was only eleven very turbulent years.

On the day of Mary's death, Elizabeth saw the ministers approaching to declare her Queen and Prince regent of England. She famously misquoted Psalms 118 in Latin, *"a dei et mirabile in oculis nostris"* which translated into: *"What the Gods have done is marvellous in our eyes!"*

The Witch Queen Social Reformist and The Catholic Jihad

Elizabeth immediately began work correcting the economy of the bankrupt country she inherited. The biggest drain on the nation was the heavy dues paid to Rome. As soon as she came to power, she ousted the Roman Inquisition and she continued the work of her father by removing the Catholic Church, its heavy tithing and civil unrest. She then formed the Church of England, as an act of uniformity, to keep England's economy closed and appointed herself as its head. The Catholic Pope immediately pronounced her a heretic, a Witch, and a bastard usurper and put a bounty on her head to be paid to the person who killed 'the usurper Witch queen.' Pope Sixtus V's issued two papal bulls against Elizabeth 1st in 1570 and in 1588 that effected what was essentially a Catholic jihad against her and her reign.

Elizabeth, in the manner of all true Witches, had a way of taking the energy of whatever was thrown against her and turning it to her advantage. She mastered the art of owning and empowering abusive slurs. She transformed the title "Witch Queen" to the more poetic "Faery Queen." She employed magicians at her court and passed laws that no law-abiding citizen could be imprisoned or executed for their beliefs. The Catholics in her realm, no longer afraid of being subjects of political persecution, relaxed and began to sing her praises. This law kept The Inquisition out of England. Free thinkers, philosophers, mathematicians and scientists flooded into her court that was hailed globally as truly embracing democratic principles.

The Queen's Magicians

The world became fascinated by the miraculous rule of Elizabeth and wanted to know more about her magicians. There were two main court magicians. One was Francis Bacon. He coined the phrase *"knowledge is power,"* in his work "Sacred Meditations" in 1597. He established and popularized an inductive methodology for scientific inquiry. He derived his methods from his study of hermetics and alchemy. He demanded a planned procedure of investigating all natural things, which is still used today, simply referred to as scientific method. Bacon wrote a theory explaining magick as an active force in matter that he calls *"Cupid"* in his "De Principiis Atque Originibus." In "De Augmentis," he refers to Pan and his nymphs to illustrate atomic movement in matter. He expresses the idea of magick as *"the knowledge of the universal consents of things ... . I ... understand (magick) as the science which applies the knowledge of hidden forms to the production of wonderful operations; and by uniting actives with passives, displays the wonderful works of nature."* For Bacon, "magick" is more than a craft, it is applied science. To him there is nothing black about magick; it was natural, since it represents the *"ultimate legitimate power over nature."* For him there were two divisions for investigating philosophy and the sciences, Metaphysic and Physics, split up by Bacon into Mechanics, and Magick.

Francis Bacon

He was also responsible for "Colours of Good, Evil," and "The New Atlantis," in 1627, about an ideal society where "generosity and enlightenment, dignity and splendour, piety and public spirit" were the commonly held qualities of the inhabitants. He was fiercely nationalistic to the point of extreme prejudice. When the Spanish armada sailed on a holy war to attack this 'heretical nation' ruled over by a Witch queen, it is thought more likely that it was Francis Bacon helped Elizabeth summon a storm that smashed the vast fleet against the rocks of the English coast with minimal losses to the English than Dr. John Dee. This was to be later repeated by English magicians during WWI and WWII.

The British Secret Service

A protector of Elizabeth before she came to the throne was a man with abilities as an excellent mathematician, cartographer, astronomer, and astrologer. This was Dr. John Dee. He was also skilled in ciphers and codes and was eventually hired to gather intelligence for her. His former patron was the British foreign minister and his neighbour was Francis Walsingham, the Queen's bodyguard and head of intelligence, who had already recruited him for their espionage ring. He became a firm friend of Lord Dudley Elisabeth's favourite. Before Elizabeth came to power, he was sent on missions by Lord William Cecil and welcomed in four European royal courts including England's main enemy Spain. He was tried for Witchcraft by Elizabeth's predecessor and Catholic half-sister Mary and was miraculously released due to "insufficient evidence" and pressure form his influential friends.

Dr. John Dee
Though he studied at Cambridge no formal doctorate was issued. It is believed that his honorary doctorate came either from the Catholic Arch Bishop of London or from Queen Elizabeth

While Dee was in Antwerp, he became a member of a secretive group run by the author Hendrick Niclaes called "The Family of Love." It was a non-aligned group based on the Pagan philosophies of Pythagorean/Shambhallic government being to take the second way of the "Pythagorean Y," not the way of the tyrant. This way is a form of government that was not to be based on any one-belief system. It was to have no arbitrary commands, articles of doctrine, church, or congregation. It was to be without office or territorial claims, without a visible place of government, and exist without moral or military coercion. It was to impartially cherish and love every race and religion on earth. It would endured successfully precisely because its authority was invisible and could never be attacked and could achieve impregnability by appearing to yielding to conquers yet eventually over coming them with this love. Thus, government would be freed from its chains to its own machinery. This non-self-interested form of government was first suggested in the Tao Te Ching.

Because he was a self-confessed Pagan, in all but name, with no religious allegiance to neither the Catholics nor the Protestants, he was recruited for a short time by the Catholic persecutors, with the archbishop of London going so far as to give him a job as his chaplain. This mercurial quality made him invaluable as "intelligentsia."

Together John Dee and Queen Elizabeth devised a cover story that her reign was aided by a method of magick delivered in code by God's angels directly to John Dee. The Catholic Church could not decry this cover story without discrediting half of the Bible cannon. This story was so successful that John Dee gained audiences with the Roman Emperor in Austria. This allowed John Dee to be sent 'on loan' by Elizabeth, to the Royal houses of Europe, who eagerly sort knowledge of this miraculous advantage of the English court. They happily told all their secrets to Dr. Dee and he sent them back to Elizabeth written in the supposed angelic script. Many of these angelic script espionage files have been translated using Dee's own 'angelic cipher.' Many of these are available to the public. The messages contained therein are very mundane however; they allowed Queen Elizabeth to head off many plots and threats to her reign before the plans could be put into action. It was the most brilliantly successful misinformation and espionage ruse in history. This was the beginning of "The British Secret Service" and what was later dubbed "The Great Game." John Dee assigned members of every royal court in Europe a number, denoting their importance in the balance of power. Elizabeth was number one and John Dee assigned himself the number 007. He was the first super spy. His trusty sidekick, Edward Kelly, was a likeable rogue whose personality has come to be popularly associated with that number. Dee's personal diaries reveal that he was fascinated with philosophy, mysticism, and magick. However, his astronomical entries in his diaries were also used as a method of passing on information, dates and details about past present and future events.

Dee's "Sigillim Aemeth" that he designed for his code key displays the ratios of 7:5

Dee cracked the code in the legendary Stenographia a pseudo-magickal text designed for espionage. Upon breaking this code Sir William Cecil immediately employed him in the Queens espionage ring. The code in the Stenographica was not broken again until 1990

Goddess Feminism

After witnessing her mother and other family members killed by Henry, Elizabeth refused to marry and place her life precariously under the whim of any man. She assumed the indomitable role of the larger than life "Goddess Gloriana" to her people.

Elisabeth created a mystical air about herself. She was deified as a living Protestant saint and a truly divine ruler. She took every opportunity to be seen as magickal. When she rejected the marriage proposal of the King of Spain, he threatened that there was 'a wind arising in Spain that would wipe away her arrogance.' To which Elizabeth replied, 'But I command the winds and if I choose they will wipe away the might of Spain in a night.' After that very thing happened, when a storm destroyed his armada whilst it attempted to attack England, the King of Spain became superstitiously afraid of her for the rest of his life.

Her virginity was highly prized and highly praised by the people of England, and Elizabeth missed no opportunity to catch the veneration due sacred virginity. From the start of her reign she nurtured this myth. She drew attention to the fact that one of her titles at coronation was Queen of France, and that her aunt on her mother's side had been Queen of France, her mother, Anne Boleyn had grown up in France, added to and tales of her receiving her notification of her accession whilst reading under a large and stately oak tree. This eluded to the 900 year old "Prophecies of Merlin" in Geoffrey of Monmouth's "Historia," the Sibyl's predictions, and the prophecies of Saint Bede. These legends had served Joan of Arc in her campaign one hundred years before and served Elizabeth just as well. They had foretold the coming of a maiden out of an oak-wood that would save her country. *"It was said that after nearly a century of war this young maiden would unite her divided people and lead them to freedom."* The French mystic, Marie of Avignon, adapted this to her own country and added: that which had been *"..lost by a woman, should be saved by a maid..."*

Queen Elizabeth in all the glory of her magically successful reign

Elizabeth acted as the Protestant replacement of the Virgin Mary in the newly converted England. Indeed literary allusions were drawn between the many mythological or Pagan images of virginal female deities and Elizabeth. Many songs were written declaring Elizabeth to be Gloriana. She was called the Queen of Heaven, Diana, Cynthia, and Belphoebe amongst others, which added to the rich imagery of the pageantry of the time.

"Who's Afraid Of The Big Bad Witch?" - by - Dr. S. D'Montford

Royal Magick and Miracles

Thaumaturgic rulership where the king or queen, after their mystical coronation and anointing ritual, can perform miracles or magick, has a long history in Europe. The ultimate manifestation of the divine in Monarchy was the cases of spontaneous healings especially of Tuberculosis, swelling of the neck glands, and casting out of demons, with a touch of their hands. Elizabeth often quoted her ability to use this power as a sign that her much debated rulership was in fact ordained by God. William Tooker in his 1597 book "Charisma Or The Gift Of Healing," site cases of Elizabeth exhibiting this divine power to the point where she even healed Catholics. The royal healing touch miracles made the public view her with holiness. Elizabeth experienced extreme glorification.

When the Catholics quoted St Paul in the book of Corinthians saying: *"Let your women keep silence in the churches: for it is not permitted unto them to speak; but they are commanded to be under obedience... let them ask their husbands at home: for it is a shame for women to speak in the church."* As reasons why she could not be the head of a church and should be married, Elizabeth countered with: *"Honour the physician with the honour due him, according to your need of him, for the Lord created him."* Alluding to her healing touch being given as a sign of approval from God. Elizabeth was venerated as God's handmaiden on earth. This aided the queen to justify her unmarried state, and when *"this scriptural figure was turned to glorify Elizabeth; it fused prettily with her conceit that she was the virgin mother of her people, joined in holy wedlock to the state."* suggests the 1939 book "England's Eliza" by E.C. Wilson.

A Craft Positive Reign

Under Elizabeth's rule, Shakespeare wrote Craft positive plays, like "A Mid-Summers Night's Dream" and "The Tempest." He reversed this line and produced the anti-Witch proPaganda of "Macbeth" under the rule of Elizabeth's successor, James 1st who mistranslated the bible to include a bias against Witches and had instigated a Witch-hunt in his homeland of Scotland that killed 4000 innocents. Macbeth was a thinly veiled retelling of the story king James used to instigate his Scottish Witch-hunt.

Elizabeth's reign became named after her, called the Elizabethan era. Elizabeth remained on the throne of England for forty-five years, longer than any English monarch, except for the present. Her reign was peaceful and under her rule the country prospered and the arts and sciences flourished. During and because of this era, the way we view the world changed drastically. The playwrights William Shakespeare, Christopher Marlowe, and Ben Johnson all wrote and presented plays that have become the foundations for the moreés and social conduct of our western society; Francis Bacon wrote his milestone philosophical and political works; Francis Drake became the first man on record in western civilisation to circumnavigate the globe, crushing forever the Catholic idea that the world was flat; and Sir James Huckle, Sir Walter Raleigh, and Sir Humphrey Gilbert established firm free trade routes with the east and founded the first English colonies in North America overturning the Catholic religious monopoly on the new world.

It was interesting to note the many references to these things in the movie "Elizabeth, The Golden Age." Though they kept any direct references to Witchcraft out of the movie, the final image makes a not so subtle reference to her reputation as The Witch Queen. The last and enduring image of the movie is as Elizabeth turns to the camera, declaring herself to be 'Queen in truth,' she reveals delicate pentagram earrings.

Elizabeth 1st was undisputedly the greatest Queen in history and is a positive role model of what could be achieved when a group follows the universal principles of The Craft.

The King James Version of Events

James was a conflicted man with double standards. He was grateful to Elizabeth for not naming another successor, yet still sort revenge for her part in his family's downfall. Then a safe way presented itself.

James beat off a Catholic revolt in Scotland in 1588. He was faced with a conspiracy mounted by John Ruthven, 3rd Earl of Gowrie. He had enemies everywhere. He needed an excuse in legislature to do away with these enemies quickly, without causing another Catholic/Protestant bloodbath. In 1589, James married the protestant Princess Anne of Denmark. On his return, with his now wife he came

The excuse for the Scottish Witch hunts, King James 1's bride, Queen Anne of Denmark

King James personally examining the Witches

up with a master plan. A group of people were placed on trial for Witchcraft in North Berwick. They were said to have summoned a storm to try to sink Anne's ship on her first attempt to come to Scotland, and again when he had travelled back with her. The King's political opponents were supposed to have paid these people for this act. They were all charged with "Witchcraft and High Treason" as Anne Boleyn, the woman who replaced James' grandmother, had been when King Henry 8th had wanted an expedient divorce.

Scottish Witch Hunts Kill Over 4000 Innocents

King James took a close interest in the trial when it looked as though the accused would be acquitted, examining some of those accused under torture himself. They were all found guilty and executed. James was then instrumental in launching a major Witch-hunt across Scotland in which, during the following century, over 3,000 Witches would be "discovered" and executed. Scotland is estimated to have been Europe's biggest persecutor of Witches. By the end of the 18th century, Scotland had put to death over 4,000 alleged Witches not including those people who died in custody after they were tortured or who killed themselves in despair. These innocents, and their cats, were considered acceptable collateral damage as this new law meant that Gowrie, and many of King James' other enemies, could now be executed expediently.

A Scottish wood cut of the time depicting the accused Witches as upper middle class

Forfar's Witches Fountain

Forfar

Forfar is synonymous with what is officially considered to be the final Witch hunt between 1661-1666 that contributed forty-two deaths of people suspected of being Witches, of whom nine were officially executed, three of whom were men. Witch-Hunts were not Women-Hunts as has been repeatedly postulated by the feminist agenda. The Witch-hunts worldwide were not exclusively against females. About a third of all deaths were males in political positions. One of the first Witch-hunts on record occurred in Shandong, China in 91 B.C. and of the several hundred political opponents, including the king's son that were arrested and confessed to working black magick against the Emperor Wu under torture, none were women. Before that in 475BC Pythagoras and 40 of his male followers, (the women and children were let go,) were burnt as Witches, whilst staying at the house of Milo at Crotona, Italy, for suggesting a better form of government. It must be remembered that political opponents were the true targets of the Scottish, and indeed all the Witch hunts, the rest were considered acceptable collateral damage such as the widow Katherine Porter and young Elspeth Bruce whose torture extracted testimonies were used to condemn other political opponents.

There were three periods of intense Witch hunting in the British Isles. The first took place in Scotland the during the reign of James VI in the late 1580's, the second during the Civil War of the 1640's and the third after Charles II was restored to the throne in 1660. All for political, not spiritual, reasons.

By the end of the 17th century, burning had gone out of fashion, so most of those accused of being Witches were hanged instead. A small well (pictured), on the eastern corner of the esplanade of Edinburgh Castle, marks the spot of the Forfar Witch trials where, many women accused of Witchcraft, were executed.

Rich Witch Hygiene

These women were not from the lower socio-economic rungs of society or randomly chosen and singled out because of minor differences as is commonly believed. Minor differences were often used as excuses. However, true reason they were chosen to be collateral damage was that they were women with property that would be forfeit once the trial started and could be sold to finance the expensive inquisition process. Professional persecutors made large sums of money and were given extravagant gifts by the local townships. Successful midwives and those well to do healers with a knowledge of herbal medicine were often accused of heresy and Witchcraft by the practitioners of burgeoning medical profession who saw them as competition. Accusations of Witchcraft were easily brought as most traditional healers practised hygiene. In those days, Hygiene was a belief system. Hygiene is an ancient Pagan goddess of cleanliness. She was Pythagoras' main deity at his school at Crotona. Those healers, who worshiped Hygiene, thoroughly cleaned their house, front door stoop, and businesses ritually every Thursday. Their 'superstitious' Pagan cleanliness made them an obvious target. They taught that hands must be washed and a sick room kept clean. This was considered superstition by the new medical universities. The result of the removal from society of those who practised the ancient arts of Hygiene as represented by the broomstick, was the Bubonic Plague. The cat holocaust, that accompanied the burning of Witches, allowed for a plague of rats, whose fleas bit humans and rapidly spread the plague.

Mathematical Witches

Pythagoras was not only associated with mathematics, he was also attributed with many healing miracles and his traditions were held dear by many healers. He was called the pre-Christian Christ. More on him later. His mathematical teachings had become very unpopular with the early Church because of the Pagan origins of these teachings. Many mathematicians were also accused of Witchcraft for this reason.

Galileo Galilee was imprisoned in his home by the sceptics of his time. They refused to believe that his Pagan based teachings, of the world moving around the sun in an elliptical orbit as proved by Euclid over 500 years before Christ, could be possible. Additionally, the idea that the earth was not the centre of the universe was hearsay. It was not until October 31st of 1992, that the Roman Catholic Church finally admitted that it had erred in its 359-year-old persecution of the 17th century astronomer and physicist.

On The fifth of March 1616, the Roman Catholic Church, through Scottish Cardinal Robert Bellarmine, declared Nicolas Copernicus' "De Revolutionibus," detailing the mathematics of ellipses and how the earth revolved around the sun, was not the centre of the universe, as heretical, and was placed on its "Index of Forbidden Books." In this book, Copernicus openly encouraged a return to the ancient Pagan sciences, as they existed before Aristotle. These ancient practitioners of Hermetics, the works of Hermes Trismegistos the Alti-shaman and the Hindu Suraya, all showed that the Sun was the centre of our Solar system. For this The Church accused him of being a Witch and a sun worshiper.

Witchcraft accusations were brought for political reasons against these men and not just against the lowly and the female. The lowly and the female were really no threat to the Church's power of themselves. They were, and remain, acceptable collateral damage in authority's persecution of perceived threats. The Church had a lot invested in the belief that the Earth was the centre of the universe and that the pope was the centre of its power. It was to their benefit to keep the masses believing without question that it was right. To them the elimination of enquiring minds was a noble cause. This was the cause of the dark ages the height of The Churches power through its feudal overlord system. To maintain its power, it viciously persecuted anything that challenged its cosmology and doctrines. To The Church's credit, if the local minister did not believe in persecuting innocent people on trumped up Witchcraft charges, then a Witch-trial could not happen in that locality. In Forfar however, was an enthusiastic young minister called Alexander Robertson. He believed that Witches existed and should be eradicated. Whether his belief was personal or encouraged financially by local politicians is still not clear. However, he took the matter of accusations to the town council who would set the ponderous forces of 17th century justice into motion.

Lies To Stay Alive

The first woman accused by Robertson, is someone that a community would understandably want to be rid of. Her name was Helen Guthrie. She was, by her own admission, a drunken and wicked woman who had murdered her own stepsister when they were both children. Helen and her 13-year-old daughter Janet Howat were accused of being Witches. Without her, the Forfar Witch-hunts would not have lasted so long or encompassed so many. She played a vital role in the mounting prejudice and intolerance. She aimed to keep herself and her daughter alive as long as possible by claiming to be able to identify another Witch simply by seeing her. She agreed to help the Witch hunters. She became the star witness for the prosecutors. She told stories of drunken midnight Sabbats held in Forfar churchyard, desecration of graves, cannibalism, ship sinking at Carnoustie and destruction of bridges at Cortachy. She boasted of her prowess under the name of The White Witch, claiming the devil tried to rescue her from imprisonment during the trial by levitating her up through the rafters. Her imaginative stories were published and they stirred a new Witch-hunt to a frenzy in which she personally named eleven others including Isobel Shyrie, Helen Alexander, Girsel Simpsone, Agnes Spark, Katherine Porter, John Tailyeour, and Janet Stout. Helen Guthrie finally outlasted her usefulness to the Witch hunters and was the last Witch to be executed in Forfar in December 1662. Witch-hunting ceased quite abruptly in the burgh. Its demise coincided with Alexander Robertson's removal as a minister by the Privy Council for excessive zeal in his Witch hunting. It appears that Helen did save her teenage daughter Janet, as a plea appears in the records of the Privy Council. They held another trial and no one spoke against her. This plea is dated 1666, 4 years after her initial arrest.

Witchcraft Charges Found to Be False - Witches Pardoned 400 Years Late

Oct 31st 2006, posthumous pardons where given to those that had been condemned to death on such flimsy evidence as, owning a black cat or brewing home made remedies.

A bit late for them though!

"Who's Afraid Of The Big Bad Witch?" - by - Dr. S. D'Montford

A gathering at Prestonpans, a small Scottish town, enacted its now abolished baronial rights to pardon eighty-one people, and their cats, executed during the wave of anti-Witch hysteria in the 16th and 17th centuries.

About thirty-two descendants, namesakes, and supporters came together. They hoped that this occasion would become an annual "Witches Remembrance Day" to be held in the town each Halloween. The Barron's Courts of Prestoungrange and Dolphinstoun granted the pardons as their final act of their last sessions before abolition. The democratic power of a Barron's courts for a local township to countermand a decision made by a remote King or centralised government was established by Simon de Montford, when the barons imposed the reform programme known as the Provisions of Oxford in 1258, and the Forma Regiminis in 1264 upon King Henry III, under which royal government was to be scrutinised by a baronial council of fifteen. This beginning of the democratic process in England is commemorated by the white cross on the Union Jack and unfortunately; it was abolished on the 28th of November 2005. The final Halloween 2006 session of the court declared, *"...pardon to all those convicted as well as all the cats concerned."*

Local historian Roy Plugh, who helped secure the pardons by presenting evidence to the court, said "It is too late to apologise for what happened for-hundred-years ago, yet, it is an important symbolic gesture... it is making some amends, for the unjustness, prejudice, hysteria and paranoia that led to those deaths." Mr Plugh has written a book called "The Devil's Aim" in 2001 that strongly criticised the Church of Scotland for its persecution of many supposed Witches that lead to the deaths of between 3500 and 4000 Scots, mostly women and children. The last execution for Witchcraft in Scotland was in 1727. The English Witchcraft Act was changed in 1735 making it a crime only to pretend to be a Witch.

The Mayor of Salem, Mr Usovicz is reported as considering holding a similar pardoning and annual ceremony of remembrance for its nineteen people hanged for Witchcraft.

Similarly, it took 400 years for The Church to officially pardon and canonize Joan of Arc from the charges of Witchcraft.

So much misery, intolerance, blood, and carnage because of the deliberate mistranslation of a word in the bible, a book that openly approves of Witches.

Chapter 10

Witch Hunts in Australia

In Australia, and its territories, the Witch-hunts have continued until the last few years.

Witchcraft was not legalised in NSW until the 1970s. Legal social bias against Paganism and Witchcraft officially ended in Queensland as late as 2001. Victoria did not decriminalise this religious belief system until 2003. This makes Queensland one of the last places on the globe, including 3rd world countries, to recognise that practitioners of the oldest religion on the planet have an inalienable human right to worship according to their deeply held beliefs.

Laws Relating to Witchcraft in Australia

I have included this section on the laws, lobbying, political and legal discussion of Witchcraft as a reference for any unfortunate who may still find them selves in a court room having their faith thrown in their face. This still frequently occurs as an adjunct to custody cases,; being married to a Pagan is one of only two grounds by which you may gain a Catholic annulment; or disputes with a neighbour. The law most often used against Witches in Australia was Section 13 of the Victorian Vagrancy Act 1958 which is entitled 'Fortune Telling and Pretending to Exercise Witchcraft, etc.: - *'Any person who pretends or professes to tell fortunes or uses any subtle craft means or device by palmistry or otherwise to defraud or impose on any other person or pretends to exercise or use any kind of Witchcraft, sorcery, enchantment or conjuration or pretends from his skill or knowledge in any occult or crafty science to discover where or in what manner any goods or chattels stolen or lost may be found shall be guilty of an offence. Penalty: 5 penalty unitsits..*

Fortunately this law along with others sited below has been abolished or decriminalised. However, vexatious charges may still be brought.. I have found myself in court charged with witchcraft by a disgruntle neighbour (with whom I refused to have sexual relations). Many solicitors do not know how to handle Paganism or witchcraft accusations.. This information will help.

There were versions of this in other states of Australia: -

"Who's Afraid Of The Big Bad Witch?" - by - Dr. S. D'Montford

Australian Capital Territory

The Discrimination Act, 1991, makes it unlawful to discriminate against a person on the basis of a person's religious convictions.

New South Wales

The Witchcraft Act of 1735 was repealed by the Imperial Acts Application Act, 1969 (NSW),

The offence of fortune telling, [Section 4(2)(n) of the Vagrancy Act, 1902 (NSW)] was through many submissions and changes finally repealed by the Summary Offences Act (Repeal) Act, 1979 (NSW).

Queensland

Until recently it remained a criminal gaolable offence to be a Witch in Queensland under The Criminal Code -Section 432 - This was repealed on 10th November 2000 - Though they have been decriminalised they are still not legalised.

The Queensland Government recently repealed the separate Vagrants Gaming and Other Offences Act 1931. The Summary Offences Act which takes it's place has been enacted effective 21st March 2005.

South Australia

The Statutes Amendment and Repeal (Public Offences) Act, 1991 abolished the Witchcraft laws in SA

However the 1991 Act came with a new section, Section 40. A person who, with intent to defraud purports to act as a spiritualist or medium or to exercise powers of telepathy or clairvoyance or other similar powers, (was) guilty of an offence. Summary Offences Act as Section 40.

Tasmania

The Constitution Act 1934, Section 46, provides for freedom of religion.

This document includes a legal guarantee of the religious liberty and equality of Tasmanians. Every citizen is guaranteed freedom of conscience and the free exercise of religion under Section 46(1) of this Act. Section 46(2) declares that no person is required to take any oath on religion or religious belief, and that no religious test is required for any public office.

Police Offences Act 1935 (Tas) section 8(1): ' A person shall not pretend or profess to tell fortunes or use any sul3tle craft, means or device, by palmistry or otherwise, to defraud or impose on any other person. Penalty: $500 or imprisonment six months.'

Northern Teritory

Summary Offences Act (NT) section 57(1)(d): 'Any person who pretends to tell fortunes, or uses any subtle craft, means, or device, by palmistry or otherwise, to deceive or impose upon any of her Majesty's subjects shall be guilty of an offence. Penalty: $1,000 or imprisonment for 6 months, or both.'

Western Australia

Police Act 1892 (WA) section 66(3): 'Every person pretending to tell fortunes, or using any subtle craft, means, or device, to deceive and impose upon any person ... shall on summary conviction be liable to a fine not exceeding $1000 or to imprisonment for any term not exceeding 12 calendar months.'

On The 3rd of September 2002, it was recommended to the Attorney General by the Scrutiny of Acts and Regulations Committee in Victoria that these laws should be repealed. In July 2005, this law was finally repealed with the "Vagrancy (Repeal) and Summary Offences (Amendment) Act 2005." However, the police laws remain to be enacted at their discretion. There are no standing Witchcraft laws in Australia now. Yet, the extreme Christian right movement in both Queensland and Victoria seek a reestablishment of these laws.

However, the Australian Constitution Section V chapter 116 states that: *The Commonwealth shall not make any law for establishing any religion, or for imposing any religious observance, or for prohibiting the free exercise of any religion, and no religious test shall be required as a qualification for any office or public trust under the Commonwealth.*

This means that no religion can be recognised and no religion can be made illegal. This is for all religions including the organised ones. However, the Attorney General's Department does keep a register of officially recognised religions and the government does enact legislation in regards to religious institutions and bodies.

Paganism and Human Rights

The following information is taken from the report Article 18 - *Freedom Of Religion And Belief* issued by *The Human Rights and Equal Opportunity Commission.*

3.10 Paganism

Pagans see divinity expressed in every part of the universe. The Earth, the planets, the stars, the void - all are parts of one great, divine source to the Pagan. Pagans do not "worship" trees or rocks, however they do revere the divine life force, which is contained within trees and rocks, and within every part of the universe. Paganism is a general term which covers a variety of spiritual beliefs centred upon harmony with the Earth. The umbrella term embraces beliefs such as Celtic Paganism, Druidry, Shamanism, Wicca and Witchcraft. Wicca is described by the Pagan Alliance as ... a modern revival of the ancient folkloric and magical practices of Europe. Wiccans generally perceive divinity in the form of a Goddess and a God, who have many different aspects. Most Wiccans celebrate eight Festivals each year, and hold meetings in accordance with the phases of the Moon.93 Practitioners of Witchcraft are also described by the Pagan

"Who's Afraid Of The Big Bad Witch?" - by - Dr. S. D'Montford

Alliance as 'often skilled herbalists and healers; their practices and techniques are similar in many ways to those of the tribal shaman, the village Wisewoman and Cunningman'.

The Commission received a large number of submissions from Pagans and Wiccans. They complained, in particular, that the free expression of their practices and beliefs are unnecessarily limited by the criminal law of Queensland which deems the practice of Witchcraft, fortune-telling, sorcery or enchantment an offence.... A number of submissions from individuals in the Wiccan community who practise magic and Witchcraft in the expression of their beliefs stated that the criminalisation of their practices is an unnecessary limitation on their beliefs and violates the right to freedom of religion and belief.

...A submission from R L Akers to the 1996 Queensland Criminal Code Review suggested that the illegal status of Witchcraft and fortune-telling (was) evidence of State endorsed discrimination against Wiccans. He stated that the laws may be used to perpetuate the unfair stereotyping and stigmatisation which already exist against people who engage in these practices.98

The practice of fortune-telling, including tarot card reading and astrology, may be the expression of the spiritual beliefs of certain Pagans and Wiccans. The criminalisation and prohibition of these practices limits their rights to express their beliefs freely.

Mr Akers alleged that these laws have been used to arrest tourists engaged in fortunetelling in Queensland, especially backpackers who are unaware of the State's laws in this respect.

Over the decades there have been numerous reports of tourists being harassed, even arrested for Vagrancy, after reading cards in coffee shops in an attempt to raise living expenses...

The rationale for retaining the offences prohibiting Witchcraft or fortune-telling for gain or payment appears to derive from the view that the practices are fraudulent, dangerous, and undesirable. In 1996, in response to questions in Parliament concerning the continued relevance of the provisions, the Attorney-General, the Hon. Denver Beanland stated that he was aware of representations to have section 432 of the Criminal Code, and section 4(1)(o) of the Vagrants Gaming and Other Offences Act 1931 (Qld) repealed. He stated, however,

"Who's Afraid Of The Big Bad Witch?" - by - Dr. S. D'Montford

"These provisions ... are there to protect the gullible and to discourage the practice of not only fortune-telling but, as, section 432 also provides, Witchcraft, sorcery and practices in the occult ... these practices therefore are not archaic... it was accepted that the South Australian Parliament had outlawed fortune-telling 'because it was in itself a fraudulent practice and necessarily deceptive whether or not the defendant genuinely believed in his ability to foretell the future.'"

...This provision appears to be the relic of a more superstitious age and if to be retained at all, it should be set out in legislation other than the Criminal Code. There are summary offences relating to fortune telling for gain in the Vagrants, Gaming and Other Offences Act 1931. If the relevant conduct involves fraud, it would be sufficiently covered by the new fraud offence.

Submissions To The Commission On Paganism
A submission by Ms Louise Bowes on behalf of the Servants of the Elder Gods, however, alleged that the laws prohibiting Witchcraft and fortune-telling are retained because of ignorance about the practices.

\The law was retained largely on the basis of ignorance, marrying violent activities and deliberate deception with the practice of Witchcraft and the adoption of the religion known as 'Wicca" ... What this meant for the many Wiccan followers in Queensland was obvious - they experience an immediate inability to follow their faith for fear of arrest and incarceration.109

To comply with human rights requirements the right to manifest Wiccan or Pagan beliefs in Witchcraft and fortune-telling can be limited by law but only if the limitation is necessary to protect public safety, order, health, morals or the fundamental rights or freedoms of others.

No submissions provided any evidence that Witchcraft or fortune-telling practices of themselves present a threat to the safety or well-being of members of the community. Practitioners refuted such allegations.

Pagans do not perform sacrifices (other than of their own time and energy) and are not opposed to any other religious beliefs. Pagans do not sexually abuse children; quite the contrary. Despite many hysterical claims of sexual abuse by Witches and other occultists, none has ever been proven to be true.

Wicca followers do not worship Satan; we don't even believe in his existence. We do not sacrifice animals or virgins, and we don't engage in debauched sex orgies ... we ask the Queensland government exactly what it sees as so dangerous in our religious practices. Could it be the use of alternative medicines, herbalism, and the horoscope? Could it be self-awareness they are objecting to? Or perhaps the respect and reverence we give our Earth?

As Ms Bowes pointed out, if Wiccans engaged in practices which were harmful to others, they would be subject to the same general laws as the rest of the community.

Like so many alternate religions, none of our Wiccan practices contravene any state or federal law as far as violence, stealing, cruelty to animals, abuse of children etc. are concerned. Should a religious group partake of activities which do break laws of this nature, then obviously the participants in that religion would and should be open to prosecution.

Many members of the Queensland Parliament agree. For example, the Hon T B Sullivan stated

"If there are abuses, let us deal with that abuse. If people practising Witchcraft abuse a young child, let us oppose them for the abuse of the young child, not for their faith, be that different from our own. If those who are of a non-Christian background believe in the spirit or spirits and abuse a person in some way they should be attacked for the abuse and not for their beliefs."

Findings And Recommendations On Paganism

* Wiccans and Pagans have the right to manifest their beliefs 'either individually or in community with others' in the practice of Witchcraft and fortune-telling subject only to 'such limitations as are prescribed by law and are necessary to protect public safety, order, health, or morals or the fundamental rights and freedoms of others' (ICCPR article 18.3).

* There is no evidence to suggest that individuals or the community require specific protection from Witchcraft or fortune-telling practices. There is no evidence that the practices of Witchcraft and fortune-telling in Australia require limitations as permitted by the ICCPR.

* Any practice associated with Witchcraft which might result in physical or mental injury to other individuals or loss of or damage to property can be dealt with under general criminal and civil laws dealing with conduct of that kind.

* Similarly, any fortune-telling practices found to constitute fraud or deceptive conduct can be dealt with adequately under the general criminal law.

* Section 432 of Queensland's Criminal Code 1899 and section 4(1)(o) of the Vagrants, Gaming and Other Offences Act 1931 (Qld) and the equivalent legislation in Victoria, Western Australia, South Australia, the Northern Territory and Tasmania are not necessary to protect public safety, order, health or morals or the fundamental rights and freedoms of others.

* Laws prohibiting Witchcraft and fortune-telling unnecessarily discriminate against members of the Wiccan and Pagan communities and contravene the right of practising Wiccans and Pagans to express their religions or beliefs in accordance with ICCPR article 18.

The Commission recommends

* R3.13 - The federal Attorney-General through the Standing Committee of Attorneys General should encourage Queensland and Victoria to repeal legislation criminalising the practice of Witchcraft, fortune-telling, sorcery and enchantment.

* R3.14 - The federal Attorney-General through the Standing Committee of Attorneys General should encourage Queensland, Western Australia, South Australia, the Northern Territory and Tasmania to repeal legislation criminalising the practice of fortune-telling.

Indigenous Aboriginal Spiritual Traditions Are Still Illegal.

Though the politically correct appearance of acceptance of indigenous spirituality is given in Australia, the practise of aboriginal magick under Australian law is still illegal. These anti-indigenous magick laws stemmed from an incident in 1840 at Port Phillip, Victoria. Aborigines, angered at an unprovoked capture, temporary imprisonment, and killing of two of their men, channel their anger into magick in order to unleash the power of Mindye, the local name for the rainbow serpent, on the whites and blacks who were friendly with them. Various state governments were so terrified by this that they reacted by out-lawing indigenous sorcery and its main practitioners, the Kurdaitcha men.

Kurdaitcha means the clever men, whose traditional job among other things was to deal with law breakers even to the point of issuing capitol punishment in the indigenous community. This Australian legislated Witch-hunt of this group saw an increase of serious crime among the aboriginal people. An example of Kurdaitcha dealing with injustice occurred very publicly on 20 April, 2004 when a member of the aboriginal community defied these laws by invoking an ancient curse on Australian Prime Minister John Howard by "pointing the bone" at the right wing politician, to protest against his decision to scrap a top aboriginal council. Aborigines believe that to point a kangaroo bone at someone is to bring that person ill fortune, and the black magic is strong enough to cause death. However, preliminary discussions with indigenous council representatives at the 14 March 2007 Cairns to suggest law reforms about law and order matters encompassed Aboriginal Magick. It will be interesting to see what results from this symposium.

The Kurdiatcha Men

Kurdiatcha magick is neither black, pardon the pun, nor white, it just is!

The magick was used in every aspect of their lives and is prevalent in their past and present dreaming. Few people realize that the term "black magick" originally referred to the colour of the skin of the magick practitioners. It was originally a slang term for Obia practitioners, the indigenous African religion of the black slaves in the US, and Voodoo its Christianized form. These religions were also banned by law in the United States until relatively recent times, because it was used by the Negro

hunters and wise elders. They could travel freely between tribes and over tribal boundaries with impunity as they were often asked to judge on difficult tribal disputes with the power of life and death called 'singing.'

"Who's Afraid Of The Big Bad Witch?" - by - Dr. S. D'Montford

Magickal Justice

For instance at the turn of last Century, early 1900s, over 100 aboriginals, a whole tribe of men women and children, were poisoned by a Gold Coast dairy farmer for taking the occasional cow to eat, from what used to be their land. This was over looked by local authorities and this mass murderer was never brought to white justice. Therefore, his land was cursed by the Kurdiatcha Men of several surrounding tribes. The result was that his business failed and no other enterprise ever attempted on this prime land, right beside The Pacific High way at Mudgeeraba, has ever succeeded. Consequently, for years this land has been left fallow. A few years ago, a famous Australian golfer purchased the land very cheaply to build an exclusive golf course. From that day he started loosing his golf matches, his wife has left him, claiming a huge chunk of his wealth, with the papers saying he has been having an incredible run of bad luck. The new golf course is not doing too well either.

A few of us offered to negotiate the release of the curse from the golf club land, but the managers are not willing to acknowledge the indigenous heritage of the area, so the curse remains.

There is also a very similar story in the Daintree rain forest near Cairns. Seventy-five aboriginal men women and children were herded off a cliff at Mt Mulligan. The Kadaitcha cursed this deed and an earthquake happened soon after. A portion of the cliff face fell away clearly revealing large numbers etched into the new face. 19111921. On September 19th 1921 the township responsible for the massacre lost 75 men in Australia's worst mining accident to date. Military men, who whilst camped on that cliff, have reported being visited at night by the spirits of the massacred people. All of the men in the group saw the tortured aboriginal spirits. These tough men were scared at first but they claim that the spirits gave them a form of teaching.

Rumour has it that in areas around Golburn on the Victorian NSW border, one of the local sports, has been 'hunting the blacks'. This 'sport' takes the form of a group of white men taking one aboriginal male out into the bush, giving him a short head start and then they hunt him with utes and dogs, kill him and drop his body down the old mine shafts. In the past local law enforcement has turn a blind eye to this local 'tradition'. Local legend says that there is a Kurdiatcha curse on Golburn and its surrounding areas, that says for every Aboriginal shot by a white man, a white man will be killed by a white man also.

Most of rural Australia is renown for its friendliness yet this is a very violent area of Australia. Ivan Milat, one of Australia's most notorious serial killers, was based out of Berrima, not far from Golburn, taking his victims to the Belanglo State Forrest, where some of these hunting parties are believed to have occurred. Seven caucasian bodies were recovered. Milat is believed to be connected with many other disappearances in that area. In 2010 Milat's 17-year-old nephew was charged with the thrill killing one of his best friend's with an axe in this forest. Though it is a beautiful highland forest, it is eerie and well known for violence and disappearances. A sign at the entrance to the forest asks all visitors to "Please Be Careful."

If these stories are true, do they show this form of magick to be evil or "black magick?" Is it wrong? Alternatively, is it Justice? However, with numerous stories like these about the power of indigenous sorcery it is understandable that the government is so afraid of them.

Royal Commission Findings

Royal Commission into Aboriginal Deaths in Custody had this to say on "the ideas of 'singing' and sorcery" *"... the spiritual dimension to Aboriginal people is an integral part of the overall reality. ...The phenomenon of sorcery (being 'sung') usually serves for regulating, in a culturally appropriate and accepted way, groups, intrafamily or personal conflicts. In this way regulating possible antagonisms and threats of communal disorganization. As sorcery traditionally leads to the involvement of a healer ('wise man') the belief system and the healer's participation serve to reinforce the stability and integration of the society/group...Aboriginal people are still subject to traditional punishment. He explained that 'singing' may be used as an alternative to traditional punishment when the accused refused to attend and face traditional punishment....it would make no difference if the reason that the accused was unable to face his community was beyond his control, for example, if he was in prison. A victim of singing can only be released from the influence of the singing with the assistance of a Mabam man. However, on being released, he would still be required to face traditional punishment. ...a Mabarn man is 'a magician' as distinct from a 'Kadaicha man' or 'Featherfoot'. ...where someone is dying through singing and asks for help, the Mabarn man (or traditional healers, - marpantjarra) may be ... called in to cure this man from some spell that has been put on -or has been sung. He is able to cure this man ... He is also a very clever man. He knows what is going on, or what has happened, why he has been sung, therefore he is the man that could be called upon, the mabarn man...an accused would know he had been sung 'because he feels -his conscience tells him that he has been sung'. While 'white law' had abolished the death penalty, ...there is no change in Aboriginal law..."*

New Guinea's Current Witch Hunts

Australian established anti-Witchcraft laws were enacted to protect Witches after the murder of two people accused of Witchcraft in the mist-shrouded highlands of Papua New Guinea, claimed the Sun Herald of December 10, 2007.

"We ran after them and we chopped their heads off with an axe and a bush knife," said the perpetrator, a 27-year-old farmer from Goroka, in Eastern Highlands Province. *"I felt sorry for them but they were Witches, they deserved to die. If they were still alive they could hurt people with their magic."* Two more men were arrested by police under The Act Of Sorcery incorporated into Papua New Guinea's criminal code.

Norman Lindsay's controversial "Venus Crucified" depicted the witch-hunt of his former model, his fellow author, artist, and Pagan, Rosaleen Norton.

Amnesty International claims that hundreds of people each year, mostly women and children, have been subjected to horrific torture like being dragged on ropes behind vehicles, burnt with hot wire and heated metal pipes, have had hands and fingers chopped off before being hanged, thrown off cliffs or buried alive.

"Who's Afraid Of The Big Bad Witch?" - by - Dr. S. D'Montford

When Papua New Guinea was an Australian colony, they suppressed sorcery killings. However, since independence in 1975, this practise, the seed of which was originally planted in the minds of indigenous communities by missionaries who taught them that Witches were evil, has undergone a gruesome renaissance. "Villagers believe they have to kill the so-called Witches, otherwise the whole clan is at risk from black magic," said Jack Urame, a member of the Dom tribe who has researched sorcery killings for the Melanesian Institute in Goroka. "What is disturbing is that children are witnessing these things. The belief in Witch killing is being passed on to the next generation." Urame said.

Rosaleen Norton - The Witch of Kings Cross

After decades of a successful working relationship with the media, a public affair with famed conductor Sir Eugene Gossens was scandalised by the press. Rosaleen was arrested and subjected to psychiatric examinations numerous times, though she was never incarcerated. After the initial furore died down, Rosaleen became a recluse. People kept finding out where she lived and turning up on the doorstep or anonymously leaving anti-Witchcraft slogans for her. In 1974, a new Witch-hunt erupted against Ms Norton and Norman Lindsay whose painting; "The Crucifixion of Venus" was an allegory of this persecution of her by The Church Rosaleen Norton was eventually harassed to death in 1979

The Woman Behind the Myth

Rosaleen Norton has become one of modern Australia's great urban legends. But who was the woman that was a both fragile genius and a terrifying whirlwind under the self-created persona of "The Witch of Kings Cross?" Rosaleen Norton was always good copy for such sensationalist publications as Australasian Post and Truth. Her artwork and her legend still captured the imagination of the public in the new best seller "Rosa Marie's Baby" by Robert Barrett. In it, her mythos is entwined with the rambunctious Les Norton, a fictional character, in the most recent book in that Aussie adventure series.

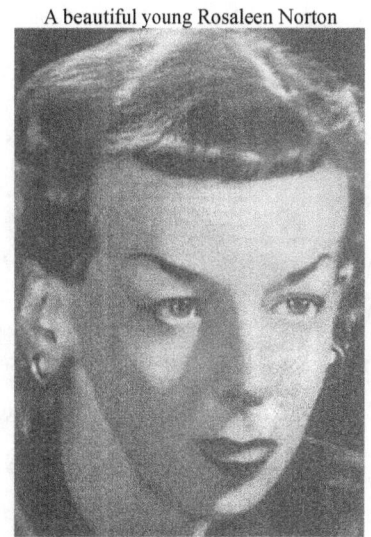

A beautiful young Rosaleen Norton

"Who's Afraid Of The Big Bad Witch?" - by - Dr. S. D'Montford

The Façade

Rosaleen relished the early media limelight that she created by being Australia's first media Witch. Only Aleister Crowley has been able to generate more media attention. Moreover, Roie as she was affectionately known, used similar shock tactics as Crowley to keep the media talking about her. She began working as a journalist and an illustrator for 'Smiths Weekly' at the tender age of fifteen, and later for 'The Bulletin'. By 1950, at 33 years of age she began to promote herself. After, eighteen years in the media, she knew exactly how the system worked. With books and artwork to promote, she used the journalist maxim of: 'No publicity is bad publicity, but bad publicity is great for sales.' She made her works as controversial as possible. By 1951 she had become locally well known and flourished in the atmosphere of bohemian inner Sydney and Kings Cross, where her artworks adorned cafés such as the Kashmir and Apollyon at which people would gather hoping to meet her. Many galleries did a brisk trade in her popular and provocative works. To a large extent Rosaleen, like Crowley, became the victim of her own cheap publicity stunts that played to public fears misconceptions rather than attempting to correct then. This was a mistake that haunted her to her grave. Predictably, in those pre permissive-60s days, her work was banned. The bans were temporary and the publicity was huge. Yet, the seizure of her work in Australia prevented her making a living from sales. She fought back against such censorship saying. "This figs leaf morality expresses a very unhealthy attitude." Many in the academic community originally supported her in her fight. She wrote an ode to censorship called "*Odium Psychopathologicum*"

Behold my friends the empty space
That doth this volume thus disgrace
The drawing that should fill this space
Hath Vanished:
Banned
and
Banished!
O Puritanic Harpies, rage!
Thy Breed alone doth this disgrace
That mirrored saw its own fowl face
With mind as empty as yon space
Whose culture (O enlightened age)
Is even as a missing page.....
Enraged Caliban
(Whose knowledge is, to thy perdition,
Limited as this edition)
Snipping Art in art's expression
Secrets of thine own repression
Howl thy malice! Ban...
Yet, know O ape of little sense
"Honi soit qui y pense!"

(That Latin phrase is the motto on Queen Elizabeth 1st coat of arms and the motto of the 'Order of the Garter' Meaning: *Evil to him that thinks it...*)

Rosaleen's gift with words was as great as her gift with art. A limited edited collection of her beautiful writings, some unknown art work, personal memoirs has recently been published.

When she was unable to sell her works, she made a living by becoming Australia's first woman pavement artist. She worked as an artist's model for, among others, Norman Lindsay, did odd jobs such as kitchen hand, waitress, postal messenger, and of cause, sold her Witchy publicity story to other magazines. She encouraged such headlines as, "Devil Worship Here!" in the Australasian Post, Sydney, 6 October 1955 and 'I Was Born a Witch,' in the Australian Post, January 3, 1957, where she was quoted as answering the question, "Have you ever seen the Devil?" by replying, "If you mean the being whom I know as the God Pan, I frequently have that privilege." She played up to the publics fear and expectations of the occult, to the point of accompanying one such story with a cheesy picture of her in a black pointy Witch's hat. She appeared to live beyond respectable society, apparently flouting all moral and social conventions. She was hounded by the media who seized on her alleged satanic rituals, sex orgies, and drug taking. When asked whether she ever considered leading an ordinary life, she exclaimed: *"Oh God no, I couldn't stand it! I'd go mad or sane. I don't know which."*

Despite all of the tacky publicity stunts and quick quips, Rosaleen was deeply devoted to her spiritual path.

Her chosen deity was the God 'Pan,' the fertilising principle of nature. She credited him with stirring her creative abilities. Pan's other attribute, the ability to cause hysteria, from which we derive the word 'panic' also manifested itself in her later life. Her artwork accurately reflected the overly sexual and frenzied aspects of this deity as well as the deeper mysteries of occult practise. When one reporter arrogantly demanded to know "…if being a Pagan was worth all the scandal, and what she could possibly be getting out of a life of magick?" Rosaleen Norton answered for all Witches when she replied: *"I get a life that holds infinite possibilities and is entirely satisfactory to me on all planes of consciousness."*

The Protector

Yet, she protected those close to her. She refused to sell the press a story about her co-author and lover Gavin Greenlees when his mental health failed and he was admitted to Callen Park in 1955. Nor when erotic photos of them were stolen from her home by her coven members and sold to the press, who were unable to publish them because of their erotic depictions. (See Bert Travenar's statement below) Upset at Rosaleen not giving him a story on Greenlees, a reporter broke into her home, stole her private love letters, and handed them over to police. There was nothing illegal in them, just an obscure reference to S.M., which, as every good Witch knows, means Sex Magick, but the reporter was hoping it meant something more. Nor would she do a tell all on her next lover, the famous conductor Sir Eugene Goosens, when in March 1956 he was searched at Mascot Airport as a result of his association with Rosaleen. Some of his letters to her had been in the stolen love letters and as a result, the police deicded to have him watched and searched. He was accused of trying to "smuggle" into the country some of Rosaleen's banned books, ritual masks and 1,166 art study photographs deemed "pornographic" by Australian customs. However, he was only fined £100 for that. He was forced to leave the country because of a voluntary statement he gave Detective Bert Travenar about his private life. Rosaleen never revealed this secret though she was offered lots of money for the story and was in necessitous circumstances. She took the secret of the love letters with her to her grave. Today we know the secret as it was revealed on the ABC's "Rewind" programme of 5 September 2004 by Michelle Arrow

> Here is a portion of the transcript: -
> BT: "Do you know a woman named Rosaleen Norton?"
> EG: "Yes. I've known her and Gavin for some time."
> BT: "There was repeated mention of 'S.M.' rites between you and Norton and Greenlees made in your letters. What is that?"
> EG: "That is sex magic. It is a symbolic ceremony involving sex stimulation."
> BT: "How is that rite conducted?"
> EG: "We undressed and sat on the floor in a circle. Miss Norton conducted the verbal part of the rite and I then performed the sexual stimulation on her."
> BT: "How did you do that?" He said,
> EG: "I placed my tongue in her sexual organ and kept moving it until I stimulated it."

If he remained in Australia, he was to be charged with 'Scandalous Conduct' for the act of having oral sex in the privacy of his own home mentioned in a private letter, for which he could do several years in prison. Today it would be laughed out of court. He could not have been convicted of 'Scandalous Conduct' anywhere else in the world. Yet, Australia retains this law to this day! There followed a huge scandal with lots of misinformation. Goosens returned to England disgraced and never came back to Australia. The scandal involved many other socialite friends of Goosens, which Rosaleen protected and refused to name. She carried herself with resolve and dignity and refused to compromise her morals, though her morals were not the morals of the rest of society. She remained noble, loyal, and protective even when she was betrayed. Instead of the juicy story the press hoped to get from what they thought would be an easily bribed, morally bankrupt, desperate, destitute and media hungry Rosaleen, the 11th March Sunday Telegraph had to run a sensationalised trumped up story: "Big Names In Devil Rite Probe." in which an unnamed police investigator supposedly disclosed that "black masses and other devil worship ceremonies had taken place in luxurious homes on the North Shore" …involving a prominent "…banker, a lawyer, and …two radio artists who are said to be among those involved." However, there were no names to be printed. Rosaleen would not tell. Her modest home was raided in the middle of the night. She had not expected this backlash. The jilted media turned against her and were inciting legal persecution of her. The people who she had protected did not risk their reputations by trying to assist her.

"Who's Afraid Of The Big Bad Witch?" - by - Dr. S. D'Montford

The Recluse

Rosaleen was arrested and subjected to psychiatric examinations numerous times, though she was never incarcerated. After the initial furore died down, Rosaleen became a recluse and attempted to live a quieter, more private life. She simply stepped out of the public light for the next 10 years. She kept away from anybody who might like to use her for publicity or notoriety or magick. She kept to herself, lived quietly and in poverty. People kept finding out where she lived and turning up on the doorstep or anonymously leaving anti-Witchcraft slogans for her. Suddenly in the 60s, the things that she was doing did not seem so weird any more. Later in the 60s, she would occasionally let a reporter into her coven to do a story.

One amusing story of people trying to hunt her down was published June 15, 1967 issue of Australian Post. Journalist Dave Barnes describes how he and a colleague looking for a story, started to search for Rosaleen at her 1950s, address. Locals directed them to her new front door through which they dropped a note requesting that she ring their office to arrange an interview. The following day they received an invitation. When they entered, they were surprised that Rosaleen was living in what looked like a darkened nuns cell that was only 10 foot by 6 foot. It was adorned with all sorts of esoteric artwork and paraphernalia "and growing creepers..." that they did not think had enough light to grow. She was cheerful and playful but would not answer any serious questions. Instead, she kept asking them how they tracked her down, and at what time? Puzzled, they told her they left their office just before 4 pm and dropped the message through her door at approximately 4.45pm. She began to laugh but they could not understand why. When they got back to their office and check their messages, they found that Rosaleen's call to them had been logged at 4pm the previous day - before they had actually delivered it.

Despite being illegal, discriminatory, ignorant, ill-informed lies, displaying jealousy and just plain bad taste, defamation like this, clipping from the "Liverpool Champion" still appear in the news papers on a regular basis.

Satanic 'bias'

IT has been happening for a long time – Christophobia is alive and well.
The front cover and page four article of the *Champion* (March 19) is offensive to Christians.
Where is the "fair go" of tolerance and respect for Christians?
Let's not fool ourselves, this worship of nature is satanic.
The goddess Dana is recognised by various names across the world – Anu, Danae and as Don (masculine).
She also is associated with child sacrifice and this is satanic.
Satan is not a Christian creation, he is real.
He deceives people into not believing in him.
On March 6 to 8, all the local Anglican churches ran for eight nights the *Good Life – Now* festival at the

Whitlam Centre, Liverpool.
Where was the front page coverage for this? Fair go, please.
"Jesus is the light of the world" (John 8:12).
This pagan festival is darkness.
Now is the time for Christophobic practices to cease.
Please stop giving offence to Christians.

REV GEOFF TAYLOR
Anglican area dean for Liverpool
Sadleir Anglican Church minister

Sydney's Witch Trials in 1974

Things soured again in 1974 as, a new Witch-hunt erupted lead by the Right Rev. Marcus Loane, Anglican Archbishop of Sydney, who set up a "Commission of Inquiry into Occult Practices" in the wake of the movie "The Exorcist." This was only the second such enquiry held in a Protestant country since the middle ages. The

Commission reported, on the sinister modern "crazes" of Occultism and Satanism and their dangers. This report spurred the press to point out supposed Satanists everywhere. Many fingers pointed at Ms Norton. Rosaleen's contemporary, Norman Lindsay, weathered his own inquisition against his similarly styled artwork because of his more conservative nature.

Rosaleen came forward to address the 'findings' of the inquiry. She stated that she agreed with the findings in that *"... Magic can send you around the bend – It's as dangerous as drugs,..."* She declared that magic should not be used as a parlour trick and that armatures that just dabble without learning their craft properly, could stir up forces that they might not be able to deal with. Yet, she did not see this as a reason nor a cause for censorship or prohibition of sales in a free country.

A media frenzy Witch-hunt erupted. People became frightened of her on the street, in busses and in cabs. The police were often called to remove her from public places. Rosaleen was harassed to death quite literally as she contracted colon cancer from the stress. She died less than five years later, in 1979 at the Roman Catholic Sacred Hearts Hospice for the Dying, in Sydney, still worshipping Pan; a Pagan until her death. Shortly before she died, she is reported as saying: *"I came into the world bravely; I'll go out bravely."*

The People Who Knew Her and Whose Lives Were Touched by Hers

Friends who knew Roie remember her with fondness, and invariably refer to how kind and gentle she really was, quite the opposite of the demon so portrayed in Press.

Richard Moir,

Has published a memoir about her in 1994 that paints a vivid picture of her final days. *"When I arrived at the hospital I was ushered into the visitors lounge room, strange I thought, as Roie couldn't walk. I waited in the lounge room for some time patiently, suddenly Rosaleen Norton appeared physically standing on both legs, welcoming me, escorted by two sisters. The vision I beheld was, mind blowing. It was Rosaleen Norton (the persona,) not Roie (my friend) standing there in full garb, her hair flaming back, carefully arranged in her look. Her make-up had been very carefully applied, the face powder, the Rosaleen Norton full eye makeup and eye brows, the red lipstick. It was the Rosaleen Norton as I had always remembered - but even more so. She stood for only one minute... The last words Rosaleen Norton ever said to me were "Darling; I can't stay too long, I just came to say hello. Ah! I must go Darling." And with her head in a proud position Rosaleen Norton was escorted away out of my sight forever."*

"Who's Afraid Of The Big Bad Witch?" - by - Dr. S. D'Montford

Norm Sweeny

"My girl friend and I befriend Roie later in her life. I was just a teenager. We lived in Victoria St, near the Cross, close to where Roie lived. We visited her tiny place and met tall Gavin who was an absolute genius. Her home was small and filled with taxidermied animals and a big goats head. Roie's place did not have a bath. We told her that she could use our facilities anytime she needed. She used to come over to our place once a week, bring candles, oils, herbs, oranges, and Strega liqueur, and perform this elaborate ritual around taking a bath. She would sit in the tub for along time singing happily and enjoying herself. She was a sweet, soft, fragile, person."

Norman Lindsay, whose work her own was often compared to called her: -

"...a grubby little girl with great skill who will not discipline herself."

Anna Hoffman

"When she died in 1979 Rosaleen Norton was a legendary figure, but for the wrong reasons. Her art, representing supernatural imagery has now become more acceptable following the revival of interest in fantasy and surrealistic art. But in her own day her paintings were regarded as bizarre, obscure and pornographic, and she was not accorded the recognition she deserved. She was certainly one of the most interesting, intriguing persons I have ever known and that is why I have chosen her character as the central figure of my novelette, Tales of Anna Hoffmann: part two."

As an adolescent girl in 1955, Anna Hoffman was picked up by the police in Kings Cross for vagrancy. She blamed her sorry state on one of Rosaleen's "Black Masses." She later admitted that she had made all this up, but not before the newspapers had taken the story and run with it. It appears that her penchant for fictional stories about Rosaleen continue to this day!

Bert Trevenar. – N.S.W. Vice Squad Detective:

"Well, two young fellows were hawking some photographs around amongst the newspapers, trying to get the papers to buy them. And eventually, they went to the 'Sun' and the fellow from the 'Sun' got in touch with the chief of the Vice Squad of the day and he detailed me to go down and collect the photographs and then continue on with the inquiry. And I found out that they were photographs of Rosaleen Norton and Gavin Greenlees and that they had come from their Witches' coven at the Cross."

(Re the black-and-white photos of Rosaleen Norton, naked, in various bondage scenarios with Gavin Greenlees, dressed in ceremonial robes)

Ken Wills - as a young Constable detailed at Kings Cross 1976-77

"As a young 18-19 year-old constable working at Kings Cross from Paddington Station, I was called several times to remove 'The Witch Of Kings Cross" from public places. People were scared of her in public as she looked just like an old storybook Witch, with straggly hair, exaggerated makeup, and a baggy green dress. The Anglican 'Inquiry in to the

Occult' was going on at the time, there were some bizarre stories in the paper and the public were getting very nervous. With the public reacting this way, it was easy to see how the Witch burnings got started. Restaurant owners world ask for Rosaleen to be removed as the patrons were complaining. She would get into a bus or a cab and they would refuse to drive her anywhere. She got understandably vocal when this occurred and when she was riled she could swear like a trouper and be very creatively uncooperative. I felt very sorry for her. To me, at the time, she was just a little old eccentric hippy lady that no one liked."

At 50 years of age, Ken Wills has come full cycle. He is now a Pagan and a practising Magician.

Lionel Conroy

"*...Beresford* (Rosaleen's 1st husband) *is actually my father. His full name is Beresford Lionel Conroy the son of Dr Lionel Bigoe Conroy. Dad was born in Crookwell in 1914 so in 1935 he must have been 21 when he married Rosaleen Norton. ... their marriage lasted until after the war, Beres spent two years as a Commando in the A.I.F. in Northern New Guinea. After WWII dad remarried* (Patricia Roberts) *and sired three children. Beres was a very private person who died in 1988, and rarely spoke of his first marriage...*"

Sir Eugene Goossens - In A Letter To Rosaleen

"*RoieWitch, You came to me early this morning, about 1:45. I realised, by a delicious orificial tingling that you were about to make your presence felt. We have many rituals and indulgences to undertake. Even now, my bat-wings envelop and lift you.*"

Kenneth Anger,

During a visit to New Zealand in 1993 said: "*...she inspired the **Rolling Stones** song "Sympathy for the Devil".*" In addition, announced his intention to make a feature film about her life. He said "*Her life has all the ingredients of a good film - sex, black magic, high and low society, drugs and melodrama.*"

Keith Richmond

Who is an editor of both Aleister Crowley and Rosaleen Norton, and has just completed a biography of Aleister Crowley's Australian disciple, Frank Bennett said:

" *... Without doubt the most famous Australian occultist was **Rosaleen Norton**, ...*"

Apuleius' "Defence On Magic"

Apuleius is best remembered for his humorous classical work on magic called "The Golden Ass" or "Metamorphoses." He lived in the early part of the second century CE in Roman North Africa. Apuleius wrote a short work called "Apologia," or, "Apuleius' Defence on Magic." It is a 'transcript' of a lawsuit against Apuleius'; being tried in Sabrata in 158, before Claudius Maximus, the proconsul of Africa on the charge of "Casting Spells On His Own Wife." In it, he made the strongest argument ever against Witch-hunts and Witch-trials being:

IF THE ACCUSERS WERE TRULY AFRAID OF THE MALEVOLENCE OF MAGIC, THEY WOULD NOT BRING THE MAGICIANS/WITCHES TO TRIAL FOR FEAR OF MAGICAL REPRISALS, AGAINST WHICH, THERE IS NO DEFENCE.

Therefore, when someone publicly accuses a person of Witchcraft, they are lying, and the accusers must have other motives rather than believing that magicians/Witches were doing evil magic. History has shown that Witch-hunts are politically motivated.

The Apologia Verse 26

"...But, if these accusers of mine, after the fashion of the common herd, define a magician as one who by communion of speech with the immortal gods has power to do all the marvels that he will, through a strange power of incantation, I really wonder that they are not afraid to attack one whom they acknowledge to be so powerful. For it is impossible to guard against such a mysterious and divine power. Against other dangers, we may take adequate precautions.

He who summons a murderer before the judge comes into court with an escort of friends; he who denounces a poisoner is unusually careful as to what he eats; he who accuses a thief sets a guard over his possessions.

However, for the man who exposes a magician, credited with such awful powers, to the danger of a capital sentence, how can escort or precaution or security guards save him from unforeseen and inevitable disaster? Nothing can save him, and therefore the man who believes in the truth of such a charge as this is certainly the last person in the world who should bring such an accusation..."

Many celebrities due to public and private persecution have gone back into "The Broom Closet." After basing a music career on Craft themes, Ms Nicks now publicly denies Craft connections. Image used with permission from the official Stevie Nicks website.

If They Have Nothing To Hide, Why Do Witches Practise Their Rites in Secret?

After all the things you have just read is it any wonder?

Witch-hunts in one form or another continue today. Many public figures, entertainers, and private citizens find it necessary to go back into the 'broom closet,' as it were, to avoid serious consequences to themselves and their families.

Still there are many open public workings in each year. Members of the public are welcome to attend these to experience the truth about Witches, Pagans and their workings, as long as they follow simple, respectful, guidelines. Many covens have closed workings, as a coven is a close unit like a family. Entry to an established coven can take years.

Witches are essentially shy as a group. This is understandable after 500-years of Witch-hunts and intense persecution in Europe and Asia, added to the fact that the persecution in Australia has only recently officially been repealed but has not in truth ceased.

Chapter 11

Isn't the Pentagram the Symbol of the Devil?

No!

It is a symbol of the creative & reproductive forces in nature

Then what does the Pentagram REALLY mean? Where did it originate? Moreover, why has it been adopted as the highest symbol of the craft?

The pentagram has been used since the beginning of civilisation as a symbol of spiritual significance. Though Pentagrams have been found in the ancient temple art of the east, Çatyul Hüyüak, Samaria and Babylon, like it or not, today's, Magickal use of the pentagram began with the ancient Greek Pagan philosopher and mathematician Pythagoras. Yet, few craft practitioners know this, or if they do that are not willing to admit it. Lets have a brief and honest look at its true significance.

Pythagoras

Six hundred years before Christ, and way before the dark ages, the Pythagoreans used the pentagram as a sign of recognition. To be admitted to Pythagoras' school, a student had to be able to draw a pentagram with out lifting the stylus, combined with a secret password "Hugiaine!" which means, "Be sound, whole and blessed!" In this sense, it first became a banishing pentagram, as this symbol was used to keep the bad elements and the idly curious out of the school and prevented the discussion of the mysteries with the uninitiated. Thus, it became associated with banishing the negative to promote soundness, wholeness, and health. The Pythagoreans called the symbol Hygia from which we get the word "hygiene" and was synonymous with the Goddess of health and cleanliness by that name, the daughter of the God Aesculapius. The Romans called her Salus and associated her cleanliness aspects with water (i.e. sluicing) and the banishing

Pythagoras

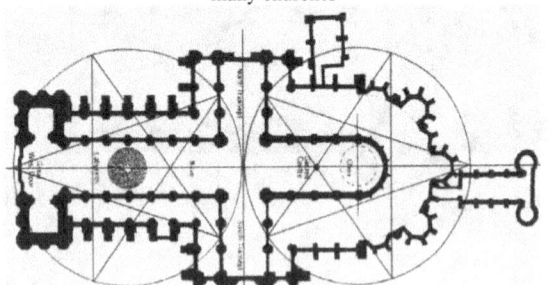
The proportions of the pentagram were used in the floor plans of many churches

qualities with salt. When Witches use their circles of salt with a pentagram, they are directly invoking Pythagoras' main deity Salus/Hygeia.

Hygiene comes from the same Indo-European root word that gives us "viva," "vital," "bios" "vigour," "vigil" and the Latin words "vegetus," i.e. lively, vigorous and "vegeo" i.e. to quicken as well as the Anglo/Germanic words "Wicca" and indo-European word "Witch" originally pronounced with a 'V' sound instead of a 'W' sound.

Christian Pentagrams

Pythagoras is often referred to as the pre-Christian Christ, and was heavily referenced by early church fathers. It is not surprising therefore, to find that pentagrams abounded in early Christianity. According to Heather Child's "Christian Symbols, Ancient and Modern," medieval Christians believed it to symbolize the five wounds of Christ, the five senses, five fingers and the five joys

1) The Annunciation,
2) The Nativity,
3) The Resurrection,
4) The Ascension and
5) The Assumption.

Therefore, the pentagram was believed to be a Christian protection symbol. The pentagram featured in the heavily symbolic Arthurian romances. It appears on the shield of Sir Gawain in the 14th Century poem, "Sir Gawain, and the Green Knight." In which, the five lines of the star are given multiple meanings, but most profoundly, they represent the five virtues of knighthood which Gawain hopes to embody:

1) Frankness,
2) Fellowship,
3) Purity,
4) Courtesy and
5) Compassion,

The Sheild of Sir Gwain

which were also the five virtues of the Pythagoreans. In addition, to this day, it is still a sacred symbol in many Mormon churches.

Labelling the Pentagram

The Pythagoreans labelled the points or angles of the Pentagram with the Greek letters arranged counter clockwise from the top thus: U-G-I-EI-A. Agrippa did the same in his *"De Occulta Philosophia."* Pythagorean signet rings and coins have been found that label an upright pentagram with *both* Hugieia and Salus.

The Elements

The letters labelling the corners of the Pentacle are the first letters of Greek words for the Elements. (See Table)

The Planets

The four 'attributes' correspond to the suits of the Minor Arcana (See Table) by way of the Powers: Intuition-Hot-Swords (Ares), Feeling-Wet-Cups (Aphrodite), Sensation-Cold-Pentacles (Zeus), Thinking-Dry-Wands (Hermes). The Higher-Self corresponds to the Major Arcana (the Divine or Archetypal Realm), associated with your notions of divinity

The Great Work of the Alchemists

The later alchemist began to play with more co-respondances, which are still debated today. They were the first to attach colour and directions to the elemental attributions. Tables of co-respondances became lengthy and varied greatly.

The Tetractys

Pythagoras associated a divine spirit to the first 10 digits, called the Decad, believing that the spirit of these numbers want to help humankind solve every problem known. The first five numbers completed the first cycle. The Tetractys, the first 4 numbers, in the sequence 1+2+3+4, which together adds to the Decad, or 10, was another holy symbol of the Pythagoreans. The second century Neo-Platonist Theon, the father of and co-author with Hypatia, gives a set of correspondences to the Tetractys, based on the properties of the first four numbers. The first four numbers also represent processes of growth or development. The addition of the fifth number, 5, which Pythagoras felt was the hub of everything, gives the sequence a total of 15, which is the sum of any straight line in the magic square of 3x3. Plotting the points from 1-9 on the magick square of 3x3 gives the shape from which the unicursal hexigram and the Masonic symbol is derived. The lead line on the magic square of 3X3 is 618, the decimal of the phi ratio. Pythagoras believed that the magic square of 3x3 and the pentagram were intrinsically linked.

The Phi Ratio and the Pentagram

The Pentagram has over 200 expressions of the Phi ratio hidden within its simple geometry. Where any two lines intersect, the proportions happen to be this ratio. When you draw a smaller Pentacle inside the larger Pentacle, it reduces or compresses to that same ratio. This can continue endlessly in either direction, diminishing into the micro atom or enlarging to the macro universe. When mapped out or plotted, this can produce a graceful spiral, similar in shape to a nautilus shell or a twisting animal's horn. Unfortunately, over time, this sacred symbol of the 3-Dimensional Phi Spiral was demonized by being placed as two twisting horns on of the head of the pictographic representations of the notorious Christian Devil and by placing an inverted pentagram on the devil's third eye. This stained the pentagram and sacred spiral's divinity with fear. Fear means that no access to this memory can be achieved, which keeps the masses in the dark ages.

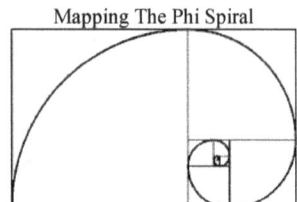
Mapping The Phi Spiral

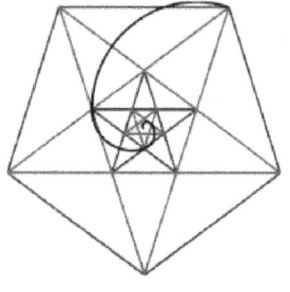

Understanding the Phi Ratio

The masses are beginning to understand that the divine symbol of the Witches Pentacle has been smeared. Most people are now aware of the importance of the Fibonacci sequence, thanks to the best selling book, "The DaVinci Code," by Dan Brown. However, millennia before there was the 'DaVinci Code' there was the Witches code. The success of this book means that a few million more people have heard of the once weknown Fibonacci sequence of numbers: 0, 1, 1, 2, 3, 5, 8, 13, 21, 34, 55, 89, 144, etc. They are derived by having a starting point of zero and one. Adding the two beginning numbers together: 0 + 1 = 1 this gives

the third number of the sequence: 0, 1, 1, then add the previous "1" to the last "1" which gives: 1 + 1 = 2, giving the fourth number of the sequence: 0, 1, 1, 2. It is like adding the Past, to the Present, to give the Future, a veritable Trinity of numbers. Thus, the next number would be: 1 + 2 = 3 and the continuing sequence becomes 0, 1, 1, 2, 3, and so on. When we decimalize the ratio of these numbers to each other, they approach the number: 1.618. We call this relationship, the Phi Ratio: 1:1.618 and is symbolize it by using a Greek letter of the alphabet that gives the "f" sound, called "Phi" or "φ"

The Phi Ratio is the living mathematics of nature. The pentagram is a geometric representation of this. We see these Fibonacci Numbers in the pentacle form of many flowers like the passion fruit; we see it in the pinecone, eight spirals going one way intercepted by thirteen spirals going the other way. In the sunflower, we see twenty-one clockwise spirals versus thirty-four anti-clockwise spirals. We also see these numbers as the approximate distances of the planets from the sun, and the proportion of the human body, from the proportional measurements of the DNA through to the outer proportions like ratio of the limb where the elbow and the knee bends creating beauty, grace and functionality. Architects reflected these proportions in sacred structures like the Parthenon of Greece and the Pyramids of Gizah. These beautiful temples are an outer reflection of this inner divinity in humankind. For thousands of years, great artists used this Fibonacci sequence as the blueprint for their canvass. That is why we are attracted to the proportions of the famous Mona Lisa, as the outer rectangle that contains her form as the blueprint of the Golden or Phi Rectangle in the ratio of 21:34. The graceful phi spiral is often produced as pictured here from nesting the golden rectangle. However, it is easier to reproduce the phi spiral from nesting pentagrams. The overlaid nested phi spirals produced from each arm of a pentagram give us the graceful mathematics and compaction of reproduction that are encoded into the petals of every flower. (For more information on the phi ratio see the writings of Jain or visit www.jainmathemagics.com)

Invoking the Higher-Self

Samael Aun Weor used these proportions in the human body and the pentagram to invoke the Atman or higher-self. By assuming the posture, when a person's limbs are outstretched to create the symbol of the pentagram, and then reciting the mantra *"Klim, Krishna, Govindaya, Gopijana, Vallebayah, Swahah"* 108 times, the higher-self is said to be awakened and will come to the initiate's aid.

Using Pentagrams in Ritual

Therefore, a pentagram is a fractal representation of the larger universe and should be present in all craft rituals as a symbol of this. A fractal is a small part of something that looks just like the larger object. e.g. broccoli braches, tree branches and lightning forks, with the fractals occurring at phi ratio intervals. The pentagram is a map of this fractal nature of creation. As the emerald tablet states: *"As Above So Below As Within So Without."* Thus, all of the elements that we include in our sacred circles create a small universe with in a larger one.

Newtonian law also states that if you drop the apple to the earth, it does not just fall. The apple and the earth move proportionally towards each other. *"For every action there is an equal and opposite reaction."* **So, when you produce a change in your ritual, within your small representation of the elemental universe that you have created, the outer world must move correspondingly. This is the true and deeper meaning of the pentagram. That within ritual space, the individual can create, co-create, and recreate their world according to their will.**

TABLE OF CORESPONDANCES AND SYMBOLISIM FOR THE POINTS OF THE PENTAGRAM									
ELEMENT	**DIRECTION** for the southern hemisphere	**PLANET**	**DEITIES**	**POWER**	**TAROT**	**LIFE STAGE**	**SEASON**	**QUALITY**	**COLOUR**
Spirit	Up	Jupiter	Zeus	Divine	Major Arcana	Change of state	The in between time, reincarnation	The Divine	Octerine
Air	South	Mercury	Hermes	Cold	Wands	Child	Spring	Intelligence and the arts	Red
Fire	North	Mars	Ares	Hot	Swords	Youth	Summer	Courage and daring	Yellow
Water	East	Venus	Aphrodite	Wet	Cups	Maturity	Autumn	Emotions and intuition	Blue/green
Earth	West	Saturn	Chronos	Dry	Pentacles	Old Age/ Death	Winter	Stability and physical endurance	Black

Chapter 12

Are There Pagan Foundations To Western Society?

Did Pagans and Witches try to undermine the foundations of our western society?

No!

Far from it! Many of the noble tenants of society that we hold dear were founded upon Pagan concepts. We owe a far greater debt to Pagan society than acknowledging their philosophers and mathematicians.

Plato said *".. and the ancients, who were superior to us and dwelt nearer to the Gods, have handed down a tradition that all things that are said to exist consist of a One and a Many and contain in themselves the connate principles of limit and unlimitedness."* In this chapter, I would like to examine a few of the people that Plato was referring to who were indeed the pro-generators of society.

Athens – Cradle of Western Life

Five centuries before Christ, a small city of only 70,000 people, during a period of only fifty years, influenced the rest of history, architecture, medicine, politics, philosophy, science, sport, and many other things, in such a new and positive way. At that time Periclase (495 - 429 B.C.), the elected leader of ruler of Athens, gathered the greatest minds in history to form a city that was a living temple to the Goddess of wisdom, Athena. The city was called Athens after its patroness. That short fifty-year rule of Periclaes over the people of Athens was the Golden Age of Greece.

The great minds gathered there included Socrates, the founder of Socratic inquiry, whose successors were Plato and Aristotle that established the first academies. The word academy means "Sacred Grove," in which their students gathered for discourse and learning. Also in this group was Hypocrites father of modern medicine, Pindar the play write, Sappho the first love analyst, Asphisia the slave girl who became first lady and the glue that held this gifted company together, and many others. These were just some of the great minds he cultivated during his rule. Pythagoras (570- 490 B.C.) before this period, laid the conceptual foundations upon which the golden age of Greece and therefore our modern society was built.

The School of Athens

Ironically a painting entitled "The School of Athens," intended to show a harmony between Pagan philosophy and Christian theology, was the first painting completed in 1511 by the Italian renaissance artist Raphael, as a part of a commission to

The School of Athens 1511 by Raphael

decorate the Apostolic Palace in the Vatican. It is framed by two sculptures. The one on the left is the god Apollo holding a lyre he is the God of music, medicine, healing, light, and truth who was said to be Pythagoras father. The one on the right is a statue of Athena herself, the patroness of this golden Pagan age. Though the painting is anachronistic, depicting fifty-five famous Pagans through out classical history, it highlights the debit that society owes Pagan culture. Of the total, at least ten of are female, twenty-one are identifiable. Some of those depicted in this Vatican painting are:

- Epicurus, father of atomic theory,
- Empedocles, the father of cosmogenic theory of the four classical elements,
- Pythagoras, famous for mathematical and musical theory, is the person whose teachings are held to be the foundation of this golden Pagan age, we shall discuss in depth,
- Alexander the Great, the conqueror, who drew the east and the west together,
- Hypatia, who we shall discuss in depth, the first Pagan martyr whose death marked the beginning of the dark ages, was painted in the likeness of the renown beauty Margareta, Raphael's mistress.
- Socrates, who described himself as 'the pricking thorn that inspired forward motion,'
- Heraclitus, painted to look like Michelangelo he was the father of the western doctrine of change being central to the universe, and that the Logos is the fundamental order of all.
- Diogenes, father of anarchism, made a virtue of extreme poverty.
- Euclid, the father of geometry,
- Archimedes, the father of the lever, simple machinery, hydrostatics and displacement theory,
- Strabo, a land mark Greek historian and geographer,
- Apelles, a renowned painter who Raphael egotistically depicted as himself.

The two in the centre of the painting, are: -

- ◎ Plato, on the left designed to resemble Leonardo DaVinci and his student
- ◎ Aristotle, on the right.

Both are holding copies of their own Pagan philosophy books that have been responsible for the formation of western thinking. Plato is holding "Timaeus" in his left hand with his right arm pointing to the heavens and Aristotle is holding "Ethics" in his left whilst his right hand gestures to the earth. This is the Pagan sign of *"As Above So Below."* This is the main phrase in "The Emerald Tablet" which is widely held to be the basis for Pagan philosophy. Indeed the "School of Athens" brought the fire of the Gods, the knowledge of life, from the heavens to earth, inspiring the world.

Despite this, and despite the Vatican containing a Pagan temple with some of the best preserved and most magnificent statues of many Pagan gods in both the Chiaramonti Museum and its Belvedere Courtyard, it continued to ban Pagan science, mathematics and philosophy that contradicted its erroneous dogma until the 20th century.

Pagan Aspirations and Advancement

Pagan philosophers asked questions about the most general and abstract features of the world and began to categorise what we think into: mind, matter, reason, proof, and truth. In philosophy, the concepts with which we approach the world become the topic of enquiry such as reality, causation, belief, right and wrong, beauty, self, the nature of the Gods, and law. Philosophy encompassed the systematic inquiry of the fundamental questions. Their answers have become integral to our modern worldview. The questioning of the nature of reality became metaphysics. The questioning of the nature of knowledge became epistemology. The examination of the conduct of life was the first studies of Pagan ethics. This enquiry extended to the point of examination of the structure of argument, which became the study of logic.

2000-year-old Baghdad Battery
This simple acid battery still emits voltage when a common acid like lemon juice is introduced.

This lead to the first categorised speciality fields of study: - biology, mathematics, anatomy, astronomy, etc. At that time, they had already measured the distance to the stars, the circumference of the earth, developed elliptic theory, and discussed atoms and atomic theory. The remains of acid batteries have been discovered in Baghdad and in Athens. Electrum jars made from the organic gemstone amber, that produce a charge from friction and rotation, dating to that period in time, indicating knowledge of electricity. All of this science and technology was lost to Europe under the Christian dark ages from 300A.D. until the rediscovery of many of these things during the Renaissance of the 1700s.

Establishing the fact that ancient advanced civilisation and technology existed in ancient Pagan culture is not the aim of this text. There are several excellent works on this. For further reading on these, see "From the Ashes of Angels" by Andrew Collins or "Secrets of the Lost Races" by René Noorbergen.

THE PAGAN ORIGINS OF DEMOCRACY

Western society arrogantly proclaims itself to be the epitome of democratic civilisation whilst deriding Pagan cultures as being barbaric, heathen and less evolved. This is a laughable statement as the origins of democracy are Pagan and many forms of pre-existing democracy were far fairer than the present paradigm.

What Is Democracy?

Democracy is a political system by which, in theory, all the members of the society have equal access to the decision making process. However, this is just not the case in western society. In representative democracy, the people we elect often vote against the majority decisions of those that elected them for their personal and political gain. This was not the case in the ancient Pagan history of democracy.

We can historically trace democracy's Pagan origins in the ancient world. It disappeared in the Christian feudal medieval period but had a re-emergence in the renaissance of 17th century.

Tribal Democracy

A tribal group is essentially a democracy. This form of near self-rule by co-operation has been termed 'true anarchy' or 'primitive democracy.' Tribal democracy can still be seen in small communities or villages with face-to-face decision making discussion in a village council or when a headperson's decisions need support by village elders or other groups. This honouring of the right to self-determination was the earliest form of democracy. It was Pagan in origin and is still widely spread.

"Who's Afraid Of The Big Bad Witch?" - by - Dr. S. D'Montford

Sumerian

Sumeria has some of the earliest written records of a democratic process. It is interesting to note that the legendary ruler Gilgamesh, in early Sumer, did not hold the autocratic power. Rather his actions had to be approved by a council of elders and a council of young men. The final political authority rested with these two groups and they had to be consulted on all major issues.

India

India appears to be the source of the western version of democracy. Pythagoras, after studying in India returned to Greece expounding these ideals along with the mathematics he encountered there. Alexander the Great and Aristotle both admired early Indian democracy in which the monarch, or Raja, from of a family of the noble *K'satriya Varna*, was elected by the *Gana*, a deliberative assembly. The assembly met regularly. In some states, or *Sanghas*, attendance was open to all free and educated men and women, and discussed all major state decisions. The Gana had financial, administrative, and judicial authority. The Raja had to coordinated his activities with this assembly and a council of other nobles.

We have records of these "republics of India," as early as the sixth century B.C. which continued until the fourth century C.E. Diodorus, a well know Greek mentions that independent and democratic states existed in India. It should be noted that these concepts arise from the *Artha' sastra Veda*, an ancient sacred handbook on how to rule, from which these concepts are derived, and it predates Diodorus' account by a thousand years.

Early Irish Democracy

Medieval Pagan Ireland used what is called the Túatha system. It was a local assembly that met annually to decide all common policies including local wars against other Túatha. One of its main functions was the election of a new King, which normally occurred during the old King's lifetime. The new King had to be descended within four generations from a previous King, so this in effect was a hereditary Kingship, alternated between lines of cousins. About 80 to 100 Túatha coexisted throughout Ireland. Each Túath was divided among its members and controlled a compact area of land that it could defend from cattle-raids and invasion.

The Elected High Kings

The election of the High Kings in Wales and Erin (Ireland) is a very ancient and exacting process dating from the Cruthin, in middle semi-mythical period, till 1541, when King Henry VIII assumed the title by force.

Many claim that Roderick the Great in 388 B.C. (Rughraidhe Mor or Rudricus Magnus) was the last true High King, however, the election of leaders clearly continued as a High King still presided over the five provinces of Ireland in medieval times. Each province had their own King, who were subject to the elected High King, which, resided at Tara. The written judicial system was the Brehon Law, and had professional jurists to administer it. Kings were the sporting heroes of their day. They were the cream of their societies and had to be free from mental and physical imperfection. King Nuda lost the top job when he lost an arm in battle after which another King, Bres, was elected to replace him.

These leaders were selected from amongst their peoples at an early age and given specialist training, not just in warfare. Prof. Frands Herschend of the University of Uppsala points out; they were expected to be like the God Odin, literate, subtle, political, slippery, and very clever. Dr Neil Price suggests that they also trained in clear thinking, compassion, foresight, courage, magick spells for giving enhanced concentration under fire, and seduction. This kingly seduction was not sexual seduction but seduction of the public for political reasons. In Gamla Uppsala, the traditional seat of Sweden's Pagan Kings, they had to campaign for allies and give good gifts to court public popularity. They also needed to be able to talk to the Gods. They were taught to be selfless to the point of sacrificing themselves, as one of their Kings, Dumald, did literally. Leslie Webster of The British Museum agrees with these findings and adds that from her examination of Anglo-Saxon burial mounds in Taplow, Buckinghamshire, from the 7th centaury AD, they were also poet musicians because of frequently finding musical instruments buried with them. Dr Cameron Lawson Archaeologist at the University of Cambridge, likens them to "...musical war correspondents and spin-doctors for their people."

Here are "Instructions from King Cormac Mac Airt," for the selection of Red Branch Knights who, one day, may be voted in as King. These include making sure that the candidate has the following qualities:

"...Goodness of his shape and family,

His experience and wisdom,

His discretion, kindness, eloquence, and bravery in battle,

And the number of his friends..."

If our present day political leaders could only retain their office because of their eloquence, generosity, self-sacrifice, and adherence to their word, would any of them make the grade? Would any of them go onto a battlefield rather than hide behind the lives of other young men presently being sent to fight their battles for them?

It is ironic that Western Christian history derides Pagan culture as uncivilized with all of this proof of democratic Pagan history that upholds the concepts of hight ethics, self-determination and the individual's rights. The first elected Christian-based parliament in Europe was not until D'Montford's (D'Montfort's- French) Parliament in England in 1265 giving back to the people through The Council of the Barrons, rights that they had lost during the Christian feudal dark ages. Simon D'Montford in 1265 introduced the idea that power holders are responsible to an electorate and established a baronial court to which the English monarchy was answerable. This Pagan institution is represented by the white cross on The Union Jack. Using this mechanism, thirty-two descendants, namesakes, and supporters sort a pardon for witches executed under the jurisdiction of the Barron's Courts of Prestoungrange and Dolphinstoun, as their final act of their last sessions before abolition of the Provisions of Oxford established in 1258, and the Forma Regiminis in 1264. Under these provision appeals could be made and the King's decisions overturned, by a baronial council of fifteen. These provisions were the beginning of the democratic process in England and are commemorated by the white cross on the Union Jack and unfortunately; it was abolished on the 28th of November 2005. The final Halloween 2006 session of the court declared, "...pardon to all those convicted as well as all the cats concerned."

Spartan Democracy

Many people incorrectly attribute the rise of democracy to the culture of the ancient Pagan Athens. The Greek state Sparta preceded its implementation by 200 years. Greece was originally a collection of warring independent city-states called Poleis. Many of these poleis were oligarchies; a form of government where political power effectively rests with a small elite segment of society. Sparta's rejection of private wealth as a primary social differentiator, paved the way for Western style democracy. In Spartan government, the political power was divided between three bodies:

1. Council of Gerontes or elders, over 60 years of age, elected for life, including the two Spartan Kings. This dual Kingship diluted the absolute power of the executive office. These dual Kings had to share all judicial decision with the Gerontes.

2. The Ephors were representatives from the poorest social rungs who oversaw the Kings and were capable of deposing them.

3. All were answerable to the Apella or the assembly of all free Spartan men and women above the age of 30.

The creator of the Spartan system of rule was the legendary Pagan philosopher and lawgiver Lycurgus. His drastic reforms were instituted in the second half of the 7th century BC. His reforms were directed towards the three

Lycurgus, as depicted in the chamber of the U.S.

Spartan virtues: 1) Equality among the free citizens, 2) Military fitness, and 3) Austerity. The Spartans referred to themselves as Homoioi, men of equal status. It was also reflected in the Spartan public educational system, Agoge, where all citizens irrespective of wealth or status had the same education. Spartan women also enjoyed the right to inheritance, property ownership, voting and public education. Spartans were free to criticize their Kings and they were able to depose and exile them. Lycurgus' written list of reforms were called Great Rhetra; from which we get the word rhetoric, meaning to debate. It is the world's first written constitution.

Athenian Democracy

A form of democracy did not begin in Ancient Athens until 508 BC when "the many were enslaved to few, the people rose against the notables." In 594 BC Solon, a Lyric poet, acting as a mediator between the rival factions, attempted

Solon, depicted in the chamber of the U.S. House of Representatives.

to satisfy all sides by alleviating the suffering of the poor majority without removing the privileges of the rich minority. This laid the foundations of what has come to be called modern Western democracy.

Solon's theories divided the Athenians, into four economic classes, with different duties for each. All citizens were entitled to attend and vote at the Ecclesia assembly, the principle body for passing laws, electing officials and hearing appeals from the courts. Four hundred members from all socio-economic groups could serve a year at a time, to prepare business for Ecclesia. The positions of Archons and Magistrates were reserved for citizens of the top two income groups. Retired archons became members of Areopagus or Council of the Hill of Ares, and it was their responsibility to keep in check improper actions of the Ecclesia. This philosophical/political system resulted in the magickal system of the Sator/Rotas.

Previous to this, Greece had remained a cultural backwater long after the appearance of the earliest forms of democracy in the Near East, Ireland and Scandinavia

Pericalase and Asphasia

As stated earlier, Pericles, a Pythagorean student, is credited with ushering in the golden age of Athens under the encouragement from his consort Asphasia, a captured Minoan princess. She was an educated woman that rose from slavery to marry Pericles, the then elected ruler of Athens. Plato describes her as one of the few people from which Socrates would ask advice. Knossos in Minoan Crete was the centre of a once vast and peaceful Goddess worshiping democratic society. The elected Knossos king had to be willing to sacrifice himself for his people. Unlike the Greeks, they had no army, nor wars, but were artisans and traders and merchants. The Greek states, called Apolos, which included Athens, and Sparta, did not include Knossos. The Greek Apolos were very separate and in awe of the Minoans until natural disasters devastated their culture.

When asked why and how he accomplished establishing such a great city and how he fostered so many great minds, Periclaes replied: - "As the birds of prey see their trackless way in the sky so can I see my way." The owl is a symbol of the Goddess of wisdom, Athena, patroness of the city of Athens. Today the placing of the outline of an owl formed by roadways and other city works by town planners is considered a clever nod to the golden era of Pagan Athens that birthed the concepts of our democratic western society.

The Pagan Way

Pericles's way was a magnificent ideal. In this one city alone, Pagans developed modern theories of science and architecture that enabled beautiful structures like the Acropolis and the Parthenon and many of the other major buildings of ancient Athens to be built. Some of these were centrally heated and cooled through the marble floors. They had running water and flushing sewerage systems. Additionally, the Pagans of this region established the first international peace games now called the Olympics. The word athlete was first used during this time. In this Pagan city dedicated to the goddess of wisdom, fields of learning were first divided into specialist areas and academies formed. Using advanced mathematics they measured the circumference of the globe and calculated the elliptical orbits of the celestial bodies in our solar system. They first theorised on the atom and dark matter most of this knowledge was lost due to the Church's persecution of all things Pagan and had to be officially rediscovered in the last 300 years. Yet, under Pericles, the term "philosophy" was first used derived from a combination of the Greek words "philo" meaning love and "sophia" meaning wisdom; literally the love of wisdom or knowledge. Socrates, Pericles teacher and the most influential man in Athens is famous for encouraging the growth of philosophy with his constant badgering questions and his statement that "The unexamined life is not worth living."

Accepting what is spoon-fed to us in a society that has repressed knowledge for over 1500 years, with all of its prejudices and manipulations is not living "an examined life." The ancient Pagan way is a proud heritage that birthed the wonderful things in our modern society. By examining our Pagan heritage we can find the elements that make our life worth living.

Later Scandinavian, Norse and Other Pagan Democracies.

From our earliest written European records we know that no communal undertaking, from raid to cropping to shipbuilding, was commenced in Norse communities without a vote in an assembly in the community great hall. These were formalised assemblies were called *Things* and are still found all over Northern Europe.

The *Althing*, the parliament of the Icelandic Commonwealth, was founded in 930. It consisted of the 39 to 55, *Goðar*. Membership, which could be lent or sold. However, each hereditary goði was kept tight hold of by the owner. Each independent farmer in the country could choose what goði represented him. The Althing has run continuously to the present day.

The "Thing of All Swedes," was held annually at Uppsala in the end of February or early March. Like in Iceland, the assemblies were presided by the lawspeaker, but the Swedish King functioned as a judge. In 1018, when King Olof Skötkonung wanted war against Norway Þorgnýr the Lawspeaker reminded the King that the power resided with the Swedish people and not with the King. The people used to obey the King only when they thought his suggestions were good, although in war his power was absolute.

Most of the procedures used by modern democracies are very old. Because of this antiquity the city-state of Milan, lead by the elected ducal Saforzas, rebelled against the feudal Medici Popes in the time of Leonardo DaVinci. Many of his paintings reflect the loss of this system of democracy to Papal theocracy.

Indigenous peoples of the Americas and Australia had democratic systems. The early American philosophies of democracy propounded by Thomas Jefferson, Benjamin Franklin, and others, were inspired by indigenous peoples of the Americas, Historian Jack Weatherford claims that Americans learned democracy from the indigenous peoples of the North America.

South Ameriacn Aztecs society practiced elections, and the elected officials were elected as a supreme speaker, but not a ruler.

Elizabeth 1st removed Catholic theocracy in 1625, and passed laws that no law-abiding citizen could be imprisoned or executed for their beliefs. This law kept The Inquisition out of England. Free thinkers, philosophers, mathematicians, and scientists flooded into her court that was hailed globally as truly embracing democratic principles.

Where Is Modern Advancement?
It is interesting to consider, how far have society really advanced in the 2500 years since Athens? Considering the rate of advancement that occurred during that 50-year period, what have we really

achieved since then? This is an interesting question, which has been debated by many. We have the internal combustion engine. Yet, the Romans first invented the steam engine before the fall of their empire. The self-declared non-aligned Pagan Leonardo DaVinci revisited it 1200 years later. However, in the last hundred years that we have been commercially using the internal combustion engine, it has not really changed much. We have aeroplanes. The ancient Hindus had flighing machines thay called Vimana. Apparently so did the Pagan Maya and the Inca of Peru. Nevertheless, our aeroplanes are basically the same as when the post WWII generation started to jet set. Where is the real advancement? Even our so-called advancements in space are debated. The question has been raised many times, "Was Mr. Armstrong really the first on the moon?"

We have mechanised mass production. This has resulted in an insatiable greed than has made our society slaves to consumerism. A thing that our ancestors successfully avoided. Even our electronic toys are on the "slow release technology" plan. That is, up dates released every three to six months but this is not in any way representative of our latest technologies. The object of this is to maximise the electronics company's profits and thus many remain constantly in debit to the credit card companies and banks. Individuals willingly hock their souls, to keep themselves amused and distracted away from achieving their full personal power potential.

Is the propaganda line that we are now the most advanced civilisation that ever existed on the planet true? On the other hand, is it just the arrogance of the conquerors that wish to discredit the cultures that they have destroyed? If our new academies and think-tanks are superior to those of the golden age of Paganism then where is the evidence of progress in our society? Are we still living in a form of controlled release information, akin to, (but shinier, with more flashing lights,) the social control of the dark ages? Alternatively, have we reached the limits of advancement in mundane technology? Has our society hit the same wall of the physical plane that other ancient civilisation have hit before us? As the ancient Pagan philosophers realised, the non-hysterical exploration of magick, metaphysics, and quantum mechanics is where our next great innovations will take place.

'The Dark Side Of The Force' And 'The Fifth Element' In Modern Astrophysics!
Recent research shows that ancient alchemists did know what they were talking about after all! It is very refreshing to see modern scientist admit that they have come to the point in their research where they now

know that they really don't know much at all and acknowledge, that for all of their technological toys, the universe remains a 96% unsolvable mystery to them. It is lovely to see them tip their hats to their very early predecessors and admit that alchemical theories of earth, air, fire, water and quintessence/spirit - a sublime fifth element may, have been right all along.

In 1998, astronomer Brian Schmidt published a paper on supernovas that concluded that the universe is filled with a dark energy that is causing galaxies to move away from each other at an accelerated rate. The expanding universe is sometimes compared to a currant cake rising in the oven, with the currants representing galaxies and the dough of the cake representing expanding space.

Since the supernova data was gathered, two other observations have independently confirmed that the universe is expanding at an accelerated rate. One of these was made by an award winning team of astronomers working at the Anglo-Australian Observatory near Coonabarabran in NSW.

Supernovas are spectacular eruptions that occur at the end of a star's life. Astronomers use them as signposts or 'standard candles,' which help them calculate the size and age of the universe. Schmidt says ".. they allow us to look back in time." The universe is now believed to be about 13.7 billion years old, with a 5 per cent margin for error.

Geometry Is Destiny.

It was believed that if the shape of the universe were known, astrophysicists would be able to predict how it would eventually end. If the shape was an open curve, in which the two ends point away from each other, then the universe could, theoretically at least, expand forever. However, if space was found to curve inwards, like a snake biting its tail, which is the ancient alchemical symbol the Oroubus, the universe could end in a final crunch; an event Schmidt calls "The gnaB giB"

Astronomers have observed that the rate of the universe's expansion was not slowing, as expected, but speeding up. They found the galaxies were moving apart at 'a much faster rate than the laws of physics are able to explain' and cannot account for the phenomenon. Scientists have dubbed the force that is responsible for this expansion "Dark Energy," dark because it fills the blackness of space and because it is obscure, unknown and mysterious.

"Who's Afraid Of The Big Bad Witch?" - by - Dr. S. D'Montford

Physicists believe that only 4 per cent of the universe is made up of matter that can be measured by conventional instruments now at humankind's disposal. This means that 96 per cent of what makes up the universe is in a form that has never been detected directly in a laboratory: 73 per cent is believed to be 'Dark Energy' and 23 per cent an enigmatic substance known as "Dark Matter." The twist is that nobody knows what dark energy is and dark matter has never been seen because it emits no light. Its existence is inferred by the gravitational pull it exerts, e.g. this is why the outer arms of a galaxy travel at roughly the same speed as the dense centre. Yet, the question of 'what this dark stuff is,' remains unanswered. The all-encompassing "Theory of Everything," describing the universe and all its wonders, that physicists speculated we would soon reach, is looking less likely now.

A dark galaxy, which emits no starlight and is composed predominantly of dark matter, seems to exist in the Virgo cluster and has been labelled VIRGO H21. This may explain why a near by galaxy, NGC 4254, is lopsided, with one spiral arm much larger than the rest, as this is usually caused by the influence of a companion galaxy. Astronomers believe that dark VIRGO H21 is responsible.

Looking At The Past To See The Future

Einstein, and the 5000-year-old Hindu Vedas, theorised that energy and matter are essentially interchangeable. Dark energy and dark matter may be related, although most astronomers do not think they are; at this stage not enough is known about them to say.

Schmidt and his colleagues understood that their observations would change our understanding of how the universe operated. He says. "I like the idea of a finite universe that has a life cycle that begins with the Big Bang and ends with the gnaB giB, but this doesn't seem to be the way of the universe."

In the Melbourne Sun Herald, Saturday, February 4, 2006, Schmidt's went so far as to say that it would take more than 50 years or a generation for the nature of dark energy to be understood by scientists. It took about 130 years before scientists grasped the counter-intuitive world of quantum physics in which the observer influences the behaviour of subatomic particles, which are inherently unpredictable. Physicists agree that another revolutionary leap, or a good long look at the past, is what is required now.

"Who's Afraid Of The Big Bad Witch?" - by - Dr. S. D'Montford

In 1917, Einstein proposed the existence of a cosmological constant that he called "Lambda," the 11th letter in the Greek alphabet, to explain the force that kept the universe in a steady state. He theorised that the cosmological constant was a force that exerted negative pressure. Since the supernova data has been accepted, lambda has gained new respectability as a way of solving the problem and of describing dark energy. Seventy years later, lambda is being revisited because, in Schmidt's words, "it tells us what the energy of nothing is." Ancient mystery traditions have expressed this value in a way that modern physicists were previously unwilling to examine. The Pythagoreans postulated on forces and particles smaller than an atom, 500 years before Christ. The Taoists before them called the lambda force "The Tao." Thousands of years before that, the Hindu Vedandic scientist called the dynamic dancing dark energy "Shiva." Celtic mythology called it the "Silver Net."

There are difficulties with the cosmological constant. One is that the rate of the universe's expansion has not been constant but has changed over time. It is theorised that micro-seconds after the Big Bang the universe experienced a moment of hyper-expansion, when space and matter increased at an extraordinary rate. Then the rate of expansion sped up again about 5 billion years ago, which also happens to be the time our own sun came into existence. This coincidence makes astronomers and physicists uncomfortable. "Why did it happen, just when we happen to be around?" asks Schmidt. "It begs the question that maybe we are missing something." Creationism may be popular among religious conservatives, but astronomers are wary of any science that may suggest an anthropocentric universe. However, most creation myths from different religious traditions, follow the same patterns that science has only relatively recently reconfirmed.

An alternative theory calls the unknown force that is causing the universe's expansion "Quintessence." In ancient Greece, Egypt, India, South America and Asia it was believed that the world was made up of earth, water, air, fire and quintessence, a sublime fifth element. Western Alchemists, who were the predecessors of our modern scientists, took up these theories much later. All of these ancient theories state that quintessence also exerts negative pressure, but has the capacity to change over time, depending on conditions as has recently been recorded with the supernova data. Theoretically, at least, this means the nature of quintessence could also change in order to bring about the renewal of the universe at some distant future date. This is stated most memorably in the Hindu Vedas and ancient Inca and Aztec writings.

For us, the advent of dark energy marks the official return of mystery to its traditional place at the centre of the universe. Moreover, you do not have to be a physicist to appreciate that where mystery lurks, awe and wonder are not far behind.

> *"In science it often happens that scientists say, 'You know that's a really good argument; my position is mistaken,' and then they would actually change their minds and you never hear that old view from them again. They really do it. It doesn't happen as often as it should, because scientists are human and change is sometimes painful. But it happens every day. I cannot recall the last time something like that happened in politics or religion." - Carl Sagan*

NEW WAYS VERSES OLD WISDOM

Why Crystals Work

Why do esoteric people feel drawn to crystals? Is it just a superstition or science? Psychics, Shaman and Witches, without the use of technology, demonstrate that crystals can be used as tuners for the complex human instrument, and can amplify the resonance of these fields, which they then attempt to interpret.

Dr. Oldfeild's work is demonstrating that crystals have individual intelligences that chose to work with their owners. In the simplest terms, the work they do is to act as an energy tuner. The human organism has an unlimited capacity to receive information through the five senses, represented by the five-pointed star, via input that science, at present, does not fully understand. However, it works on principles that are long established scientific facts.

Crystal Radios

Crystal Radios do not run on an external power source. They use a crystal detector to attract tune and convert radio wave electricity back to sound electricity. The detector is made from a rock crystal in a holder. Earphones convert the electricity to sound you can hear. The natural mineral crystal forms a side of the junction. This functions in a similar way to the human crystal relationship, working on more subtle energies. We know that certain crystals can be an open channel to a broad range of frequencies and resonances. Crystal radios can be designed to receive almost any radio frequency since there is no fundamental limit on the frequencies the crystals will receive. Crystal radios can receive spark signals as low as 20 kHz and below. Although crystal radios are designed to detect AM, they also frequently detect FM, which is in the 100 MHz range.

A crude crystal set can be made from a coil of salvaged wire, a rusty razor blade and a pencil's graphite for a diode. By lightly touching the pencil lead to spots of blue on the blade, or to spots of rust, they form what is called a point contact diode and the rectified signal can be heard on earpieces. How much more can a trained complex human receiver pick up when aided by crystals?

The crystals with fine radio wave detecting properties are: galena, iron disulfide which is pyrite or fools gold, vitreous, i.e. clear or see through, crystals were found to work the best including carborundum zincite with bornite in a rock-to-rock junction and silicon. Bornite is a copper ore sulfide mineral with chemical

Vitreous Zincite
Used in Crystal Radios

composition Cu5FeS4. It has a brown to copper-red colour on fresh surfaces that tarnishes to an iridescent purple. Its purple to bronze iridescence gives it the nickname peacock copper or peacock ore. Zincite is the mineral form of zinc oxide (ZnO). In nature, its crystal form is rare. Like quartz, it has a hexagonal crystal structure, and colour that depends on impurities. As an early radio detector, it was used in a junction with another mineral, chalcopyrite, and the combination was known as the Perikon detector.

Crystal Silicon's ability to access and store information has had a great impact on the modern world's economy and lifestyle, because of the development of crystal silicon wafers being used in the manufacture of devices such as transistors, integrated circuits boards and computer chips. Silicon carbide (SiC) or Moissanite, is a compound of silicon and carbon bonded together to form ceramics, but it also occurs in nature as the extremely rare mineral. Pure α-SiC is a semiconductor with band gaps of 3.28 eV (4H) and 3.03 eV (6H). It is used extensively for this application in NASA's space programs. Silicon carbide is also used as an ultraviolet detector and was observed to have electroluminescence by

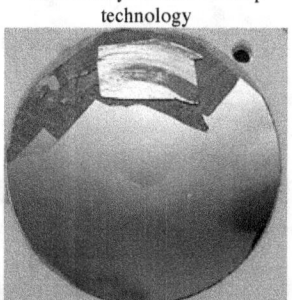
Synthetic Crystal Silicon Wafer
Used in Crystal Silicon Chip technology

Captain Henry Joseph Round, in 1907. Silicon carbide is used for blue LEDs and has the potential to be used as a power device material. Moissanite has become popular as a diamond substitute, and may be misidentified as diamond, since its thermal conductivity is much closer to that of diamond than any other diamond substitutes. It can be distinguished from diamond by its birefringence and a very slight green, yellow, or grey fluorescence under ultraviolet light. Moissanite is similar to diamond in several important respects: it is transparent and hard with a refractive index between 2.65 and 2.69, that is close to the 2.42

for diamond. It is lighter, density 3.22 vs. 3.56, and much more resistant to heat. This results in a stone of higher lustre, sharper facets, and good resilience. Loose moissanite stones may be placed directly into ring moulds; unlike diamond, which burns at 800°C, moissanite remains undamaged by temperatures up to twice that. However, it remains cost effective enough for the ground formto be used as impregnated sand grips on things like skateboard decks and steps ledges. Silicon carbide is also used in ceramic plates in bulletproof vests. Dragon Skin, which is produced by Pinnacle Armour, utilizes disks of crystal silicon carbide.

Resonance

Resonance is a way of taking a little bit of energy, and using it repeatedly, at just the right time or frequency, to accomplish a big task. Crystal radio sets take a little bit of resonance registering on crystals and transform it into other forms of registrable or workable energy; like taking radio waves and turning them into electrical impulses strong enough to power an audio headset. We use resonance when we push someone on a swing. It would take a lot of work to lift someone several feet in the air, but we can do this easily on a swing by giving a little push repeatedly at just the right time. Timing is important; if we push at the wrong time, the swing can actually lose energy instead of getting higher. When an opera singer uses their voice to shatter a wine glass, they are using resonance. their voice gives the glass molecules a little push at just the right time, repeatedly, until the glass shape is moving so far that it shatters. Subtle energy waves can act like the sound waves of the singer's voice. The energy waves picked up by the crystals rise in resonance in the human instrument until they can do the work of registering a message with the receiving person's consciousness.

Bioelectric And Radio Frequency Generation

It is well known that large electric eels have an electric organ that extends almost the entire length of their body. The organ consists of hundreds of thousands of electrocytes capable of generating electric discharges. Study has shown that electric eels also have high-frequency sensitive receptors patchily distributed over their body, which are useful for detecting their prey. These eels transmit direction-finding pulses at a frequency of 50 hertz and are capable of producing shocks reaching one amp and 600 volts.

Human Electricity

It is also well known that the human body generates an electrical current by changing chemical concentrations in and around the nerves. The brain is an electro-chemical organ. When a nerve signal is sent, potassium ions flood out of nerve cells and sodium ions flood in. Both of these ions have slightly different charges and so the difference in concentrations inside and outside the nerve cell of the ions means that a charge is created inside the nerve cell. However these impulses vary so much with fluctuation in human activity it has proven elusive to quantify. Every cell in the body is a sub-microscopic electromagnetic device. Every chemical reaction involves an electromagnetic transaction. The human body's electro-chemical nervous system can be in balance with the earth's electromagnetic frequencies of 7.9 cycles per second called the Schumann cavity resonance. Crystals must resonate to this field before they are removed from the ground. In a relaxed state the alpha brain wave can sink to 8.0 Hz cycles per second. The Theta brain wave state cycle is slower.

The nervous system not only conveys messages from the different parts of the body to the brain, but also serves to convey the energy of motion to the various parts. In short, there can be no motion of any part of the body without the electrical signals from the nerves. The nervous system is a part of the great energy-producing system of the body, as much a part of it as is the brain. This nerve-energy spreads itself beyond the limits of the body and thus crystal receivers can register this energy. The nervous system of the human being is a very intricate mechanism far more sensitive than any man made devise. Like the electric eel, the main human electrical feature, the spinal cord, runs along an opening in the spinal column, this is directly connected with the brain matter in the skull. From the spinal cord, emerge many sets of nerves, in pairs, which branch out in smaller and smaller filaments, until every part of the body is supplied with a direct connection with the main nerve trunk. There are other large cables of nerves descending into the trunk of the body, apart from the spinal cord system, although connected with the latter by nerve links. In different parts of the body are found great masses of nerve-substance, matted knots or tangles of nerves. These centres are called plexuses or chakras. Like the electric eel, these centres can also receive information from the outside world. The principal, the "solar plexus," is well known for being the major receptor of feelings about others or our gut feelings. Picking up this information can be enhanced by the receptive properties of crystals.

Added to this human body electricity, is the static electricity generation gathered by your body. Static is not generated by the body, but simply by things passing over the skin. This knocks electrons from whatever brushes against the skin, or even from the skin. These electrons build up until there is a great enough charge for them to discharge across to something else, which we see as a spark. In normal daily activities, people can easily generate charges on their bodies in excess of 10,000 volts in an insulated state. Charges of 3,000 volts or more can cause sparking to occur. These events can degrade or destroy devices, erase logic or data banks in computers and cause sparking, which can be extremely dangerous near explosive or volatile chemicals or gasses.

Human Skin Battery Potentials Measurements of transcutaneous voltage have been made by Dr A. T. Barker, Department of Medical Physics, and Clinical Engineering, in the Hallamshire Hospital, Sheffield England on seventeen normal volunteers. The results show the presence of 'skin battery' voltages comparable in size to those previously reported for amphibian and mammalian skin. Biological cells and tissues are much more complex systems than physicists are used to studying. To quote Fukada, whom others regard as a pioneer in the subject, "... electricity ... is caused by both piezoelectricity in collagen and streaming potential in micro canals in bone." Williams speaks of a recently developed polymeric device that responds to an electric field.... He remarks: "It is interesting that biological tissues, which have been on earth for millions of years, utilize this same feature, displaceable bound charge, for generating unusually large electric fields."

The Human Crystal Set

Using this information along with the simple crystal radio theory, N.T.T., the Japanese communications giant, has recently developed a technology called RedTacton, which it claims can send data over the surface of human skin at speeds of up to 2Mbps, the equivalent of a fast broadband data connection. Though this method has been used esoterically for millennia, your own body, arms and fingers, could soon be the key enablers of mundane data exchanges with other people, communication devices and in some cases with components within the body. In this form of technology, a transmitter is attached to a portable device, such as an MP3 player, which then uses the human skin electrical field to send data to another receiving device as long as they are on or within a 20cm distance from your body. The transmission is achieved by minutely modulating the electrical body field in the same way that a radio station wave is modulated to carry broadcast data. This is how psychics describe what happens to them when they use crystals to amplify and receive data from another human or the surrounding environment. Interestingly enough, the Japanese telecom company is not the first company to utilize the human body as a vehicle for data transmission. IBM itself pioneered research in this area in 1996 with a system that could transfer small amounts of data at very low speeds, and then last June, Microsoft was granted a patent for "a method and apparatus for transmitting power and data using the human body."

Experimentation verses Replication

It is distressing that over the last 200 years people have rushed to experiment water down or crush these ancient crafts of the wise. Though many of these are well intended, much damage has been done and much has been lost. Many have founded new movements that have broken down these thousands of year old, tried and proven traditions, in what was left of the true mystery schools. The rituals taught by these schools are a way of maintaining exact replication. Those mystery schools stood the test of time for thousands of years because what they taught worked. Now many of them are gone. This has left our knowledge and power in a degenerative state, rather than giving us the evolution of personal-power we had hoped for. People who stood up in defence of the loss of this knowledge have been laughed at as traditionalist. Others, who radically altered, experimented with and vandalised these wisdom traditions have been hailed as geniuses even though there were no tangible results to display for their efforts but only new theories.

The Changed Tarot

"Modern" western society has decried those remaining guardians of concealed wisdom and forever altered and played with their ancient written records. Even the "Tarot" deck was arrogantly altered at the turn of the 20th century. This hermetic repository had remained the same for over 700 years. It is said that the Tarot is the ancient book of the Templar Knight's wisdom, dating far beyond the circulation of the first Tarot decks. Others say it is the code of the gypsies, cleverly turned into a deck of playing cards when the censers burnt their books. It is very ingenious that the wisdom of the Tarot was concealed as playing cards, which survived those who wished to destroy it. By being very ordinary and unassuming, its ancient subconscious symbols and numbers were to be preserved for all that time. Now, however, it is in debate because it was arrogantly altered last century by Mr Arthur Edward Waite of "Order of the Golden Dawn." As an initiate of this order, A.E. Waite was forbidden by his vows from revealing any of the "true" secrets.

Therefore, he introduced deliberate errors, the result of which was that the Tarot's symbols and mathematical correlation's are now confused and dis-empowered. The elemental attributions were and still are, swapped around. The correlation's to the Hebrew alphabet were confused. The numbers and attributions of card number 8, "STRENGTH," one of only two immortal cards in the whole deck, and card number 11, "JUSTICE" were swapped. The other immortal card is "THE MAGICIAN," card number 1. If 'STRENGTH' is placed in its original numerical position, number 11, it is much easier to see these two cards as representing the relationship between the magician and his higher self. ie: - 1 ∴ 11. As we have seen this is the key to releasing your full magickal potential.

A.E. Waite relates his own arrogance this way in "Pictorial Key to the Tarot" written by himself about his "new" deck: -

"For reasons which satisfy myself this card has been interchanged with that of Justice (now 11) which is usually number eight. As the variation carries nothing with it that will signify to the reader there is no cause for explanation..."

In other words we are all so ignorant we could not possible understand these divine mysteries for ourselves. Sound familiar? Think about what other groups use this by-line and why? Moreover, why would he be trying to use those same control and manipulation techniques here? He does go on to highlight that

"...Strength or fortitude is one of the most exulted...cards in the deck and it correlation's are far reaching and sublime and ...operates on all planes and draws on all of its symbolism."

So, why muck around with it then? Why would he do this? Just for a fast buck? So that he could publish something that he was not allowed to because of his vows? Or for more sinister reasons? After the advent of this deck, aided by the "Ryder" publishing house it became the most successful and popular Tarot deck. Due to its popularisation, nearly every deck released since has been based on these deliberate errors, to which further individualised and so called creative errors have been added. It is a relief to know that the old "Marseilles Deck" by Grimaud or Jean Dodal remains unaltered, as do a few other "Classic" traditional decks.

These "purveyors of change" have been heralded as heroes by a "new system of things" that would keep us from ever fully realising our potential. Could it be that this new system would like us to remain confused so that we can never see "the ships in the harbour?" Are they afraid that if they share the knowledge of their power they will have less? The fact is if they are so afraid then they have no true power at all. Also question whom are they aiming to control and how? We now find the majority of society trapped and stagnating in a new system of theories, social moreés, and new rigid Hollywood / media based "beliefs" which hold and regulate us more tightly than any dictator could.

PAGAN HEROES OF MODERN SOCIETY

Pagan heroes are people who broke through this kind of control. Apart from the prominent Witches and Pagans we have already highlighted in this text such as Isaac Newton, Frances Bacon, John Dee, Capercunicus, Elizabeth 1st and many others I would like to highlight a few other amazing Witches whose Pagan contributions to our modern society are often overlooked.

Pythagora

Pythagoras

Pythagoras was a wanderer, and a magickal, mathematical gypsy of sorts. Born in 570 B.C.E. in Samos, this is now in Turkey. His mother was a Phoenician, his father a Greek stonecutter. His family moved to Syria for

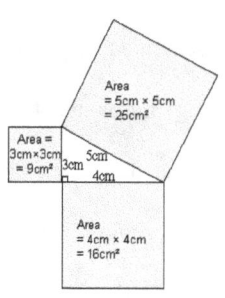

business reasons. They were successful. He was a rare, truly gifted genius. He had an unquenchable thirst for all the knowledge he could find. Therefore, his father sent him back to Greece for his schooling. There he studied the concepts of geometry with a Greek named Thales. At eighteen years of age, encouraged by Thales, he decided to travel the entire known world and study learning at its source. He learnt everything he could find. He did this for the next 22 years.

He travelled to all the known parts of the Mediterranean world. He learnt navigation and cartography form the Phoenician navigators. Pythagoras went to Babylon and studied with the Chaldean astronomers. He went to Egypt and studied the magick of the priests at Memphis and Diospolis. There he also studied with the engineers who built the pyramids, known as "the rope-stretchers." They held a secret in the form of a rope with 12 evenly spaced knots tied in a circle. If the rope were pegged to the ground in the dimensions of 3-4-5, a right angle triangle would emerge instantly. This enabled them to create accurate right angles for their buildings. Pythagoras wrote this down in an accessible Greek mathematical format and his theorem of the right angle triangle was born.

Music Of The Spheres

There are three branches of the medieval concept of music:

- Musica instrumentalis - sounds made by singers and instrumentalists
- Musica humana - the internal music of the human body and
- Musica universalis - the music of the spheres

Block cut from the 11th Century Depicting Pythagoras Musical Experiments

"The Music of the Spheres," is this "Musica Universalis," an ancient philosophical concept that regards proportions in the movements of the Sun, Moon, Mercury, Venus, Mars, Saturn, and Jupiter. The subtle sound generated as the spheres rotated is considered a resonating harmonic form of music. The spherical ellipse created by each orbit corresponded to a note in the musical scale. Thus, planets could be said to sing. By attuning to the music of the spheres, one could place oneself into harmony with the cosmos. The orbits of the planets were thought to be related to the number ratios of musical intervals, creating musical harmony.

Orbital resonance

Indeed the dance between the Earth and Venus in their 253-year-cycle of transits occurs in the phi ratio, producing beautiful crystalline patterns. In celestial mechanics, an orbital resonance occurs when two orbiting bodies exert a regular, periodic gravitational influence on each other, usually due to their orbital periods. Ever since the discovery of Newton's law of universal gravitation in the 17th century, it was not known whether they might add up over longer periods to significantly change the orbital parameters and lead to a completely different configuration, or whether some other stabilising effects might maintain the configuration of the orbits of the planets.

Listening In

Whenever a sound wave is doubled or halved in frequency, it yields another pitch similar in 'flavour' to the original one. Using this principle in 2006, Greg Fox divided the orbital periods of the planets in half again and again until they were literally audible. This allowed very large octave shifts from periodic cycles of the orbits of celestial bodies, inaudible to human ears to a cycle that humans could hear. He called the collective sounds "Carmen of the Spheres." Recent attempts to record and synthesize these resonances have been successful producing a mechanical grinding sound rather than the expected ringing bell like tones.

Pythagoras and Celestial Music

The Greek mystic Pythagoras is the first to have written about the concept in the west, after his encountering it whilst travelling in India. There it is known as "Shabda," the 'audible life stream.' According to the Surat Shabda Yoga gurus, with whom Pythagoras studied, this first word that Brahma uttered, eventually solidified and became the planets and all life, chanted as the 'OM' mantra. Pythagoras' version of this philosophy of the music of the spheres stemmed from his study of music.

Harmonics

Pythagoras developed his musical theories from real heavy metal. Whilst pausing from his travels in a town he noticed the different pitches made by six blacksmiths all hammering a single piece of metal. He related the difference in the tones of the sound to the differing weight of the hammers being used. That is, a hammer half as heavy produced a note twice as high. He discovered the numerical basis of musical octaves. Pythagoras is credited with modern musical theory. He devised expressions that are common musical terms we use today. His ratios established the relationship between: -

Diagram showing the music of the spheres as a vast celestial monochord

- Whole Notes
- Fourths
- Fifths
- Sevenths and
- The Octave

Pythagoras developed a theory of harmonic relationships that began with his theory of music and extended to the whole universe. He called this his music of the spheres. This theory has been verified by quantum theory. Pythagoras developed his theories on a single stringed musical instrument he invented and called the monochord.

Harmonic Nodal Points and Overtone Series for the Monochord

These diagrams illustrate the reciprocal relationship between string length and vibration frequencies. By stopping the string at geometrical points, the harmonic overtones can be individually emphasised. Interestingly humans are the only creature that can make harmonic sound naturally, with out the use of any

A Monochord

instrument. A harmonic note is a bell sound that peals in a rainbow like spectrum over the top of a pure tone. This is produced in humans, due in part to the shapes held by the mouth and the amount of resonance generated by the entire body. The human body is mostly empty space and makes an excellent resonance board. Harmonic sounds seem to transcend dimensions. It opens up the spaces in the individual, the environment and in atomic fabric of matter. Harmonics are a magickal thing often used to cast circle and open up doorways to other realms.

Nearly every magickal spiritual system uses music and song as a means to transport practitioners between the worlds. From Gregorian chants to mantras by monks, affirmations by the new age, spells by Witches and the song lines of the Australian aborigines. Harmonic overtones as used by Pythagoras and the Alti-Himalayans easily open the trans-dimensional gateways.

Kepler

Johannes Kepler in his "Harmonice Mundi" in 1619 believed that the music of the spheres is the connection between sacred geometry, cosmology, astrology, harmonics, and music.

Max Heindel's Rosicrucian writings state that the heavenly music of the spheres is heard in the region of concrete thought, the lower region of the world of thought, which is an ocean of harmony. Esoteric Christianity says that this occurs in the state of consciousness called the "Second heaven."

Ray of Creation

The Ray of Creation is an esoteric cosmology based on Gurdjieff's laws of octaves. It is a reflection of an older Egyptian teaching. Do Re Me Fa Sol La Si Do, was a song that was sung by the Egyptian priests as the sun was rising.

This scale indicates all levels of matter, and laws of the universe. A diagram of the ray of creation shows the place, which Earth occupies in the Universe. It has eight levels, each corresponding to Gurdjieff's laws of octaves. The first level is "The Absolute" is formed by all the worlds put together, followed by "All Worlds" – to which all galaxies put together belong, "All Suns" the Sun belongs to the Milky Way galaxy or all of the Suns combined, "Sun"- to which the planets belong or the solar system, "All Planets" - all of the planets in our the solar system of which the Earth is one, "Earth" - our planet, "Moon" - the Earth's satellite, and "The Absolute" - the heaviest and last level. This also equates with the Tibetan eight levels of existence.

String Length	Vibrational Frequency	Tonal Value
1/10	10	e2
1/9	9	d2
1/8	8	c2
1/7	7	b#1
1/6	6	g1
1/5	5	e1
1/4	4	c1
1/3	3	g
1/2	2	c
1/1	1	C

In his cosmology, "The Absolute" has only one law or force, which, as with magick, is "the Will." "All Worlds," has the three holy forces to form a whole and there by has three laws. "All Suns" has six laws. "Sun" has 12 laws, "All Planets" has 24 laws, "Earth" has 48 laws, "Moon" has 96 laws, and the next level of "The Absolute" has 192 laws. Each octave level after the original Absolute has a bigger number of laws, which govern it.

Number Monads

Pythagoras is famous for teaching that numbers are alive and are part of nature. That number wants to help you solve all of life's problems. The first 10 digits were especially sacred and thought of as deities called monads and Pythagoras attributed them the following personalities: -

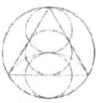 

THE MONAD	THE DYAD	THE TRIAD	THE TETRAD	THE PENTAD
Male-Female	Female	Male	Nature of Change	Androgyny
Obscure	Inequality	Proportion (analogia)	Righteousness	Wedding
Not-Many	Indefinite (aorlstos)	Harmonia	Hercules	Marriage
A Chariot	The Unlimited (apeiron)	Knowledge (gnosis)	Holding the Key of Nature	Alteration
Ultamate Prime	Growth Birth	Peace	Death	Immortal
Immutable Truth and Invulnerable Destiny	Appearance	Every Thing		Lack of Strife
A Seed Fabricator (demiurge)	Anguish	Hecate		Aphrodite
True Happiness (eudaimonia)	Equal	Good Counsel		Boubastia named after the Egyptian divinity
Zeus - Life God	Isis	Piety		Double
Memory	Movement	The Mean Between Two Extremes		Manifesting Justice
A Ship	The Ratio (logos) in Proportion (analogia)	Oneness of Mind		Demigod
Essence (ousia)	Revolution	The All		Nemesis
The Inkeeper (pandokeus), "that which takes in all"	The Thing with Another Rhea (the wife of Kronos, but also "flow")	Friendship		Pallas
The Pattern or Model (paradeigma	Selene	Purpose		Five-Fold Forethought
Prometheus - The Moulder	Combination			Light
The First (Proteus)	Boldness, Audacity (tolma)			
Darkness	Matter			
	Obstinacy			
	Nature			

  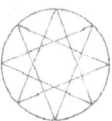 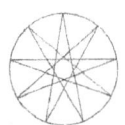 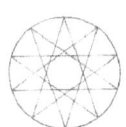

THE HEXAD	THE HEPTAD	THE OCTAD	THE ENNEAD	THE DECAD
Resembling Justice	Virgin (parthenos)	Mother	Brother and Consort	Father
The Thunder-Stone	Sister	Untimely Born	Helios	Eternity (aeon)
Amphitrite (Poseidon's wife; a verbal pun: on both sides [amphis] three [triasl])	Revered Seven (septas + sebomai heptas)	Steadfast	Far-Working (epithet of Apollo)	Untiring
Finest of All	The Forager (epithet of Athena)	Seat or Abode	Hera	Necessity
In Two Measures	Athena	Euterpe	Hephaestus	Atlas
Form of Forms	Citadel (akropolis)	Cadmia	Maiden (kore)	Fate
Double Peace	Reaper	All Harmonious	Of the Kouretes	Helios
Far-Shooting (name of Apollo)	Hard to Subdue		Assimilation	God
Thaleia	Defence		Oneness of Mind	Key-Holding
Kosmos	Due Measure (kairos)		Horizon (because it limits the series of units before returning to the Decad)	Kosmos
Possessing Wholeness	Bringing to Completion (Telesphorus)		Crossing or Passage	Strength
Cure-All (panacea)	Fortune.		Bringing to Perfection (Telesphorus)	Memory
Perfection	Fate		Terpsichore	Ourania
Three-Fold Health	Preserving		Hyperion	Heaven
Reconciling			Oceanus	All
				All Perfect
				Faith
				Phanes

Asian Travels

India and the 5000-year-old Vedic sciences deeply influenced Pythagoras, so much, so that upon his return to Greece he continued to wear Oriental dress, including a turban. Many of the Atharva-Vedas, which means "Knowledge of the wise and the old," especially the Sthapatya-Vedas which contain the sciences related to Vedic Mathematics, engineering, temple building, sacred geometry, mathematical and engineering techniques, as well as concepts of mystical monads, number magic and reincarnation arrived back in Greece with him.

Pythagoras even made the journey to the source bad the Ganges, Mt. Kaliash in the Himalayas to a hidden city where 'men were like Gods and knew everything'. Here he is said to have reached the mystical eastern kingdom of Shambhallah and attributes most of his knowledge and learning to his time spent there. It should not come as too much of a surprise that the foundations of western civilisation arose from these Alti-Himalayan concepts. It appears that Shambhallic doctrine might have given birth to humanity's intellectual development, providing some of its first and most complex conceptions of number, natural law, and an ordered, understandable cosmos. What is surprising is that these are concepts on which science still depends but does not want to acknowledge the source.

A turban wearing Pythagoras

Pythagoras' close friend Abarls, followed him back to Greece from this region. Iamblichus, describes Abarls as 'a man to which Pythagoras could teach nothing except a knowledge of the Greek language.' Abarls possesses many magickal and scientific abilities. He studied time and worshiped the sun, continually collecting money for the building of a temple to this knowledge. He is also described as having a magickal flying phurba (dagger). At the time when Pythagoras made his journey to Shambhallah, Buddhist writings describing the pre-Buddhist kingdom's magickal priests called 'the Suraya,' similarly, to how Abarls is described by Iamblichus. Pythagoras left a map to Shambhallah in safe keeping for Apollonius to use centuries later. Apollonius was born approximately 600-years after Pythagoras. It was accurate and Apollonius' used it to successfully journey to the mystical land. Apollonius' secretary recorded his journeys.

The Pythagorean Cosmos

There is little doubt that Pythagoras received much of this cosmological knowledge from an Altaic source. This is why he is often referred to as an Orphic or Greek religious Shaman. This would be quite literal. Apart from doctrinal similarities, his "Hyperborean" friend Abarls was said to ride through the air on a golden arrow (phurba). Arrows as magical vehicles or emblems of magical or astral flight are part of Siberian lore to this day. Today's race of Alti-shamans have inherited a much degenerated but still complex system that arose from their geographical ability to be able to observe, enumerate and record the ordered pattern of the polar stars and relate their observations to a complex astrological and numerical system which they then relate to all things on levels of existence. Pythagoras instance that *"all things are numbers"* reflects this theology.

Along the lines of the beliefs of the Alti-shamans, Pythagoras was amongst the first to postulate that all things are made of the same substance and put forward the idea of the atomic basis of matter. As such, he was the first to write about concepts that would later be explored in molecular theory, quantum mechanics, and the unified field theory. Pythagoras described the universe as a single organism possessing a soul and intelligence. He had outstanding astronomical knowledge for his period Explaining that *"the planets coming from the sun revolve around it, that the stars are so many solar systems governed by the same laws as ours, and that each has its appointed place in the vast universe."* He was more explicit than the Gnostics about the extraterrestrial origin of both Gods and human beings. He described the human soul as emanating *"... from an unchangeable and higher spiritual order as well as from a former material evolution, from an extinct solar system."* Pythagoras believed that humanity was on an eternal journey from star to star and in wave upon wave of races diverging in a Y pattern. Some peoples taking this fork in the road some taking the other. Indeed this doctrine seems to be reflected in the later writings of Jesus about the narrow and the wide path.

Pythagoras also adopted the Altic-Pagan culture's beliefs that the earth is round. History, credits him as the first person to spread this idea.

The Beginnings Of The Pythagorean School

At 40 years of age, he returns to starts his first school in Greece. He was the single most educated man on the face of the earth at that point. He wanted to share what he knew, but the people of his hometown Samos were less than enthusiastic, unwilling to trust their education to an unknown quantity. Therefore, Pythagoras decided to buy a student. He went to the slave market and bought a homeless child. The child was not keen to learn so Pythagoras offered to pay him three obli for every lesson the boy mastered. The slave boy agreed to this instantly, thinking that sitting in the shade of a tree all day and listening to this obviously crazy old man was better than making a days wages working in the hot sun. Slaves were paid in Greece in those days. He proved to be an apt student wanting to master as many lessons as he could for three obli.

Soon the boy realised that the lessons were valuable and began making extra money from his new skills. The boy began to bring others to attend Pythagoras' classes free. Eventually Pythagoras announced that he could not afford to pay anyone to attend his classes anymore. Therefore, the slave child, and the others, realising the value of the education they were receiving, began to pay Pythagoras for his lessons. As this story spread the value of his teachings increase in the eyes of his fellow Grecian citizens, and this school of the man cleaver enough to get his slaves to pay him, soon filled up. Pythagoras admitted men and women equally to his schools

The School at Crotona

Eventually, due to persecution by a tyrant, Pythagoras left the island of Samos and settled on the Isle of Croton. He arrived in Italy during the 62nd Olympiad. This is where he formed his 'Secret Brotherhood.'

As discussed previously, the Pythagorean mystery school is where the pentangle originated as the symbol of mathematical and spiritual perfection in nature. Students had to be able to draw a pentangle with out lifting their stylus in order to gain entry to the school. The Catholic Church about 1500 years later, during the first inquisitions, began to associate the pentangle with Witchcraft and dark rites in an attempt to eliminate men with great learning who were teaching others. This proved very successful. This Pythagorean Secret Brotherhood was far more than just a school of mathematics.

The Goddess Hygia

Pythagoras main deity was Hygia, the Goddess of cleanliness, of both the physical and the mental. Pythagoras students first year was a year spent in a vow of silence, to clean away the clutter and ego of their minds. They could listen, learn, and not ask longwinded questions to display how much they knew, which according to Pythagoras was nothing. They needed to just listen and learn. They wore simple clean white linen and followed dietary restrictions the most notable of which was a diet with a prohibition on eating some types of meat and beans. The bean prohibition was most likely for social reasons in the confined spaces of communal living in addition to the avoidance of 'favism' being diseases induced by the high sulphur content of Italian beans which include: low resistance to infections, headaches, anaemia, diabetes, cancer, porphyria, periods of insanity and prolonged neonatal jaundice. During that first year, they had to learn the code of conduct by heart. It is now referred to "The Golden Verses Of Pythagoras" and shows that the school at Crotona was much more than a school of mathematics. These also show why Pythagoras was referred to as the pre-Christian Christ: -

"Who's Afraid Of The Big Bad Witch?" - by - Dr. S. D'Montford

1. First, worship the Immortal Gods, as they are established and ordained by the Law.
2. Reverence the Oath, and next the Heroes, full of goodness and light.
3. Honour likewise the Terrestrial Dæmons (spirits) by rendering them the worship lawfully due to them.
4. Honour likewise thy parents, and those most nearly related to thee.
5. Of all the rest of mankind, make him thy friend who distinguishes himself by his virtue.
6. Always give ear to his mild exhortations, and take example from his virtuous and useful actions.
7. Avoid as much as possible hating thy friend for a slight fault.
8. [And understand that] power is a near neighbour to necessity.
9. Know that all these things are as I have told thee; and accustom thyself to overcome and vanquish these passions: --

First gluttony, sloth, sensuality, and anger.

10. Do nothing evil, neither in the presence of others, nor privately;
11. Above all things respect thyself.
12. In the next place, observe justice in thy actions and in thy words.
13. In addition, accustom not thyself to behave thyself in any thing without rule, and without reason.
14. Nevertheless, always make this reflection, that it is ordained by destiny that all men shall die.
15. The goods of fortune are uncertain; and that as they may be acquired, so may they likewise be lost.
16. Concerning all the calamities that men suffer by divine fortune, support with patience thy lot, be it what it may, and never repine at it but endeavour what thou canst to remedy it.
17. Consider that fate does not send the greatest portion of these misfortunes to good men.
18. There are among men many sorts of reasoning's, good and bad; admire them not too easily, nor reject them.
19. Nevertheless, if falsehoods be advanced, hear them with mildness, and arm thyself with patience.
20. Observe well, on every occasion, what I am going to tell thee: -- Let no man either by his words, or by his deeds, ever seduce thee nor entice thee to say or to do what is not profitable for thyself.
21. Consult and deliberate before thou act, that thou mayest not commit foolish actions.
22. For it is the part of a miserable man to speak and to act without reflection.
23. However, do that which will not afflict thee afterwards, nor oblige thee to repentance.
24. Never do anything, which thou dost not understand.
25. Nevertheless, learn all thou ought'st to know, and by that means thou wilt lead a very pleasant life.
26. In no wise neglect the health of thy body;
27. Give it drink and meat in due measure, and also the exercise of which it has need.
28. Now by measure, I mean what will not incommode thee.
29. Accustom thyself to a way of living that is neat and decent without luxury.
30. Avoid all things that will occasion envy.
31. Moreover, be not prodigal out of season, like one who knows not what is decent and honourable.
32. Neither be covetous nor niggardly; a due measure is excellent in these things.
33. Do only the things that cannot hurt thee, and deliberate before thou dost them.
34. Never suffer sleep to close thy eyelids, after thy going to bed, till thou hast examined by thy reason all thy actions of the day.
35. Wherein have I done amiss? What have I done? What have I omitted that I ought to have done?

36. *If in this examination thou find that thou hast done amiss, reprimand thyself severely for it;*

37. *In addition, if thou hast done any good, rejoice.*

38. *Practise thoroughly all these things; meditate on them well; thou oughtest to love them with all thy heart.*

39. *'Tis they that will put thee in the way of divine virtue.*

40. *I swear it by him who has transmitted into our souls the Sacred Quaternion, the source of nature, whose cause is eternal.*

41. *Never begin to set thy hand to any work, till thou hast first prayed the gods to accomplish what thou art going to begin.*

42. *When thou hast made this habit familiar to thee,*

43. *Thou wilt know the constitution of the Immortal Gods and of men.*

44. *Even how far the different beings extend, and what contains and binds them together.*

45. *Thou shalt likewise know that according to Law, the nature of this universe is in all things alike,*

46. *So that thou shalt not hope what thou ought'st not to hope; and nothing in this world shall be hid from thee.*

47. *Thou wilt likewise know, that men draw upon themselves their own misfortunes voluntarily, and of their own free choice.*

48. *Unhappy that they are! They neither see nor wish to understand that their choice for good is near them.*

49. *Few know how to deliver themselves out of their misfortunes.*

50. *Such is the trick by which mankind blinds itself, and takes away his senses.*

51. *Like huge cylinders, they roll back and forth, and always oppressed with ills innumerable.*

52. *For fatal strife, innate, pursues them everywhere, tossing them up and down; nor do they perceive it.*

53. *Instead of provoking and stirring it up, they ought, by yielding, to avoid it.*

54. *Oh! Jupiter, our Father! If Thou would'st deliver men from all their own evils by which they oppress themselves,*

55. *Show them of what dæmon they make use.*

56. *Nevertheless, take courage; the race of man is divine.*

57. *Sacred nature reveals to them the most hidden mysteries.*

58. *If she impart to thee her secrets, thou wilt easily perform all the things which I have ordained thee.*

59. *Moreover, by the healing of thy soul, thou wilt deliver it from all evils, from all afflictions.*

60. *But abstain thou from the meats, which we have forbidden in the purifications and in the deliverance of the soul;*

61. *Make a just distinction of them, and examine all things well.*

62. *Leaving thyself always to be guided and directed by the understanding that comes from above, and that ought to hold the reins.*

63. *And when, after having divested thyself of thy mortal body, thou arrivest at the most pure Æther,*

64. *Thou shalt be a God, immortal, incorruptible, and Death shall have no more dominion over thee.*

Other mystical and scientific acts attributed to Pythagoras are described by Aristotle. He paints him as a wonder-worker who had a golden thigh, which he showed to Abarls, and exhibited in the Olympic games as a sign of his divinity. Aristotle and others believed that he had the ability to travel through space and time, and to communicate with animals and plants. He and his student's prophesied earthquakes with infallible accuracy, stilled the wind, stopped hailstorms and calmed violent waters so that people could safely cross. Pythagoreans cured disease by ointments, herbs, willpower, magick, and music. He made no distinction between these methods seeing them all as arising from an understanding of Nature. In what appears to be an early attempt at photography, Pythagoras asserted he could write on the moon. His plan of operation was to capture its image upon a treated looking glass. One account says that Pythagoras met some fishermen pulling ashore a large net of fish. They teased him for being a great teacher who taught others to not eat fish. Pythagoras bet then that he could tell them exactly how many fish they had caught and that if he was right they must gran him a wish. Pythagoras then wrote a number in the sand. They agreed and set about counting the fish. The fish totalled the number that Pythagoras had written. His wish was for them to return the fish to the sea. They derided him for this as the fish had been out of the water too long and would die, as would their families if they came home empty handed. Nevertheless, they did as they had promised. All the fish lived and Pythagoras produced enough money to pay for their whole catch. This miracle is so similar to the one in the biblical account of John written some 500 years later, that it appears to have been an act of ideological plagiarism included in the gospels to draw comparison and give added validity to the new religion.

At age seventy, Pythagoras married a persistent young female student who fell in love with him. She bore him two daughters. Her name was Theano, the daughter of Brontinus an Orphic initiate. She was a mathematician in her own right. She is credited with having written treatises on mathematics, physics, medicine, and child psychology, although nothing of her writing survives. Her most important work is said to have been a treatise on the principle of the golden mean. Theano and their two daughters lead the inner advanced group of Pythagorean students called the mathematikoi.

In the year 500 B.C.E. violent persecutions of the Pythagoreans begins due to a published theory of a better form of government. Numa Pompilius, the second King of Rome, is said to have studied this under Pythagoras himself. This theory proposed the use of invisible power as the cornerstone of an alternative form of government. It was later enshrined in Western mysticism by John Dee in his famous "Monas Hieroglyphica." Dee's book opens with a diagram of the Pythagorean Y, mentioned earlier in his cosmological theories, and applies this to possible courses of action a ruler may take: 'the broad way of 'tyrants,' or the straight and narrow way of the 'adepti' or inspired mystics.' Pythagoras proposed the states need for higher disinterested guidance and sort to place an advisory panel of initiates above the government. His followers were murdered for this. The Pythagorean's were accused of Witchcraft and trying to subvert the state. Many were burnt. Some historians say that Pythagoras met his end there.

However, records exist that Pythagoras moved his family to Metapontum where he is thought to have died at age 101.

The Female Origins of Chemistry

The Museum in Alexandria, Egypt, was founded by Ptolemy, the new ruler of this New World capital, in 306 B.C. It was something new, a large government sponsored institute devoted to research and teaching and it employed over 100 professors. As an adjunct the Great Library, a zoo, botanical gardens, an observatory and dissecting rooms were also built. The whole complex must have borne a close resemblance to a modern 'Institute for Advanced Studies'. By 85 A.D. Alexandria had became home to some of the greatest scientists of the ancient world and some of them were women!

However within 500 years, after the first flush of discovery from the golden age of Greece, the scientists themselves were becoming jaded with this brave idea of 'new' science and could barely conceive of formulating new ideas or making discoveries unknown to their predecessors. Indeed this has unfortunately proved true for us until this present age. By the beginning of the 4th century, something new had begun to happen. Whispers and rumours abounded about the transmutation of substances, of the ability to change one thing into another, of turning base metals into gold. This was exciting and something undreamed of until that time. How was this done? There was a lecturer teaching the theory and practise of this new subject at the Museum. The classes filled and the students kept returning. The educated felt they must find out about this new field. The common folk were amazed at the very idea. The lectures were filled with beautiful words of wisdom, pearls that were easy to remember and share. Who was the brilliant scientist/philosopher that had come up with a completely new field of study? Her name was Maria. She was a Jewess and a very mysterious, private person.

Where did she learn the art that she was now teaching at a 'university' level?

Women's Work

Alchemy was not the original name for this field of study; the coining of that term came later. Originally, it was called *"Opus Mulierum"* -*'Women's Work.'* It drew on several sources: the formulation and manufacture of cosmetics, perfumes, and imitation jewellery. These were major Egyptian industries but in Mesopotamia women, chemists developed the techniques used in the formulation of perfumes and cosmetics. The chemistry of the Babylonians was considered a craft tradition, in which the woman chemist took a leading role. This new science also drew from the artistic tradition of the manufacture and mixing of dyes and the theories of colour. It included the wisdom of the Egyptian women who developed the process chemistry for brewing beer and distilling stronger alcohol. It also drew on the theoretical streams of and Gnosticism, which was an esoteric mixture of Jewish, Chaldean, and Egyptian mysticism, in which, as in ancient Taoism, the male and female were equal. This precept became a cornerstone of alchemical theory. It also borrowed from Neo-Platonism and Christianity as they were centred in Alexandria at this point in history.

In Egypt, the Goddess Isis was identified as the founder of all science. In legend Isis was the first person to take chemistry to Mesopotamia where she became the Queen/Goddess Ishtar's cosmetic manufacturer in return for information on the location of her dead husband Osiris' body. When the body was located, Isis again put her art of chemistry to work to embalm and preserve the body. The embalmer's art entailed the complex preparation and purification of many substances. The main ingredient of the embalming process was 'Natron' –Sodium mono-carbonate that dried and preserved the tissue but sent the body black. The phase of blackening called "Necro," to blacken, is still central to theoretical and practical alchemy today. Interestingly Sodium bi-carbonate or baking soda is still used today as a rising agent. Try this little experiment for yourself. Rub sodium-bi-carb on any organic substance like grass or a piece of meat and leave it for 1 day and you will find it has turned the substance black and dry. It is from this part of the embalmer's art that we get the term 'Necromancer' which means one who communes with the spirits of the dead. It is also interesting to note that Neo-Platonists used natron, not salt to cast their magick circles. Though this substance is white when you place it on the ground, it leaves a black circle in the grass that is visible for approximately 1 month. The word chemistry itself comes from the old term 'Khem' which was the original name of Egypt given to her because of her black fertile flood plain soils. So chemistry literally means: - The science of Egypt

Black Wisdom

We in the West associate the colour black with ignorance and evil. In the Middle East, it was associated with wisdom. The literal etymology of the word Chemistry was "Black Wisdom."

Kem = black.

Ist = wise, as in field of study of practical science or art.

The 'Al' came from the Arabic meaning "divine" was added later to imply the added connotation of 'Divine black wisdom', to give us the present form of the word Alchemist.

The idea of associating black with wisdom was already a common concept to the people of that land and time. The Maskhara Dervishes, whose name derives form the their practise of painting their eyes and faces black during their religious rites, were commonly called "The Wise Ones." From them we derive our words mask and mascara. Arkon Daraul in his book "A History Of Secret Societies" refers to a Middle Eastern sect called The Dhulquarneni who were also called 'Wise Ones' because their high initiates and main deity wore black. Today we tend to think of most denominations of priestly classes wearing black, however this was an uncommon practise in that era.

Isis The Prophetess

Many people still believe today that Chemistry and Alchemy originated with the Arab nations some 500 years after this time. Apart form the written records, we can see by a casual observance of the derivation of these words where these arts originated. However there is a written treatise on Alchemy that predates Maria the Jewess. A woman wrote it also. She called her book "Isis the Prophetess to Her Son Horus". Her real name remains unknown. She took this pseudonym to associate herself with the celebrity of the ancient deity who was the patron of these arts in order to publish with impunity. The practical parts of Isis' writings are mostly concerned with the coloration of metals and fusing them to obtain alloys. The theoretical parts of this surviving fragment of a first century document interestingly suggests for the first time the esoteric themes of the four elements, the 'as above so below' and the sexual nature of all things as the power of creation. In it, Isis claims a spirit Amnael (The God Amun perhaps) has shown this art to her and that it could only have been disclosed to a woman at the time of a particular astronomical alignment. In the text, he reveals the mystery of his sign, which is like a bowl of shining water and a moon sign that resembles the emblem of the moon-god Khonsu of Thebes. (This has later become the Ouroboros) He then swears her to a great oath of secrecy. In this oath, we find echoes of the great mystery and the keys to its explanation: -

Comparing the 'Symbol of Khonsu' with its snake head near an overlapping end of a circle of variable width, to its contemporary symbol from the papyrus of 'Kleopatra's Gold Making,' it is easy to see why the symbol of Khonsu could easily be given as a description of the ouroboros by 'Isis the Prophetess.'

"Who's Afraid Of The Big Bad Witch?" - by - Dr. S. D'Montford

"I conjure you in the name of Fire, of Water, of Air, and of the Earth; I conjure you in the name of the Height of Heaven and the Depths of Earth's Underworld; I conjure you in the name of Hermes and Anubis, the howling of Kerkoros and the guardian dragon; I conjure you in the name of the boat and its ferryman, Acharontos; and I conjure you in the name of the three necessities and the whip and the sword."

What Is The Great Mystery Revealed?

"...that this is the whole creation and the whole process of coming into being, and know that a man is only able to produce a man, and a lion a lion, and a dog a dog, and if something happens contrary to nature, then it is a miracle and cannot continue to exist, because nature enjoys nature and only nature overcomes nature." ...and that *"one must stay with existing nature and the matter one has in hand in order to prepare things. Just as I said before, wheat creates wheat, a man begets a man, and thus gold will harvest gold, like produces like. Now I have manifested the mystery to you."* This is puzzling because it sounds like the opposite of transmutation of substances but then the fragment continues on to show you how to do just that with instructions for hands-on lab work in melting and preparing metals such as quicksilver, copper, lead and of course gold. At the end of this Isis exclaims: *"Now realise the mystery, my son, the drug, the elixir of the widow."*

There is a legend that claims the real identity of this 1st century woman known only to us as Isis, is 'Mary the Magdalene' the wife of Jesus Christ. It is not odd to think of Jesus' wife as an alchemist if you think of Jesus as a Magician himself. This however leads to her being confused with 'Maria the Jewess' who loved some 200 years later.

Maria The Jewess

Alchemists are often associated with the name of an ancient deity or celebrity. Maria herself is written about as "Miriam the Prophetess, sister of Moses" by Zosimos. This caused some historians to mistakenly to identify her as the biblical Miriam. We really know very little of her history as no surviving writings speak of her parentage or country of origin. In addition, unlike many scholars of the time, Maria only wrote of her art, not about herself. She may be called 'The Jewess' simply because Zosimos called her a Sister of Moses in his writings. That could well have been no more than a convoluted way of saying she was wise. She may very well have been Jewish or she could have been a Greek working in Egypt, or even a Syrian. Even though these silly ego games were the expected norm, her scientific importance should not be underestimated. Maier, named her as one of the twelve wisest philosophers of all time. It was she who laid down the theoretical and practical bases of western alchemy in her treatise, "Maria Practica." For instance, Maria was the first to speak of the marriage of male and female elements through the fire and in the smoke given off from 'the hermetic vase'. This is a reference to the sublimation of black lead sulphide (PbS) to create yellow lead oxide (PbO), a process that was not popularized again until Newton published his many experiments with lead compounds and amalgams from the 1670s onwards. She studied sulphur compounds. It was Maria who created the process for making silver sulphide, the substance artists call niello, a matte black compound, often used for metalwork inlays.

Additionally, she also invented some of the most sophisticated laboratory tools of her time. Maria invented many types of stills and reflux condensers. These are often simply referred to as hermetic vessels. She invented the process of 'the hermetic seal'. That being, heating a substance to purify it and create a vacuum in its storage container that could facilitate a pressurised airtight seal that helped to preserve the contents. The Egyptian alchemist Zosimos wrote, among other things about her invention of 'The Kerotakis' so that she could study the prolonged action of the vapours of arsenic, mercury, and sulphur on metals. The kerotakis device was a variation of the triangular palette used by artists to keep their mixtures of wax and pigment hot. Maria adapted it and used it for softening metals and impregnating them with colour. Maria would boil mercury or sulphur and use the condensing vapour to heat copper or lead in a pan above. The liquid flows back down establishing a continuous reflux. The sulphur vapours attack the metal alloy yielding a black sulphide commonly called 'Mary's Black'. Again, we have a black substance appearing as the first stage of transmutation. Impurities are collected on a sieve while the black sulphide flows back down. Continuing this process eventually yields a gold-like alloy. The end product can vary depending on the metals and sulphur compounds used. The kerotakis is also used for the extraction of essential plant oils. It is still used today in nearly every laboratory in the world. Another of her inventions that we see on a daily basis is 'The Bain-Marie' meaning 'Maria's bath.' It is most commonly used today in the food preparation field. It has an upper pan where you heat food, nested in a lower pan of boiling water. The steam condensing under it, at 100 degrees Celsius, keeps the food hot though at a slightly lower temperature as it is also being cooled by the air above. This device also has been an essential piece of laboratory equipment for nearly 2000 years. Maria also invented 'The Tribikos.' It is an earthenware vessel for holding a liquid to be distilled with an ambix or still-head, for condensing the vapour which collects on a rim on the inside and is then delivered down three copper spouts that take the distilled liquid to glass receiving flasks. She simply used cold sponges to cool the ambix and facilitate condensation. Maria's detailed descriptions included instructions for making copper tubing from sheet metal and using flour paste for sealing joints. She was a contemporary of Archimedes in Alexandria and was familiar with his water displacement theories, which may have helped shape some of her own inventions.

Tough she was a brilliant, astute, and logical person; she was not merely a mechanical scientist. Her beautiful way of writing and her eloquent theories show her to be a poetic philosopher as well. She believed that metals were living male and female beings, and that the substances she produced were the result of sexual generation, expressed in turns of phrase like: "… silver thus combined easily, but copper coupled as the horse with the ass, and the dog with the wolf." And "One becomes two, two becomes three, and by means of the third and fourth achieves unity; thus two are but one.... Invert nature and you will find that what you seek... Join the male and the female, and you will find what is sought..." Maria the Jewess, 300 A.D. She adopted the concept of Hermes Trismegistos' macrocosm-microcosm, and applied the 'as above, so below' concept to distillation and reflux.

Kleopatra of Alexandria

The Chrysopoeia Of Kleopatra

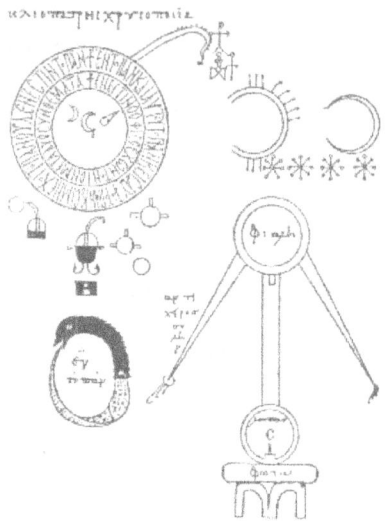

Continuing in the tradition of mystery is her successor Kleopatra of Alexandria, not to be confused with the famous Queen of the same name. Again little is known of Kleopatra the alchemist. We know that she investigated weights and measures, attempting to quantify the experimental side of alchemy. Her procedures were similar to Maria's and she used the sun and fermenting horse-dung as laboratory heat sources. She only has two surviving works. A discourse on Alchemy and a single surviving papyrus sheet with symbols and diagrams that have come to be called "The Chrysopoeia (gold making) of Kleopatra." This document shows the Ouroboros inscribed with "One is All and through it is All, and by it is All, and if you have not All, All is Nothing." Within the ring are the symbols for gold, silver, and mercury. Also illustrated are a tribikos and a kerotakis apparatus.

We know she was associated with Maria's School and may have been her contemporary, student, and successor to her titular chair in Alexandria. Jack Lindsay in his book "The Origins of Alchemy in Greco-Roman Egypt" calls Kleopatra's discourse 'the most imaginative and deeply-felt document left by the alchemists.' These surviving writings are theoretical. She placed the imagery of conception and birth, the renewal and transformation of life, firmly into the literature of alchemy. Kleopatra's vision of alchemy has a very feminine perspective and is very enthusiastic. Her passionate, poetic vision of alchemic transformation centres on the metaphor of gestation in the womb.

Here is a quote from Kleopatra's work:

"Then Kleopatra said to the Philosophers, "Look at the nature of plants, what they come from. Some come down from the mountains and grow out of the earth, and some grow up from the valleys and some come from the plains. But look how they develop. For it is at certain seasons of the year you must gather them; and you take them from the islands of the sea and from the loftiest place. And look at the air that ministers to them, and the nourishment circling round them, so that they may not perish or die. Look at the divine water that gives them drink, and the air that governs them after they have been given a body in a single being... The waters, when they come, awake the bodies and the spirits that are imprisoned and weak. For they again undergo oppression and are enclosed in Hades, and yet in a little while they grow and rise up and put on various glorious colours like the flowers in the spring and the spring itself rejoices and is glad at the beauty they wear. For I tell this to you who are wise. When you take plants, elements, and stones from their places, they appear to you to be mature. But they are not mature till the fire has tested them. When they are clad in the glory from the fire and the shining colour of it, then rather will appear their hidden glory, their sought-for beauty, being transformed to the divine state of fusion. For they are nourished in the fire and the embryo grows little by little nourished in its mother's womb; and when the appointed month comes near is not held back from coming out. Such is the procedure of this worthy art. The waves and surges one after another in Hades wound them in the tomb where they lie. When the tomb is opened, they come out from Hades as the babe from the womb." And the Philosophers, pondering what had been revealed to them, rejoiced."

Amulets, Charms and Papyri - Circa 300A.D.

The surviving amulets, charms, and papyri, both philosophical and magickal, of the era are littered with references to the female alchemists and their teachings. For the folk magick and general culture of the time to be so entrenched in this symbolism, shows how quickly these teachings became widely accepted. Worthy of note is this amulet called simply: - "Study no. 142", by Campbell Bonner, in the 1950's text "Studies in Magical Amulets, Chiefly Greco-Egyptian," It depicts an ouroboros, enclosing an inscription, characters, symbols and deities.

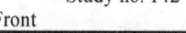
Study no. 142

Front: -

On the front, we see an ouroboros enclosing what is clearly a Tribikos with fire underneath it. Some have misinterpreted this symbol as representing a uterus. However, the idea of pro-generation does connect the two. We can also see Khnoum, the ram-headed god touching the knob of the key. Above him are Isis and Nephthys

Back

flanking Anubis and an unidentified woman

The inscription reads: -

Outside ouroboros: - soroor merpher garmar maphreiourigx.

Inside ouroboros: - iariaiaiiieôiô (Vowels sounds were sung as the song of life, to breathe life into the spell and open the divine doorways)

Sabaôth (A Jewish divine name meaning Kosmokrator or Lord of Hosts) êi

On the back: -

orôriouth (The Ouroboros) iaêôiaô Sabaôth iaêôieai borbor parphor phorbar phorphor rai.

This amulet is particularly interesting concerning female alchemy. When read with the inscriptions and obviously alchemical images on the front, it appears to be a "Key Charm" to be used for a "soroor merpher" (sister/female) only, to unlock the powers, and give birth (Tribikos/Uterus) to achieve something new.

Soror and Frata Mystica

The origins of the magickal terms Soror and Frata Mystica can be attributed to a female alchemist called Theosebeia. She had a learned friend, Zosimus of Panopolis whom called her his Soror Mystica, or 'mystical sister.' They would exchange long letters on alchemy with each other, addressing them conversely to their sora (sister) or frata (bother) mystica (magickal). Apart from the charm above, this is the first record of these terms being used. One of these letters is a tirade against the teachings of another female alchemist, Paphnoutia. Eventually these collected letters evolved into a collaborative 28-book encyclopaedia of chemistry called "Cheirokmeta" around AD 500. "Cheirokmeta" was based on the ideas and techniques of Isis, Maria, and Kleopatra.

What Happened To This Science In Alexandria?

In the 4th century, for reasons that are not clear, Roman Emperor Diocletian began a persecution and defamation of the Alexandrian alchemists and burned many of their texts, which is another reason so little information remains about Maria and Kleopatra. The Arabs adopted the orphaned science and by the 7th century, it was a male dominated art. Alchemy again reached Europe during the middle ages. There were very few advances in chemistry from the fall of Alexandria until the middle of the seventeenth century but by then

The twining serpent the symbol of the infinity of the universe represented in images of Aeon the Kosmocrator and a pre-Raphaelite image of Lilith by John Collier, 1887.

alchemy had become to chemistry what astrology has become to astronomy.

Shown here is the androgynous multiform image of 'Aeion the Kosmokrator,' the classic Alchemist's and Mithraic deity (Far Right). When compared with this later depiction of 'Lilith' by John Collier 1887, it appears the persecution and deliberate attempt to slur the female alchemists by Emperor Diocletian with sex scandals, violence, book burning, and other subversive propaganda, was very successful. Not only has history nearly forgotten these brilliant, magickal, pioneering women but socially they have been transformed into an image of a demoness. Lilith's great 'sin' was that she left her husband, similarly, the female alchemists, needing no man, gave birth to something new. Therefore, it is not surprising that the goddess Isis, who endured similar hardships, became their patron.

Why Did Female Alchemy All But Disappear?

Why did the female practitioners of this art form not retreat into solitude and continue to practise their beliefs in private? Perhaps the penalty for the broken oath of Isis came true. The secret was revealed after the promised had been made to keep it secret and obscurity was the penalty. Perhaps, because substances new to nature were sort by the alchemists, it was the fulfilment of "Isis' Prophecy." *"...one must stay with existing nature and the matter one has in hand in order to prepare things. If something happens contrary to nature, then it is a miracle and cannot continue to exist..."* So perhaps the transmutation of substances was never meant to last! Perhaps like all things that take on a life of their own, it has travelled its time around the wheel of life and is now waiting, in its black out state, for a rebirth again from the tender hands of the female mystics.

Hypatia Of Alexandria

In 415 AD, targeted by her jealous rivals, Hypatia of Alexandria became the first public Pagan martyr at the hands of the newly formed Christian church. She was 42 years old.

Just as Leonardo DaVinci has come to symbolize the beginning of the renaissance, Hypatia has come to symbolize the end of ancient science. After Hypatia came only the chaos and barbarism of the Dark Ages.

Hypatia was a prominent Pagan philosopher of the fourth century who lived in Alexandria the then capitol of Egypt. She was a respected philosophical and political figure with great beauty and magickal ability. Her writings, teachings, inventions, and academic accomplishments rival those of Leonardo DaVinci.

Her murderers were never brought to trial rather they were canonized by Rome. The sanctioning of this action opened the way for the wholesale slaughter and persecution of women and their ancient sacred beliefs. This ruse made it easy for the new church to eliminate fifty percent of its competition in one strike. Women in Alexandria at that time were becoming prominent in spearheading philosophy, alchemy, and mathematics. The church and their male rivals from within the Pagan community feared that women too easily gained prominence and political influence by the use of their "evil sensuality" and "magick."

The foremost of these was Hypatia who generated great criticisms: -

She was a person who divided society into two parts: those who regarded her as an oracle of light, and those who looked upon her as an emissary of darkness.

Why Was Hypatia So Influential?

The life of Hypatia was one enriched with a passion for knowledge, truth, and spirituality. Hypatia was born in AD 370. Hypatia's father, Theon, and her mother Euphemia took on the roles of contemporary folk heroes and are referred to in several love spells in the Greek Magickal Papyrus. Theon was a professor of Mathematics and Astronomy at the Museum of Alexandria, which was the foremost university in the world at that time. Theon was considered one of the most educated men in Alexandria. He raised Hypatia in an environment of thought and great learning. Historians believe that Theon tried to raise 'the perfect human.' This shows him to be a liberated thinker in an age when Roman policy treated females as less than human. Theon and Hypatia formed a strong bond as he taught Hypatia his own knowledge and shared his passion in the search for answers to the unknown. He and Hypatia co-authored several books. Most historians believe that Hypatia surpassed her father's knowledge at a young age. Theon also developed physical routines for Hypatia to ensure that she had a healthy mind in a healthy body. This no doubt accounted for her still being a renowned beauty until her premature death. Theon instructed Hypatia in the comparative study of religions and taught her how to influence people with the power of words. He taught her the secrets of public speaking the fundamentals of teaching, so that Hypatia became a profound orator.

Hypatia was indeed an exceptional young woman. She travelled to Athens and Italy, impressing all she met with her intellect and beauty. Upon her return to Alexandria, Hypatia became a teacher of mathematics and philosophy. She became the lover of Orestes, the Roman Prefect of Egypt, a former student, and long-time friend. Hypatia never married and during her life time and gossip has abounded among historians about her personal life.

Hypatia's life is well documented by contemporary and post historians. Some information on her comes from the surviving letters of her pupil and disciple Synesius of Cyrene, who became the wealthy and powerful Bishop of Ptolemais. Although most of her writings have been lost, numerous references to them exist. She has remained a fascination for contemporary historians who call her "…the last pagan scientist in the western world."

Hypatia was no mere shaman. Hypatia taught people of all religions and she may have held a municipal "Chair of Philosophy." According to the Byzantine encyclopaedist Suidas, 'she was officially appointed to expound the doctrines of Plato, Aristotle, and other neo-Platonist philosophers which also included their magickal texts. Students came from all over the known world to attend her lectures on mathematics, astronomy, astrology, philosophy, mechanics, and magick. Her home became an intellectual centre, where scholars gathered to discuss scientific and philosophical questions.

Most of Hypatia's writing originated as texts for her students. None has survived intact, although parts of her work are incorporated in the still existing treatises of Theon. Theon revised Euclid's "Elements of geometry" and this edition is still in use today. Hypatia worked with him on this. Later she co-authored with him a treatise on Euclid. Hypatia also wrote one book of Theon's work on Ptolemy. Ptolemy systematized all contemporary mathematical, astronomical, and astrological knowledge in a 13-book text called "The Almagest" (Great Book). Similar to the word Alchemist. (Great Work)

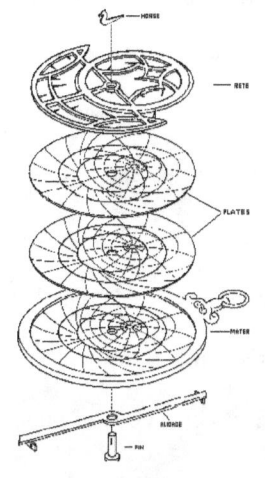

Like Pythagoras, another magickal Pagan philosopher, Hypatia's is mostly remembered for her mathematical works. What is considered to be Hypatia's most significant work, was in algebra. She wrote a commentary on-the "Arithmetica of Diophantus" in 13 books.

However, Hypatia is main passion was Astronomy and Astrology as shown by her tables for the movements of the heavenly bodies, in her work "The Astronomical Canon." Hypatia also authored a treatise on the "Conics of Apollonius" in eight books. Apollonius of Perga was a

Plane Astrolabe Images
Compliments of
http://www.astrolabes.org

third-century-BC Alexandrian geometer, the originator of epicycles and deferents to explain the irregular orbits of the planets. Hypatia's text was a popularization of his work. After her death, conic sections were neglected until Copernicus and Galileo. Then at the beginning of the seventeenth century Descartes, Newton, and Leibniz expanded on her work, realizing that many natural phenomena, such as orbitals, were best described by the curves formed by conic sections. Hypatia recognized that the geometric figures formed when a plane is passed through a cone are similar in shape to the orbits of the planets. Based on this work she invented the machine called "The Plane Astrolabe." It was used for measuring the positions of the stars, planets and the sun, and to calculate, time and the ascendant sign of the zodiac. In short this is the first astrological analogue computer and a woman invented and made it over 1500 years ago.

The encyclopaedia Britannica describes the Plane Astrolabe this way: -

The astrolabe, or "star grasper," was a very early handheld analogue computer, a great advance in the ability to find and measure time. An astrolabe contains two models of the celestial sphere, the rete and the tympan, which can be used together to solve various problems of location and distance, as well as time…For centuries, though it had no timekeeping capacity of its own, the astrolabe helped in the construction of accurate time-measuring devices, such as sundials. The astrolabe itself never caught on as a popular timepiece, owing in part to the disapproval of Christian theologians who saw it as an instrument of the devil…2

The letters of Synesius contain her designs for several scientific instruments including a Plane Astrolabe (see illustration). Hypatia also developed an apparatus for distilling water, an instrument for measuring the level of water, and a graduated brass hydrometer for determining the specific gravity or density of a liquid. Hypatia lived in a dangerous time. Alexandria was in a state of confusion. Not long before her birth, in 325 AD, Emperor Constantine at the first heads of church conference, "The Nicean Council," adopted Christianity as the new state religion for The Roman Empire. By the time of her adult life, persecution and violent conversion of the empire to Christianity had begun to occur. Up until this point in time, the Jews had been the focus of anti-sentiment. Now the Christian zealots began to view magick, mathematics and science, as heresy and evil. Three strikes against Hypatia. Christians felt that "Mathematicians were to be torn by beasts or else burned alive." Whilst the Christian fathers revived theories that the earth was flat and the universe shaped like a tabernacle, Hypatia's school was teaching people how to measure the circumference of the globe and about planetary orbits and the elliptical shape of our solar system and universe. This contradiction did not make her popular. Theophilos, the then Patriarch of Alexandria, or head of the "Holy Roman Church" of Egypt, spurred on violent conflicts among Pagans, Jews and Christians of that time. It was not a propitious era in which to be a pagan, a scientist, or a philosopher.

However, fourth-century Alexandria was the centre for neo-platonic scholars. Hypatia was a neo-Platonist in the tradition of Plotinus, as Hypatia studied at the neo-platonic school of Plutarch the Younger and his daughter Asclepigenia in Athens. At this centre, and at others in Athens and Alexandria, the mystical trends of the East, including divination, demonology, and astrology, were grafted onto the body of neo-Platonism. There was rivalry between the neo-platonic schools of Alexandria and Athens, with the Athens school emphasizing magic and the occult. Here too Hypatia found herself in the middle of conflict seeing no need for dichotomy yet unable to convince opposing factions of her neutrality. Nevertheless, to the Christians, all Platonists were dangerous heretics. Yet knowing this Hypatia came back to her hometown Alexandria, to teach the hermetic community there. Her beauty, vivacity, wise teachings and reputation for the odd wish granting miracle or two soon attracted large crowds, which included many Christians. Her contemporaries from both sides of the neo-platonic debacle and the opposing Christians rapidly became jealous of her knowledge and abilities. Those who had been refused by her publicly criticized her for her choice of lovers. The most vocal of these was a fanatical Christian, Cyril who ultimately became the one responsible for Hypatia's murder. Due to the vehemence with which Cyril opposed her and the type of rumours that he spread about her it has often been postulated that he was an embittered former lover and/or student of Hypatia's.

Hypatia, 1885, by Charles William Mitchell

Other pagan philosophers also jealous of her success and influence stirred anti-sentiment up against her. Their main accusation was that she should be charged with "Sensuality and Magick" and of being "..too beautiful and powerful.." and a "...threat to the state." Charges of magick, though rarely used, carried the death penalty.

It is indisputable that Hypatia became enmeshed in Alexandrian politics. Her student Hesychius the Jew wrote:

Donning the ragged philosopher's cloak, and making her way through the midst of the city, she explained publicly the writings of Plato, or Aristotle, or any other philosopher, to all who wished to hear ... The magistrates were wont to consult her first in their administration of the affairs of the city.

Being an influential political figure added to the danger of Hypatia's position in an increasingly Christian city. In 412 Cyril, became the Patriarch of Alexandria. An intense hostility soon developed between Cyril as head of church and Orestes as the head of state because of their very different political ideals. Cyril sort to make it a personal and dirty conflict. Because Orestes was, also Hypatia's lover Cyril publicly accused him of being *"...Hypatia's lapdog ...as Mac Anthony was to that Ptolemy!"* (Cleopatra) He used these diversionary techniques to keep public debate away from his own appalling behaviour. Soon after taking power, Cyril began persecuting Jews, driving thousands of them from the city. Then, despite the vehement opposition of Orestes, he turned his attention to ridding the city of Neo-Platonist. Hypatia, ignoring Orestes' pleadings, refused to abandon her ideals and convert to Christianity

In March 415, a Christian riot was incited by the combined efforts of a small number of bitter jealous Pagans and Parabolans, fanatical monks of the Church of St Cyril of Jerusalem, possibly aided by Nitrian monks. Edward Gibbon implied that Cyril was so jealous of Hypatia's influence and popularity that he told this rioting mob that he "…had been ordered by God to accept, the sacrifice of a virgin, who professed the religion of the Greeks'. Rist suggests that the mob was maddened because the Christians were in the middle of fasting for 40days at Lent. Therefore, they rushed upon Hypatia's chariot dragging her from it. She was stripped naked publicly in an attempt to humiliate her. She stood proud and beautiful, declared herself always naked before the eyes of the gods and that only those with things to hide, criminals and evildoers heavily covered themselves in dark robes, and went about in darkness. This being a reference to the thick robes of the monks and dark interiors of the newly converted Temple of Serapus (Osiris) into a Christian Church, and the burning of all of its ancient books. This cleaver statement only served to anger the mob further who then dragged her naked in to the church and they threw her on the altar.

Edward Hubbard describes the mob this way: -

When one sees emotionalism run riot at an evangelistic revival, and five thousand people are trooping through an undesirable district at midnight, how long, think you, would a strong voice of opposition be tolerated? Hypatia was set upon by a religious mob as she was going in her carriage from her lecture-hall to her home. She was dragged to a nearby church with the intent of making her publicly recant, but the embers became a blaze, and the blaze became a conflagration, and the leaders lost control. The woman's clothes were torn from her back, her hair torn from her head…,

It was decided to remove her attractiveness to the peoples by having the flesh scraped from her body with sharpened shells, whereby she was martyred.

Edward Hubbard Continues: -

"What was left of... her body beaten to a pulp, dismembered, and then to hide all traces of the crime and distribute the guilt so no one person could be blamed, a funeral-pyre quickly consumed the remains of what but an hour before had been a human being. Daylight came, and the sun's rays could not locate the guilty ones."

Cyril, who had organized this riot, was later canonized. i.e. made a saint for this act.

Hypatia's murder is described in the writings of the fifth-century Christian historian, Socrates Scholasticus:

"All men did both reverence and had her in admiration for the singular modesty of her mind. Wherefore she had great spite and envy owed unto her, and because she conferred oft, and had great familiarity with Orestes, the people charged her that she was the cause why the bishop and Orestes were not become friends. To be short, certain heady and rash cockbrains whose guide and captain was Peter, a reader of that Church, watched this woman coming home from some place or other, they pull her out of her chariot: they hail her into the Church called Caesarium: they stripped her stark naked: they raze the skin and rend the flesh of her body with sharp shells, until the breath departed out of her body: they quarter her body: they bring her quarters unto a place called Cinaron and burn them to ashes."

The myth attached to the legend of her death is that "Cinaron" is the "Library of Alexandria" and that the rioting crowed cremated Hypatia on a pyre of the books she loved so much whilst she lived. Moreover, that the blaze consumed the whole library in one night.

What Happened After Hypatia's Death?

Unable to take military action against the perpetrators for fear of starting a civil war, Orestes reported the murder and asked Rome to launch an investigation. He then resigned his office in disgust and sorrow and left Alexandria forever. The investigation was repeatedly postponed for 'lack of witnesses' and eventually Cyril proclaimed that there was no crime as Hypatia had made herself immortal in an unholy pact with the devil and was alive and living in Athens. Therefore, there had been no mob and no tragedy and of cause, he could not be put on trial for it. With the spread of Christianity came the rein of chaos. Interest in astrology, mysticism, and scientific investigation waned for fear of personal safety. Dogmatism as a police system was supreme. The dark ages had begun.

Hypatia's brutal murder marked the end of platonic teachings in Alexandria and throughout the Roman Empire. The anti-sentiment aroused by the jealous pagan leaders to facilitate this horror continued to fester after Hypatia's death resulting in their own demise and the demise of Hermetics and all the ideals they held dear in Alexandria in a little over a year after Hypatia's death. In 640 Alexandria was invaded by the Arabs and what was left of the Museum destroyed.

What Can We Learn Form All Of This?

These days Paganism is now the fastest growing religion in the world. The wheel turns and the cycle continues. We however have the opportunity of learning from this past cycle. The acts of gossip persecution and slander always result in self-destruction. Go about our own business quietly for whenever we attack another, for whatever reason, we are attacking ourselves.

What Would Hypatia Have To Say?

Some quotes by Hypatia:

"All formal dogmatic religions are fallacious and must never be accepted by self-respecting persons as final."

"Reserve your right to think, for even to think wrongly is better than not to think at all."

"... men will fight for a superstition quite as quickly as for a living truth --- often more so, since a superstition is so intangible you cannot get at it to refute it, but truth is a point of view, and so is changeable."

"Life is an unfoldment, and the further we travel the more truth we can comprehend. To understand the things that are at our door is the best preparation for understanding those that lie beyond.

Chapter 12

Do Witches Perform Child Sacrifice?

NO ! No! No!

Our children are sacred. They are the highest miracle of Mother Nature. It is the adult's role to watch over, care for, and protect children. The truth is that very few pagan cultures ever did this. However, the biblical cultures had this as their central theme. More on this later.

The press and indeed some academics seem determine to propagate the myth that all pagan culture was primitive, ignorant and practised human sacrifice. It seems to sell more texts or get more people into exhibits if they irrationalise and sensationalise. An example of this occurred recently in Australia.

Blood And Sacrifice In Australia

In November 2003, The Australian Museum in Sydney Australia held an exhibition on ancient artefacts from Peru. In the press releases for the exhibition were statements that this display showed categorical proof of human sacrifices depicted in "Graphic images of the Moché Sacrifice ceremony on bottles and other well preserved items…" This caught the attention of several Pagan academics, including myself and Dr. Carlos a native of South America, with a particular interest in the ancient indigenous cultures' religion and philosophy from those areas. We decided we had to attend and see this evidence for ourselves as we were of the understanding that no conclusive proof of human sacrifice has been uncovered in Peru. This race is not to be mixed up with the Aztecs, who were known for their habit of human sacrifice within a conquer religion of suppression and dominance that bore many similarities to the Catholic dogma, over a thousand kilometres away near what is now Mexico City. Nor should it be confused with the Myans who we now know practised blood letting of their royal family, without killing them to restore fertility and rains to their lands. It should be remembered that the only tales we have of continental South American human sacrifice rituals come from the written reports of the genocidal conquistadors to their Spanish King and to the Church, eager to justify their actions.

After attending the exhibit, these academics concluded that the collection was exquisite and wonderfully presented by the Australian museum. The audio tour device was invaluable in explaining what at first seem to be incongruous statements on the placards displayed with some pieces. Full praises to the Australian Museum for bringing such a display to Australia. It was a dazzling collection of ancient artefacts and a window into a very advanced civilisation that was lost to the world through greed. It stands on its own merits and does not need to use sensationalism and inaccuracies to attract crowds. My colleagues and I wanted to encourage the curators to revise some of the descriptions on their exhibitions and to use more accurate, less offensive and inflammatory methods to generate attendance for such a beautiful exhibition.

What Was Actually Depicted?

The section on human sacrifice they found to be particularly disheartening. The information placards made claims that some of the "The Stirrup Bottles" displayed have been used as receptacles in human sacrifice rituals. This was odd, as it is generally understood that these bottles have traditionally been used for the consumption of indigenous alcoholic brews including agave beer, a substance so high in mescaline that the conquistadors later distilled into a sprit that has become known as Mescal Tequila. They did not explain this apparent contradiction. Where there any traces of human blood, or indeed any blood found in any of these perfectly preserved items? If so, why did the display not site the references?

Many artefacts depicting the wrathful deities of the Peruvian peoples were displayed. Yet, this is not evidence that these people could have committed possible human sacrifice. Indeed, many classical images of the biblical God are very wrathful and bloodthirsty. Many indigenous cultures have similar images of wrathful deities to the Moché, including supposedly pacific Tibetan Buddhism.

Many images show people bound and then state that they are being taken away for sacrifice. How do we know that? An unsubstantiated statement like that is a bit of a stretch. Prisoners are bound for all sorts of reasons; war, criminal punishment, humiliation, and sometimes marriage. How can they assume that in this particular case a ritual death is intended for the incarcerated? Any assignment submitted during tertiary studies without siteing substantiating references for such conclusions would be failed. When stating a theory that is so important and on an issue that is so controversial, my associates felt that substantiating facts or in the absence of facts, cross references needed to be given for such inflammatory opinions. Are these accusations acceptable because the Moché culture is extinct and there for it is acceptable to not stick to the facts or to slander the dead? Alternatively, is it simply that academics still feel it is acceptable to not be politically correct about the Pagan subculture in general and that they are somehow not worthy of respect? On the other hand, could these opinions be put forward to appease the Vatican who funds many archaeological digs through the British Archaeology Society?

Despite press claims of "overwhelming evidence," In the whole exhibition, there were only two artefacts that they claimed actually displayed a human sacrifice being performed. If human sacrifices were as common as claimed, surely there would have been more than two relics portraying this out of the hundreds on display.

The two artefacts that the display claimed depicted a human sacrifice ritual were: -
1)"**The Mountain Sacrifice Scene**" This display made all of the academics that had children giggle as they instantly recognised smiling children at play. The scene depicted on that bottle was recognisable as the most popular form of recreation for children in a high rainfall, high temperature area. That being jumping and sliding down a muddy slope into a waterhole. There are two figures in the foreground of this bottle dog paddling in what is obviously a cross-section of stirred up muddy water. One child is floating on their back with four other children of various ages depicted smiling mid jump. One child with long wet hair is preparing to slide headfirst down the longest muddy slope into the water, which is still done today by

Mud sacrifice or mud slide?

children around the globe. A child sits at the water's edge with a pet dog in its lap. A guardian adult figure watches over them, possibly the mother of this large family or perhaps at a stretch this figure is representative

of a guardian deity. They could not see how anyone could examine this artefact and see a human sacrifice ceremony rather than children playing in a waterhole that would be an appropriate decoration for a water jar.

2) **"The Larco Bottle"** A flattened out reproduction of its images were used to promote this display. On the Larco bottle, we see an interaction between The Sun God, the Moché's main deity, and the Shaman deity, depicted with a bird's head mask. He is second in importance to the Sun God. Behind the Shaman deity is the Moon Goddess his wife and sister to the Sun God and behind her is a representation of the Moché King. These are surrounded by lesser divinities, smaller in stature. There are at least ten depictions of a particular fruit, which appears to be dripping into the cups held by the Sun God and the Moon goddess. Below them is depicted another realm. In this realm their Jaguar deity, deity of Justice is arriving on some form of aircraft. A man is bound in front of a jaguar priest. The jaguar motif is repeated at least seven times and only in the lower half of the scene. Small other worldly figures are interspersed in this lower half of the relief. The scene on this jar was felt to be very similar to the Ayhawasca ritual, similar to the Pyoté healing ceremonies of the present day Curenderos of the Andes. In this ritual, a plant-derived mind-expanding substance is used as an oracle when significant decisions have to be made. The indigenous Peruvians still regularly use this substance for all matters including the finding and trying of criminals especially thieves. The fruit depicted on this bottle is given the name "Ulluchu" but has never been botanically identified and yet this display

jumps to the conclusion that it has anti-coagulant properties to facilitate blood drinking. What is the substantiating evidence for this? In front of the man bound appears to be a bundle of clothing and goods. Recovered stolen goods perhaps? The man who is bound appears to have fluid coming from his nose, not his neck, as confronted by the Jaguar priest. Could this be mucus and tears of penitence? All of these theories are as valid as the ones put forward in the display except for one thing, we have an existing hallucinogenic shamanic ritual in Peru, often used in matters requiring justice, that is very similar to the one depicted, that definitely does not include blood drinking or sacrifice. Why is a matching living tradition ignored in favour of propaganda?

Advanced Civilisation

A serious crime has been done to the country of Peru. Genocide was committed. That can never be undone. The Catholic conquistadors wiped out an entire race of people. The Peruvian peoples were not the only losers in this sad chapter of human history. The world lost their wisdom and technology. The exhibition shows: -

- Their advance architecture that still cannot be reproduced with our technology today.
- Advanced jewellery making techniques that cannot be reproduced with our technology today.
- Advanced astronomical knowledge that today, 1500 years later, is only 3 seconds out.
- Their sciences are today forever lost to us, destroyed before they could be passed on and preserved.
- These sciences included a form of electroplating. Did they have electricity and advanced chemistry in order to perform electro plating or did they have a better technology? We will never know.
- On the planes of Nazca, they appear to have left behind vast airstrips. Did they have flying technology 400 years before the Wright brothers? This can never be conclusively answered now.

Not Primitive Bloodthirsty Savages

Nevertheless, one thing we know is that these were not the "primitive savages" as they are being portrayed. Some things in their society, displayed in this exhibition, were more advanced than now. Is it fair to portray a lost civilisation as savage and more primitive than our own just to try to justify a guilty historical conscience? Alternatively, is it that the funding given by the Vatican to the prestigious British Archaeology Society still dictates the slant to be given to history and the interpretation of such artefacts?

Yes, human sacrifice did occur in Peru. However, the only evidence to be seen of this is that the Christian conquistadors sacrificed an entire advanced Pagan culture to their lust for gold and for rewards from King and Church.

It is my hope that one day we may see exhibitions of Pagan cultures showing them as the corner stone of our present civilisation. That one day society will no longer feel need to portray them as blood lusting savages but as the brilliant scientists, artisans and philosophers that have shone the light of progress in this world, but who have been marginalised by the irrational fears of a few religious fanatics.

My call is to common sense. Keep your wits about you if you ever see the old Roman tenants of propaganda bandied about. The cry of "Blood and Sacrifice" has been used for millennia to justify genocide. It is the illusionist art of misdirection on a societal level. When you see these in an institution that is supposed to be exhibiting something for your examination and then telling you what to think about it, ask yourself, "What are they trying to stop us seeing?"

Various Christian groups for the last two millennia have thrown this type of slanderous propaganda at Witches. When in actuality, the reverse is true. Historians systematically ignore Bible verses advocating child sacrifice. The churches, for obvious reasons, no longer quote them. Yet, within their own religious writings is proof that these popular belief systems were founded on the blood of countless innocent children.

THE DARKEST SECRET - THE TRADITION OF CHILD SACRIFICE IN THE BIBLE
Harmless Religious Mysticism Or A Tradition Of Real Child Sacrifice?

Our story begins with an unseen presence talking to an old man in robes. "What is it that you want from me?" asks the entity.

"I would like to own this piece of land.," replies the old man.

"Make a pact with me and I promise that it shall be yours." answers the entity.

"What is your price?" asks the old man

"Sacrifice your firstborn son and the firstborn sons of all of your descendants, and all of your animals to me for the rest of eternity!"

Abraham's Sacrifice
by Rembrandt Harmensz van Rijn

"Done!" says the man, who later takes his favourite son out alone into the desert to begin this tradition of child sacrifice.

Is this the plot from some cheap 1970's Hammer Horror movie about a satanic cult? No! It is the well-known Bible story of Abraham making a covenant with Yahweh God that begins the Biblical tradition of child sacrifice.

Biblical Religions Record Their Own History Of Child Sacrifice

Like children telling ghost stories in the dark, historians speculate that child sacrifice lurked hidden in the origins of nearly every Pagan religion, yet can find no hard evidence of it. However, staring them in the face are writings from some of the largest religions. Some of these they hide and try to pass off as metaphor, whilst other references to child sacrifice they proudly proclaim. We are very familiar with the ones that have been around us for so long we have become hardened to the true horror of what they are actually saying.

For instance, millions gather every Sunday for the ritual of Holy Communion to individually eat the body and drink the blood of baby Jesus Christ. What is really eaten at Christian mass on Sunday is not the literal human blood and flesh, it is substituted by the Host and wine. Yet many Christian churches teach the doctrine of "Transubstantiation," a holy miracle by which the Host and the wine transforms into real human flesh and blood in the mouth of the one taking communion. Christians praise the fact that their God sacrifices his own son and are constantly encouraged by most of the New Testament to emulate his example. "No greater love has a man then to give his only begotten son...." etc.

Some historians take this knowledge for granted, and assume that it is general knowledge. For instance Maurice Bessy in his, "A Pictorial History of Magic And The Supernatural" states: -

> "The Mexican civilisation of pre-conquest times was not alone in practising human sacrifice. ...(The stories of)... 'Moloch's - mass incinerations of children ...(is)... derived, so it seems, from the Hebrews. Moloch is a corruption of the name Melech, a king of the Hebrews and one of the gods of the Ammonites. They sacrificed their children to him to obtain good harvests.... The... idea behind ritual murder is a reflection of the belief in the necessity of assimilating those forces, which, having left the dead will come to inhabit the body of the executant. It is probable that the

> *story of "The Massacre Of The Innocents," which the gospel recounts, derives from ancient Hebrew practices of ritual murder: all the children are killed so that one amongst them, the future Messiah, will take upon himself all their vigour and their virtues."*

Some, who are unaware of it, may be shocked by such statements and question: -

➢ How can historians state with conviction that the people of the Old Testament, the Hebrews, performed child sacrifice?
   o Because **they tell us bluntly in their own histories**.
➢ Why is this hidden from modern day worshipers?
   o To make the religions arising from the Bible, more palatable and proselytising easier.
➢ What are the origins of these modern rituals that enact child sacrifice so blithely?
   o Bible Law!

These are the short answers. Let us examine these questions in detail.

Bible Condones and Orders Child Sacrifice.

The entire Bible has child sacrifice as the main theme. The following are some examples.

Abraham

The first real friend of God is Abraham. He calls God by his first name, Yahweh (or popularly Jehovah). The price of this intimacy, and divine assistance for giving him a son late in his life through his favourite but barren wife, Sarah, is that Abraham is told to sacrifice his miraculous son Isaac. The Bible never shows this request in a shocking light and the text treats this as a

Persian picture of Ishmael as the chosen child sacrifice for the Islamic faith

reasonable divine request. Abraham does not question it. Though Abraham had questioned Yehweh God about his intention to slaughter every man, woman and child in Sodom, even though they were strangers, he meekly says nothing when a divine unseen entity demands the life of his favourite son. He did not say, "It is not right to kill my son given to me as a miracle by my God? No! You must be an evil entity pretending to be my God. Go away." Not at all, Abraham willingly complies and at the last moment, there is a ram with its horns caught in a tree near where the sacrifice was to be and God accepts this as a redeemable substitute. (Gen 22:1-14 -See Box) Note; the sacrifice is not cancelled only substituted. The binding and intended sacrifice of Isaac is considered by theologians to be one of the most challenging, and ethically troublesome, parts of the Bible. Jews, Christians, and Muslims agree that Abraham is the key figure to all of their faiths as he had sworn a covenant with Yahweh to give his children to him to time indefinite, in exchange for the land that he was living in at the time. All of these religious groups see his willingness to sacrifice his son as a reasonable part of that bargain. However, Muslims disagree on the identity of the sacrificial child. The Bible states that this child was Isaac. Christians agree with the Jews in this matter:

> *"By faith Abraham, when he was tested, offered up Isaac, and he who had received the promises was ready to offer up his only son ..."* (Hebrews 11:17, R.S.V.)

The Qur'an never mentions the name of the sacrificial child; yet Muslims claim it was their ancestor Ishmael, who was the only one who had the right to be sacrificed as the true firstborn son.

Through his desire to obey God at all costs, even if it meant sacrificing his son, Abraham became the definitive model of faith for the major world religions of Judaism, Christianity, and Islam.[9]

Moses

Some generations later, Yehweh God decides that he is going to kill Moses for no apparent reason whilst he is being sent back to Egypt from the land of Midian to deliver the Israelites from their slavery to the Egyptians. This is only prevented by Zipporah, Moses wife, performing a circumcision on their first-born son and then rubbing the bloody foreskin on Moses. She calls her husband 'the bridegroom of blood.' Then Yahweh is satisfied with this blood substitute and goes away. (Exodus 4:24-26)

The Sacrifice of The First Born Of Every Womb In The Land Of Egypt

This theme of the slaughter of the first-born males continues into Egypt. Moses has previously been told that this is the main reason that he is going to Egypt - to make sure that this happenes. God tells Moses that Pharaoh has no way of escaping this mass child sacrifice, it is preordained by him. Yahweh instructs Moses to ask Pharaoh to do something to prevent it, give the Israelites their freedom, and then harden his heart to not do it. (Exodus 4:21) Pharaoh is in a "Catch 22" situation and Yahweh God is torturously playing with him. Moses does not want to be party to this and makes several excuses but Yahweh gets angry with him and will not let him out of this either. (Exodus 4:22&23) God then begins to instruct Moses how to perform the plagues or curses. The last of the 10 plagues is the curse of: 'The sacrifice of the first born of every womb in the land of Egypt.' The house, barn, or stable yard was to be spared this sacrifice or passed over by Yahweh's sacrificial angel of death, if, as in the case of Abraham and Isaac/Ishmael, a lamb's blood was again substituted for the child intended to die. All of the unredeemed children die in one night as pre-ordained by Yahweh God. Egypt being the largest metropolis in the world at that time means that hundreds of thousands of children may have died as a sacrifice by Yahweh God's angel of death. (Exodus Chapter 12)

Levites

The theme of human slaughter continues when the Levites, gain their right to be the Priestly caste, only by mass slaughtering selected Israelites (Exodus 32:26 to 29), Their ceremonial robes remind them that Yahweh is a God of slaughter and they have bells sewn to their robes to remind Yahweh not to kill his own priests! (Exodus 28:31-35&36-43) The main function of the Levites continued to be slaughtering sacrifices. [20]

Here are some comments given to me by Oberon Zell Ravenheart, the father of neo-paganism on this topic: -

"Here is one of the most relevant and overlooked passages in the Bible. It is from Exodus--Chapter 32, verses 25-29, immediately following the episode with the Golden Calf. This section is referred to by title as "The Zeal of the Levites." "Zeal," of course, means "intense enthusiasm, as in working for a cause; ardent endeavour or devotion; ardour; fervour –SYN. See PASSION" (Webster).

25. And when Moses saw that the people were naked (for Aaron had made them naked unto their shame among their enemies);
26. Then Moses stood in the gate of the camp, and said, "Who is on the Lord's side? Let him come unto me." And all the sons of Levi gathered themselves together unto him.
27. And he said unto them, "Thus saith the Lord God of Israel, 'Put every man his sword by his side, and go in and out from gate to gate throughout the camp, and slay every man his brother, and every man his companion, and every man his neighbor.'"
28. And the children of Levi did according to the word of Moses; and there fell of the people that day about three thousand men.
29. For Moses had said, "Consecrate yourselves today to the Lord, even every man upon his son, and upon his brother; that he may bestow upon you a blessing this day."
(Exodus 32:25-29, Gideon Bible)

However, a far better translation of these passages is found in the more accurate and scholarly Jerusalem Bible:

25. When Moses saw the people so out of hand--for Aaron had allowed them to lapse into idolatry with enemies all around them-

26. he stood at the gate of the camp and shouted, "Who is for Yahweh? To me!" And all the sons of Levi rallied to him.

27. And he said to them, "This is the message of Yahweh, the God of Israel, 'Gird on your sword, every man of you, and quarter the camp from gate to gate, killing one his brother, another his friend, another his neighbour.'"

28. The sons of Levi carried out the command of Moses, and of the people, about three thousand men perished that day.

29. "Today," Moses said, "you have won yourselves investiture as priests of Yahweh at the cost, one of his son, another of his brother; and so he grants you a blessing today."

(Exodus 32:25-29, Jerusalem Bible)

Thus the Founding Prophet of the entire Jewish religion ordains the original Priesthood (and please understand that the Levites WERE the Priests of Yahweh forevermore) specifically because this one Tribe were willing to uncritically and cold-bloodedly slaughter 3,000 of their companions for no reason other than that Moses--their Visionary Liberator, Holy Prophet, and Heroic Leader--told them to. I guess one could conceivably consider this behaviour to be "intense enthusiasm, as in working for a cause," but to me it just sounds like unmitigated mass murder. I mean, how would such actions be regarded if performed today?

Moreover, this immediately after delivering the 10 Commandments--supposedly inscribed in stone by the very hand of Yahweh himself--containing the Law: "Thou shalt not kill." One would think that Moses' call--"Who is for Yahweh? To me!" implied "Who accepts these Laws?"

Now, some have tried to say that the Law, "Thou shalt not kill," was not meant to preclude killing enemies in battle, or "capital punishment," but was only meant to prohibit "murder"--however that may be defined and debates around this distinction have raged for millennia. Nevertheless, no matter how you slice it, how can such summary killing of "one his brother, another his friend, another his neighbour," possibly be justified as anything other than cold-blooded murder? I mean, all those people were completely innocent by this account, as Aaron--Moses' own brother--had "made them naked unto their shame among their enemies," and "allowed them to lapse into idolatry with enemies all around them."

And one might further ask:"What 'enemies'?" The Israelites were out in the middle of a virtually uninhabited desert, and they were over 10,000 strong! The Egyptian army, according to the account, had all been drowned when the Red Sea came flooding back after most of the Israelites had passed through. There WERE no "enemies"! Nor are any specifically identified anywhere in this account.

Another question that should be raised is--just who exactly were these "sons of Levi," and where did they get their swords? The Exodus story tells us that all those Israelites were escaped slaves, fleeing from bondage in Egypt. However, I cannot imagine that their Egyptian masters would have armed their slaves with swords-what is the real story here?

Nevertheless, the most important aspect of all this is that this act was not considered by Moses or the subsequent writers, compilers, editors and translators of the Bible to have been anything wrong or "sinful"! Indeed, this episode is presented matter-of-factly as a simple explanation of how the Levites earned their investiture as the Priesthood of Yahweh. Nor have I ever heard of any critique of this.

So, what does this say about Yahweh, his Prophet, and his Priesthood? Does this sound like a good God to you? Does Moses come across as a noble leader and Prophet--the inspiration for the likes of Jesus, Gandhi, and Martin Luther King? Do these Priests sound like the kind of Clergy you would want to entrust the care of your soul unto?

This is a pivotal story; indeed, THE pivotal story of the founding of the first of the three great monotheistic religions. In these few passages, we are told how Yahweh became established as the God of Israel, and the Levites as his Priesthood. This event is the point from which it all begins, and this sets the template for all that is to follow over the next 3,500 years.

If we are to fully understand the history of monotheism, holy wars, religious conflicts, and the present situation in the Middle East, I believe we need to examine and tease apart this account of how it all began, and to fully grok what happened there, at the base of Mount Sinai, at the triumph of the Exodus from Egypt, and the delivery of the great Law..."

Christ's death is in harmony with biblical laws ordering the child sacrifice of all first born males, animal and human.
Exo 13:11-15

BIBLICAL LAWS ORDERING CHILD SACRIFICE.

Moses then writes laws demanding the sacrifice of every first-born male of every womb of man and beasts, presumably, fowls were safe.

"Who's Afraid Of The Big Bad Witch?" - by - Dr. S. D'Montford

(Exodus 13:11-15 NIV) "After the lord brings you into the land of the Canaanites and gives it to you, as he promised on oath to you and your forefathers, you are to give over to the lord the first offspring of every womb. All the firstborn males of your livestock belong to the lord. Redeem with a lamb every firstborn donkey, but if you do not redeem it, break its neck. Redeem every firstborn among your sons. In days to come, when your son asks you, 'What does this mean?' say to him, 'With a mighty hand the Lord brought us out of Egypt, out of the land of slavery. When Pharaoh stubbornly refused to let us go, the lord killed every firstborn in Egypt, both man and animal. This is why I sacrifice to the lord the first male offspring of every womb and redeem each of my firstborn sons."

This law is not isolated and is not a metaphor. It is referring to death and killing for sacrifice as made apparent by the reference to the breaking of the neck of the donkey. Again, we see this requirement of redeemer price, the blood of a lamb. If no redeemer price was available then, as with the children in Egypt, it says that the child must be sacrificed. This ancient community is thereby relieved of a large percentage of orphans and other dependant low-income earners.

This makes one ponder the true meaning of the references to: "Is there no relief for the son of a widow?" in other religious, Rosicrucian, and Masonic observances. These observances imply that a son of an impoverished widow is slain in the temple. In 1 Kings 17:17-24 a widows son dies and she feels the man of Yahweh God, who is staying with her has come to exact some price for a legal error. She felt that her son's life was forfeit because she could not pay the redeemer price.

The Sacrifice of Jephthah's Daughter
Charles Le Brun 1619-1690

Again in:

(Numbers 18:15&16 NIV) "The first offspring of every womb, both man and animal, that is offered to the lord is yours. But you must redeem every firstborn son and every firstborn male of unclean animals. When they are a month old, you must redeem them at the redemption price set at five shekels of silver, according to the sanctuary shekel, which weighs twenty gerahs."

This is a very scary way to raise funds for the temple!

(Micah 6:6&7 NWT) "...Shall I give my first born son, for my revolt, the fruit of my belly for the sin of my soul?"

(Exodus 22:29&30 NIV) "Do not hold back offerings from your granaries or your vats. You must give me the firstborn of your sons. Do the same with your cattle and your sheep. Let them stay with their mothers for seven days, but give them to me on the eighth day."

This is not a reference to circumcision. The Israelites circumcised their male children on the eighth day but not their sheep and cattle. As we have seen by Moses experiences in Exodus 4:24-26, circumcision could be used as a substitute for sacrifice. As circumcision was usually performed at the same time that the redemption price was paid, it may also have served as a marker, an outward sign to let Yehweh, and his sacrificial slaughterer priests know that substitution sacrifices had been made and not to take that particular child. We can see that foreskins were used as a method of tally in 1 Samuel 18:24-27 to track the numbers of kills in a battle.

Fulfilment Of Those Laws

The concept of child sacrifice rounds out the dogma of all the religions that have arisen from the Bible. This clearly eliminates the ethical questions regarding the sacrifice of Isaac (Gen 22:2) as it makes it harmonious with Biblical law. In this context Jesus' death can clearly be seen as a fulfilment of Mosaic law as is often stated in the new testament. He was:

> '...the lamb of God that takes away the sin of the world.'
> (John 1:29)

He was to be a child redemptive substitute sacrifice himself, so that child sacrifice would no longer be owed to Yehweh God as the cost of Abraham's Covenant and the price for delivery from Egypt. So this is why, from a Biblical point of view, Yahweh God had to perform a ritual child sacrifice on his own son. In theory, this paid back the promised debt in full.

Wishing Child Sacrifice On Others

It also seems acceptable in the Bible to wish human sacrifice on others, who were not Israelites and not cursed to forever repay Yahweh God with their first-born. When Israel destroyed Jericho, Joshua cursed it with a prophecy that whoever rebuilt it would do so with human sacrifice:

> "...he shall lay the foundation thereof in his firstborn, and in his youngest son shall he set up the gates of it." (Joshua 6:26)

Crucifix is the Symbol of Child Sacrifice.
The image of the cross is synonymous with the rare instances of the concept of divine child execution in the ancient world. The Celtic cross predates the Christian cross by a thousand years. It has come to symbolise the death of little Gwion Bach, who, after tasting a magic potion, changed his shape to a grain of wheat, and was consumed by the Goddess Ceridwen, a virgin. He was reborn from her nine months later renamed "Taliesin" (Merlin) or halo.

The Spaniards were surprised to find the cross in Mexico was an implement upon which Aztec priests offered child sacrifices.[21] It is interesting to note that these childhood executions were decried in ancient legends, not glorified as in the biblical religions. The Greeks used the crucifix as the symbol of family tragedy because of its association with Dionysus' child execution by his father Zeus and resurrection by his grandmother Rhea. Early Christianity adopted it as a logical way for them to publicly identify with the biblical concept of child sacrifice.

The curse fell on Hiel the Bethelite in the early days of king Ahab. (1Kings 16:34) Another supposedly altruistic religion, Tibetan Buddhism, makes it a practise to dedicate temples, cities, and fortified courts by burying children alive in the foundations. (See article by Dr. D'Montford on the "Bloody History Of Buddhism" in Nexus vol. 12 no. 4)

In the Bible (Judges 11:29-40), Jephthah, after a victory over the Ammonites, sacrifices his daughter to Yehweh God, even though she is not a first born male, because he had vowed to sacrifice the first thing that came out of his door to greet him on his return.

In 2 Kings 3.27 During a war against the combined forces of Israel, the king of Moab sacrificed his firstborn son and heir as a whole burnt offering to Yahweh, in emulation of Abraham, atop his city walls in view of the Israelites. This is apparently effective, as the Israelites are promptly repelled, defeating the army and the many miracles of Yahweh's magic performing prophet Elijah, with a great wrath.19

Genocide as Sacrifice

Sacrifice of human children did not just take place singly or just to the first born males. Mass human sacrifices of men, women, and children were performed. In Deuteronomy 13:12-16 we read that a group of heretics and all of the people who live in the same town with them will be sacrificed to Yahweh along with all of their livestock, all their property and the town itself. 20 In Isaiah 34:5 to 7 a similar notion comes up with Yahweh promising the genocide of the people of Edom as a personal sacrifice to himself. This theme is extended to the genocide of children in Babylon in:

(Psalms 137:9 LEB) "Happy is he who shall take and dash out on the crags, the brains of the children that play about you."

How Long Did This Tradition Continue?

This human sacrificial tradition may have had a long life in Judaism. The Christ's proclamation that he is the fulfilment of this old sacrificial law and the subsequent declaration of the new Christian faith as heresy by the Jews only makes sense if these sacrifices were still going on at the times of Christianity's origins. Jesus act of redemption only makes sense within the context of the Biblical human sacrificial rites! 20

A second or third-century A.D. Neo-Punic stele from the era of Constantine, in Algeria, seems to bear out the concept that the biblical human sacrifice or

This may look like a representation of Jesus Christ but the ancient inscription tells us it is actually the God-Man Osiris-Dionysus who, in myth, was slaughtered 3 times as a child by the titans. It is dated around 500 B.C.

redemptive subsume was continuing to that time. The stele is inscribed in Latin: 'vita pro vita, sanguis pro sanguine, agnum pro vikario' which translates: "Life for life, blood for blood, a lamb for a substitute." The Qur'an condemns human sacrifice, as an ignorant and foolish act of those that have gone astray, implying the Israelites. (surah 6 ayah 140). In the Sirah (Biography of the prophet), the father of the prophet Mohammed, Abdullah, was about to be sacrificed by his own father Abd-Almutalib to fulfil an oath he had taken. A substitute of a redemptive sacrifice of 100 camels was slaughtered instead. This confirms that this was still in practice as late as 650AD. 13 & 24

Was God Only Trying to Trick Them?

To add a twist to the plot, the Bible in Ezekiel 20:25-26 speaks of Yahweh God giving his people bad laws, that they could not keep in order to trick them out of life. Specifically referring to child sacrifice, among other things. Therefore, if God is willing to admit some of the Biblical laws are bad and deceptive, then the fundamentalist literalist argument breaks down, which is a good thing where child sacrifice is concerned! 20

Nevertheless, consider what sort of God demands child sacrifice of the first-born male of every mammal in a nation into infinity? What kind of entity expects eternal repayment for the good deed of helping the great-grand-children of his friend, escape slavery that he led them into in the first place and then later tells them that he has tricked them by putting them in a "Catch 22" situation with no way out. No other God that I have ever heard of! This is not a "God of Love" as portrayed in popular propaganda about him. A close examination of the personality of Yahweh God as described in both the Old and New Testaments, shows the defining characteristics of, spite, vengeance, greed, jealousy, and a love and need for constant death. Nevertheless, THIS IMAGE OF THE GOD OF THE BIBLE RUTHLESSLY DEMANDING CHILD SACRIFICE HAS BEEN KEPT AS THE DARKEST HIDDEN SECRET OF THE BIBLICAL RELIGIONS. It is there, but it is not spoken about like so many other things in our society, which is supposed to be based on Biblical principles.

As They Have Sown, So Have They Reaped.

One has to question the foundations of faith that makes a virtue out of the willingness to sacrifice a child.1 When we think of all of centuries of war, acts of violence, genocide, misery, the abuse and betrayal of children becoming so widespread and sometimes institutionalized, it is hard not to despair. Faced with these facts and the societal consequences they imply, academics are starting to tenuously examine these issues. At a religious studies conference held at the University of Alberta in December 2004, the question of child sacrifice in ancient Israel was on their agenda. Dr. Ehud Ben Zvia, professor of religious studies and host of the conference says. *"It is the highest form of sacrifice you could possibly make."* In her book "Abraham on Trial," Carol Lowery Delaney examines the Freudian aspects of *"a recent trial in which a father sacrificed his child in obedience to God's voice."* Reviewing these acts perpetrated through out history by the many religions that have come from this book, we could expect nothing less from groups that have arisen from the karma of ritual and substituted child sacrifice. Should we continue to perpetuate this story and the lessons it teaches, viewing it from the perspective of its consequences, the results of the blind and unquestioning obedience it fosters, and the rivalry between groups to be the acknowledged as the true seed worthy of being sacrificed? Unless they awaken and consciously disassociate themselves from these shocking archetypes and cycles, and take only the best of what their faiths have to offer, we would expect more violence from them in the future.

No wonder Pagan and foreign Gods were so feared and slandered by these religions of the Bible. If the majority of Yahweh worshipers ever found out the truth, that nearly all other representations of Gods were much nicer, more friendly and helpful and didn't demand unreasonable repayment for any help they offered, there could be a new mass 'exodus' from this Yahweh imposed slavery to the rituals of blood and child sacrifice.

Did The Pagan Nations Around The Land Of Israel Perform Child Sacrifice?

Were the Israelites just following what was common practise in the area at the time? We know that human sacrifice was not practised in Egypt where they dwelt before establishing their own written laws. The Hebraic 'Ten Commandments,' which included the prohibition of murder, were a derivation of the much older "Forty-two Confessions" governing human conduct in "The Book Of Coming Forth By Day" (The Egyptian Book Of The Dead) of which the fifth was very specific: *"Hail, HaHera, who comes forth from RaaStet. I have not killed humans."* We do know that much later, fifth century Arabic nations would dispose of unwanted daughters for financial but not religious reasons. However, according to eminent scholars, human sacrifice was not practised in Canaan.

If the nations round about Israel did not sacrifice their children, why would the Bible say it was so? Indeed does the Bible say that it was? Lets examine this.

Children Passing Through The Fire

After we have the laws in Exodus demanding the sacrifice of the first-born males, we begin to have a prohibition against offering children to the indigenous fertility God, Molech. (Leviticus 18:21) Why after legislating mandatory child sacrifice of every first-born male would an issue be made over other nations regularly doing the same thing if indeed they were? Something else must be

PASSING A CHILD THROUGH THE FIRE

Thick smoke hangs in the still afternoon air as the author smudges a child for her naming ceremony. This is a protection ritual. No harm comes to the child, in fact it is often fun!

An Azande ritual of cleansing a baby with smoke, after birth, by passing it through the smoke of a fire to banish evil spirits.
The reality is very different from the Christian propaganda images below
Above image appears on page 79 "The History Of Early Witchcraft." By Susan Greenwood

the agenda here. It becomes clearer when you consider the first of the "Ten Commandments," as the law that was the most important in the nation of ancient Israel:

"You must not worship any other Gods but me." (NWT Deuteronomy 5:7)

These probations on Molech simply appear to be a ban on the worship of a foreign deity.20 The English translations of the Bible imply that the Ammonites offered child sacrifices to Molech. But close examination of the passage reveals it is an objection against a baby naming ritual where the child is passed from one parent to another over a sacred smoke, (i.e. through the fire) before the image of their God whilst the child is given its names by a priest, and dedicated to the God. This style of baby naming ritual is still practised today by many indigenous cultures and neo-Pagans. (See image.) This was confirmed by anthropologist Edward Evans-Pritchard in his book "Witchcraft Oracles and Magic Among the Azande." He carried out a study of the Azande tribe of central Africa, Sudan, very close to the biblical regions, in the 1920s. It has been confirmed many times since then. As a celebrant, I have performed many of these myself, and the child is never killed. Quite the contrary, this ritual is performed because it is believed that it will protect the child. The sacred smoke, some times called smudging, is thought to drive negative forces away by giving the child a baptism of fire, so as to speak. Some form of baby naming ritual is performed in nearly every culture right around the world. This ritual fulfils a natural desire of parents to name, protect, and connect their child to some higher power. Sacrificing your child is not a natural desire so its actual occurrence in history is very rare. Yet this remains an easily prayed upon subconscious fear that is ruthlessly manipulated in order to besmear some groups or individuals for political or religious reasons.

Blood Liable.

The legal term for this is **Blood Libel**. It is a term for a FALSE accusation, in which groups are falsely accused of killing children and drinking their blood. The 'blood libel' was then used as an excuse to attack these groups. **Pogrom** being one term for this kind of attack. There are four tenets of propaganda associated with 'blood liable':

1. The sacrificing of children
2. The drinking of blood
3. The essential non-humanness/evilness of the liabled group and
4. The undermining of the prevailing society.

These four tenets of propaganda have not changed in 4000 years since they were first employed in politics. They are still surprisingly effective. They dehumanise a group, and incite mob consciousness against those liabled. 'Blood liable' easily allays the mob's human conscience and allows it to justify any actions towards the liabled individuals or group. If you hear these things being used against any individual or section of the community BE AWARE THAT SOMEBODY IS TRYING TO MANIPULATE YOU. Hitler used these techniques against the Jews and the Romany Gypsies. This method was used against the early Christians in Rome, who threw them to the lions for it. Things turned around when the Christian Church of Rome became the political power behind the empire, the same methods of 'blood libel' were employed by them, not only against the Pagans but also against its opposing Christian factions including, the Cathars, the Knights Templar, the Gnostics as well as the Church of Carthage. All of these are historically recorded but they are beyond the scope and the constraints of this article. For now, we will just focus on Carthage as one example.

Where Living Children Sacrificed To The Gods Of Phoenician Punic Carthage?

Image of Neo-Punic Baal

Some individuals want to grasp at straws and argue that they did. There are hundreds of right-wing extremist Christian websites that loudly proclaim they did without any proof what-so-ever. I cannot understand the joy that anyone might derive from making such claims about others without proof. However, many do.

M'hamed Hassine Fantar argues that children were not sacrificed to the gods of Phoenician Punic Carthage. Seven other eminent scholars Prof. Moscati, Michel Gras, Pierre Rouillard, Javier Teixidor Arthaud, Sabatino Moscati, Hélène Benichou-Safar, and Dr. Salvatore Conte agree with him. Most other reputable scholars admit that there is no conclusive proof. Presumably, if the practise of child sacrifice was as wide spread and common as is claimed by some, there would be lots of non-ambiguous evidence. However, if these scholars, who fly in the face of popular myth, are correct then what have the popular misconceptions been derived from?16

What David Ike Was Afraid To Tell You

As I show earlier, 'blood liable' has been promulgated by groups and sometimes by individuals, for progress of their cause. It is not limited to the pages of history. Sadly, it continues today. Organisations such as the C.I.A. and dictators such as Polpot have employed it successfully in recent times. In addition, contemporary authors have been known to use the fear it generates to sell their books regardless of the consequences to the innocent. Several years ago, refusing to believe that David Ike was deliberately peddling his 'blood liable' for personal gain, I, assisted by two friends, made the effort to personally show him the information, references, and research contained in this subheading. I believed David Ike was a sincere but misguided person who just did not have his facts straight. I am no longer of that opinion. However, at that point in time I believed that if his facts were straightened, he would realise that many of his wild stories fall apart and I believed that he would stop falsely accusing the groups, whose traditional job has been to protect humanity, with 'blood liable.' Therefore, I showed him all of what follows, and several other facts. I also explained how dangerous it is for people and groups to be falsely accused of such crimes and what has been the result of doing so in the past. He looked at all I showed him with great interest, acknowledged it, thanked me for making the effort, and asked for copies to be sent to him, yet he has changed nothing. I guess that he was afraid of admitting that he had been mistaken. It is very sad that this refusal to admit a mistake has continued to promulgate so much modern fear, hatred, and 'blood liable.' I will leave you to draw you own conclusions as to why he would chose to continue doing so.

You see the Carthaginians (800BCE) arrived in history over a thousand years after the Ammonites that are mentioned in the Bible, (1500-1200BCE) in a completely different area (North Africa from Western Arabia) over a thousand kilometres away from each other. They were both distantly related Phoenician people in the same way that the British and the Germans could be both called European. Trying to count them together culturally is like trying to count apples and oranges, both fruit but very different. Due to this separation in time and space, the Carthaginians understandably did not worship the same God as the Ammonites. The

The Symbol of Tanit

Carthaginians did not worship Molech they worshiped Baal Hannan and his consort Tanit. The word Baal is mentioned in the Bible, but it is simply a generic Phoenician word for God or Lord. It is not used to indicate any particular God. It is also used as a title for the king of Tyre. (Sidonia) (1Kings16: 31) Some how David Ike has taken the God of this earlier race that is mentioned in the Bible and then liberally mixed it into Diodorus the Sicilian's account of Carthaginians. Diodorus claimed that 300 children were sacrificed in one day by the Carthaginians in an effort to get their Gods to grant them victory in a battle against Rome. There is no evidence of this. (See Box – right) He then surmised that if the Carthaginian's had sacrificial customs they would be similar to those of his home town Sicilian myths, specifically the myth of the great bronze bull, built for the Sicilian tyrant Phalaris, in which the king's enemies were roasted alive and there the similarity, between myth and fact, ends. The bull he had chosen, was representative of a God of a much earlier race, and Diodorus was looking for dirt on the worshipers of Baal Hannan, always represented as a man.16 Diodorus is well known for writing Roman propaganda in which he portrayed the Carthaginians as oriental intruders who had no right to call Carthage home. It should be remembered that the Christian Church of Carthage was in contention with Rome to be the Vatican's seat. The two cities faced each other across the narrow neck of Mediterranean Sea. They were ever at war. They wanted the same prize. The Church of Rome was well versed in using its 'blood liable' techniques against its enemies and it had good reason to use them against Carthage as it had a lot to lose. This sullied image has been blurred even further in recent popular culture by David Ike's imaginative addition of an image of an owl to represent Molech. The owl is a symbol of the Goddess of wisdom, Athena, patroness of the city of Athens. David Ike delights in displaying owl images in the plan of city streets as if it is something insidious. Yet, any architect could tell you that, the placing of an owl in the city works by town planners is considered a clever nod to the golden era of Athens that birthed the concepts of our democratic western society. Unfortunately, both Diodorus and David Ike's accounts are the stuff of fiction not history.

Molech was definitely represented as a grass eating bull not any form of fowl. The ancient Ammonites not the Carthaginians worshipped Molech. There is no evidence of child sacrifice ever having been associated with Molech. To the Ammonites, Molech was a fertilising God who dwelt in the soil and had nothing to do with fire.

IMAGES OF MOLECH
Above: ANCIENT- L: As a man seated - R: As a bull
Below: MODERN - L: As a grandfather figure - R: As a bull from the "Goetia"

It is not clear at all from the classical sources that the Carthaginians sacrificed their children to their Gods, even those seeking a reason to blacken the Carthaginians reputation, do not mention anything like this. Besides Diodorus, there is no documentary evidence for child sacrifice. Unlike the written laws in the Bible, the Carthaginians themselves left no written account of it. Though they were a highly literate race that invented the early form of what became the alphabet that we used today. It is ironic that the Phoenician word Byblos became the word used for Rome's most holy book, the Bible. There is no physical evidence for child sacrifice as such. The bottom line is

Molech was depicted as a bull or a man
NEVER AS AN OWL

that we should not read unreliable speculation into the actual evidence. The science and academia of our generation is supposed to be beyond that.

In fact, the lines oft quoted in support of Diodorus, written by the Roman Virgil in the Aeneid's sixth Book, 426-429 (T.C. Williams translation)25 do not support his theory:

"Who's Afraid Of The Big Bad Witch?" - by - Dr. S. D'Montford

"Now hears he sobs, and piteous, lisping cries

Of souls of babes upon the threshold plaining;

Whom, ere they took their portion of sweet life,

Dark Fate from nursing bosoms tore, and plunged In bitterness of death."

Note that Virgil is not explaining these children's deaths by human actions rather he attributes them to fate. He is describing a special place in the afterlife were very little children cannot be judged by "Minos, the judge of the underworld," that Aeneas encounters on his way to meet Dido the dead Carthaginian queen.

So how does the following verse fit in with that?

"He [the late- seventh-century B.C. Judahite king Josiah] defiled Tophet, which is in the valley of Ben-hinnom, so that no one would make a son or a daughter pass through fire as an offering to Molech" (2 Kings 23:10).

This is what Professor M'hamed Hassine Fantar has to say on this topic:

"The Tophet was a sacred space where urns containing the incinerated bones of children were buried. These remains, moreover, were no doubt buried ritually, in accord with Punic religious or cultic laws. Marking some urns are stélae bearing Phoenician inscriptions, along with symbols (like the triangular symbol of the Goddess Tanit).... The incinerated remains are those of very young children, even foetuses; in certain urns, the bones of animals have been discovered. The sixth-century B.C. prophet Jeremiah accused syncretizing Judahites of setting up a "high place of Tophet" in the Valley of Ben-Hinnom outside Jerusalem (Jeremiah 7:30-32), where they "burn (sharaf) their sons and their daughters in the fire (b'esh)." This is clearly not a description of sons and daughters "passing through" the fire in some sort of rite of passage from which they emerge singed but not incinerated - but they were not alive at the time. It was a dedication after death...Some historians, such as the French scholar Hélène Benichou-Safar, have proposed that the Carthage Tophet was simply a children's cemetery in which incineration was the method of burial....The Carthage Tophet, like other Tophets in Sicily and Sardinia, was not a necropolis. It was a sanctuary of the Punic God Ba'al Hammon....The texts of the inscriptions in the Carthage Tophet suggest that the sanctuary was open to everyone, regardless of nationality or social status. We know that Greek-speaking people made use of the sanctuary, for instance, since some inscriptions have the names of the Gods transcribed in Greek characters. Foreigners who visited the Tophet clearly did not offer Ba'al Hammon their offspring. Nor is it likely that visitors from other Punic settlements visited the Carthage Tophet to bury or sacrifice their children. One inscription, for example,

A Tophet Tomb

mentions a woman named "Arishat daughter of Ozmik." The inscription tells us that Arishat was a "Baalat Eryx," or noblewoman of Eryx, a Punic community in Sicily. It seems reasonable to assume that Arishat, while visiting the great city of Carthage, simply felt the need to pay homage to the Punic Gods or to utter a vow or make a request. The Carthage Tophet was a sacred sanctuary where people came to make vows and address requests to Ba'al Hammon and his consort Tanit, according to the formula "do ut des" ("I give in order that you give"). Each vow was accompanied by an offering. Some of the stélae suggest that animals were sacrificed and then offered to the Gods. For example, some stelae bear engraved depictions of altars and the heads of the animal victims."

However, not so for the children. There are no images of slaughter of children. All the evidence shows only a children's crematorium, dedicated to a foreign God, which harmonizes with the Biblical descriptions of a Tophet. The presence of foetuses contradicts the idea that these were places of live sacrifices. If the Tophet were not a cemetery, we would not find foetuses buried in the sanctuary. The reverence, with which the

The Tophet
This site in Tunisia, formerly the site of Carthage, is presumed to be like Tophet described in the Bible

Looking very much like a children's cemetery as they exist today in many parts of the world.

foetal remains are interred, shows a culture with a great love of, and a high regard for the life of children. Infant mortality was very high in the area at that time, due to the constant warring with Rome and the stressors that it placed on their society. Large families were the norm. It was not uncommon for women to give birth between 10-15 times, only half of which were expected to reach maturity. It is very common, all over the world, to find that children, who die young, and especially foetuses, are accorded special status. Many cultures believe that these are not ordinary deaths.

The Italian archaeologist Sabatino Moscati, points out that in Greek, some Islamic and present day, Japanese necropolises, children were incinerated and their tombs were located in a separate sector, quite distinct from the burial place used for adults. They are placed in special areas of the temple grounds, and carved figurines that suggest their holy status, represent them. Similarly, the Punic children who died young possessed a special status. They were buried inside an enclosure reserved for the cult of "Lord Ba'al Hammon and Lady Tanit." For

A Remains Jar and Heads Stone
Only one deceased person per grave.
No mass grave as we would expect to see in the instance of large sacrifices or mass murders

mysterious reasons, Ba'al Hammon had decided to recall them to himself. These very young children were not "dead" in the usual sense of the word; they were special retroceded servants in close contact with the God and Goddess. They could be called upon in the sanctuary to supplicate Ba'al Hammon and Tanit for the propitiator. Along with the mundane desires sort, the request most often found on these funeral stéle was from the bereaved parents for another child (presumably the reincarnation of this child) to return.

Classical Greek mythology makes reference to "The Daemon of the Dead" which is the left over life force energy when someone dies early or unexpectedly. They considered this capable of granting wishes. Similar propitiations and requests are found in ancient papyri in Greek cemeteries to this Greek 'daemons of the dead.' These Greek child cemeteries are not considered places of child sacrifice. The same styles of mundane requests to the 'daemon of the dead' were also found at the altar areas in the later Roman gladiatorial rings where child-sacrifice was not performed.

Therefore, available evidence points to the fact that the Carthaginians did not sacrifice their children to Ba'al Hammon in the Tophet.

Sincere Bible interpreters, who continue to say that the nations surrounding the ancient tribes of Israel were participating in child sacrifice, at the Canaanite Tropets, are taking a big leap of faith across a void.

What Can We Do With This Correction Of Misinformation.

There is no evidence that the Pagan nations accused, performed child sacrifice, in fact there is strong

Watching over our children, our gift to the future

evidence to the contrary. Whilst the ones who have been accusing others of child sacrifice and other 'blood liable' for the last 2000 years are the ones who do have religions based on this concept as a continuing theme down to this day. Finding out that these facts have been kept as the darkest of secrets, away from the publics view, will be quite a shocking realisation for many.

We do not want to go to the extreme with it. We do not want to start accusing the religions based on the Bible with currently practising child-sacrifice, which we know is not the case. We know that the likes of David Ike and extremist right wing Christians, who still peddle such 'blood liable' propaganda against the innocent, have an agenda to prove and they do not mind sacrificing a few facts to a few irrational fears to achieve it. They are trying to dehumanise their opposition and make themselves look better. We do not want to do that. Anyone who starts irrationally ranting that a large section of the community sacrifices-children and drinks blood, are practising the crime of 'blood libel' to push their own wheelbarrow, so as to speak. We do not want to do that with this information.

Conclusion

WHAT SHOULD WE DO WITH ALL OF THIS INFORMATION

We are living in a startling age. Information is readily available. It is becoming increasingly easy to research, check facts and discover truths, even when a falsehood has been promulgated in the popular propaganda, recently or for hundreds or even thousands of years. This information gives us the power to make informed choices, not only about how we live our lives, but also in what direction we will take our society.

Looking at the violence, the hatred, the wars, the crime and the turning of a blind eye to child abuse that has occurred in societies that base their beliefs on a book that has a theme of child-sacrifice as its basis, and then pushes its own guilt out on to other sections of the community that it wants to destroy, we have to ask ourselves: -

WILL WE CONTINUE TO CONDONE SOCIETAL MYTHS THAT RESULT IN SUCH THINGS?
- Will we continue to restrict our beliefs to a limited source?
- Will we continue to condemn others without personally examining the facts?
- Should we condemn Witches that revere nature, and hold children as sacred because of fiction and lies in the media?

WITCH-HUNTS ARE POLITICALLY MOTIVATED and were started because some minority groups in our community believe in the human spirit and believe that we can do better. Self-interested powers that seek to maintain their control, are afraid of individuals and society doing better. Yet, these small groups, at great cost to themselves, believe that each individual has the right to be fully empowered by knowledge, wisdom, magick, and an inquiring mind. Thankfully, due to these small groups, great bodies of ancient knowledge have been preserved. They don't believe in any governmental system that would take these things away and seek to control you. Like Periclase, and Socrates and Pythagoras and Gandhi and John Kennedy and countless unnamed others, they see things as they could be and ask why not? They seek the highest and best form of government, not just the same old 'only system' with the same old fears and apathy.

- Shouldn't we all be seeking the best systems to raise our families in?
- Shouldn't we all be seeking to be the best we can be?
- Does our society have the courage to change, to research, to admit that it has made a mistake?
- Individually have we been rash and made a mistake in believing the big bad stories, and unfounded saintly stories, without looking at the facts and the hearts of the individuals?
- Can we as individuals and as a society examine other modalities without looking through the goggles of fear, self-interest, and media bias, to take the best out of all of all belief systems to keep as our own?

The historical plight of the hunted Witches is useful in highlighting that there is one thing in the world more powerful than magick: - ASKING QUESTIONS AND DEMANDING TRUTHFUL ANSWERS. Doing this gives you the power to choose your own future. This is the greatest power in the universe. Don't hide from it. Don't give it away. Don't be weak or lazy and not use it. Sure it is easier to believe anything that is spoon fed to you in the media and let your power of reasoning atrophy. The power of your enquiring mind is the greatest gift of the Gods. It is the greatest gift you can give yourself or your children.

What will you choose for your future and for the future of your children?

Stay informed, stay powerful, stay awake, and you will make the right decisions!

My Blessings to you all.

Dr. S. D'Montford

Appendix:

A Witch Raised In Fear and Pain

I was raised in a tumultuous household, the oldest of three children in a super strict Christian home. We lived an affluent life in a large home on the canals on the Gold Coast. I had two younger brothers. The youngest and I are adopted. I was adopted into this family when I was eight days old. My biological mother is a tiny red-haired woman of first fleet Irish convict descent and my biological father is a tall blond Hungarian. My adoptive mother was a mean woman but very psychic. She was addicted to medicinal drugs and abused us severely. From her I learnt that being psychic does not always mean you are wise or nice. As my youngest brother often pointed out in his childish wisdom, we lived with the modern equivalent of the fairytale "Evil-Stepmother." My adoptive father is a very conservative Englishman, a well-known businessperson on the Gold Coast who worked closely with the natural health industry and championed some of its causes in its infancy here in Australia. Because of him, we wanted for nothing materially. He worked very hard, was a good provider, but was seldom there. So I guess he would be the equivalent of the absent/ineffectual father or Good King fairytale archetype. Jung could have written a thesis on our family. My father startled me with his own psychic ability of always knowing my mother was pregnant before she did. However, she had many miscarriages. In addition, he would just *know* when to turn up and take her to hospital. He always knew if we children were sick or in trouble at school. The reason why we were prosperous is, I believe, that his natural instincts gave him much success. I learnt many things from him, including his business ethic. Years later I was voted co-winner of Queensland Businesswoman Of The Year by Women in Business magazine. I suppose that being raised in that atmosphere one cannot help becoming psychic by osmosis. However, because of dogmatic religious beliefs, unexplainable psychic occurrences were swept under the carpet and generally not talked about unless it was unavoidable.

My first experiences of psychic phenomena were pleasant enough. As with every child I used to have my favourite tree that I would talk to. It was a big willow with a special large rock under it, on which I would sit and play music to the ants, snails and the fairies that live in the clover. This is nothing exclusive to my childhood though. I feel it is one of the great crimes of modern living that our society is programmed to erase children's natural connectedness to all things living.

A Companion In Spirit

Looking back on it now I think the first time I began to realise I was a little different was in my relationship with my adoptive grandmother. She was a beautiful slender redhead who was very down to earth with a wicked sense of humour. She would read tealeaves for everyone, with the exception of close family members. She was the most affectionate person I remember from my childhood. She used to hold me so tightly, rock me, and say she would protect me 'cause I was special. She died when I was four years old. Shortly after, I began to have vivid dreams of her in which she would speak to me and comfort me. I began to hear her whisper little pithy anecdotes in my ear, just the kind of thing she would have said, right at the most appropriate or inappropriate of moments. When I repeated these phrases, they would usually result in my getting into trouble for being sarcastic.

When I finally told my mother that Nana whispered these rather inappropriately adult comments in my ear, I received a sound thrashing for being supposedly demonic. This is how my family had been taught to react to the supernatural by the Jehovah's Witnesses. They had become devoted followers of the Jehovah's Witnesses version of the truth. It consumed them and became their only interest. Their truth allowed the bible to be filled with people having supernatural experiences who were declared divine. Yet anything outside their dogma, including other Christian belief systems, were considered demonic. Mind you, the things Nana said that I repeated were never swearing or gross, just things like, "Get down off the cross, someone else could use the timber" or "Never poo on your own doorstep!" nonetheless, inappropriate for a four year old to say to an adult. The feeling I remember of those thrashings was not that my mother was trying to throw out demons but rather that my mother was always jealous of the relationship I had with my grandmother. In Nana's will she left me a ring, a watch and a very unusual "Templar" style crucifix, all of which my mother flushed down the toilet in a jealous, righteous, Christian rage.

Diagnosed as a Poltergeist

That reaction was nothing compared to how the family behaved as the poltergeist activity started when I was about 12 years of age. The kind of phenomena we began experiencing was the usual for a poltergeist outbreak. There were knockings in the walls, things disappearing, and then reappearing in different places. My bedroom drastically changed temperature and was always hot. Dad called it the psychic hot spot. Some not so usual things I remember were fish jumping out of our fish tanks through the smallest opening, as I walked by, into my hands. Once when I was beaten for not eating all of my dinner, the kitchen draw flew open and the entire cutlery set landed on the floor. The draw hit the pantry, the pantry door came open, and a lot of tins and packets fell out. However, my youngest brother found this wildly amusing, clapped, and laughed and wanted me to do it again. The rest of my family was horrified. Mum grabbed me, shook me, and told me to clean it up. Dad prayed for protection from demons. Shortly after this, my mother got on local talkback radio and humiliatingly discussed the details of this event on air. My friends stopped playing with me. A paranormal investigation team heard this on-air discussion and arranged to come to our house. They wandered around for an afternoon, asked some questions, and officially diagnosed me as a poltergeist.

You have to understand that at this stage I was not sure it was in any way really connected to me. Therefore, I began to research this phenomenon. Lisa, a girlfriend at school, told me that she had read of Matthew Manning in the United Kingdom, who was a teenage poltergeist. She gave me one of his books called "The Link." It was such a relief to find out that I was not the only person in the world experiencing this; there were others like me. This gave me heart. I began to look things up in my Miami High School library, which proved to be a very good source of information. Never discount the old school library. In addition, I began to buy books with my lunch money, then I would hide them under my bed at home, as the religion did not allow us to read about such things. I became a little skinnier. Nevertheless, I felt happier as these books were telling me that I was not demonic at all and that the phenomenon of poltergeist activity is relatively common and follows a pattern. Being that: -

- It usually affects teenage girls raised in a stressful and repressed environment.
- That it will increase in intensity, usually until about the time of her first period.

Religious Abuse

The members of my church did not react well. My dad approached the elders of his Jehovah's Witness congregation. Their opinion was that we had come under demonic attack because we were such good Christians. He was told to search my room for anything demonic and burn it. He found all of my books and photocopies from the library hidden under my bed and he dragged out anything else that could have the slightest esoteric connotation, like unicorn plush toys and plastic mermaids. Mum lit a big fire in the outside barbecue, ripped the pages out one by one, and burnt the lot along with my remaining photos of my grandmother too. After which Dad and one of the elders prayed in my room to exorcise me and remove the 'evil influence'. I then went before a tribunal of the elders who praised me for being a fine young bible scholar who in the past had spoken at such a young age before up to five thousand people at assemblies of

Jehovah's Witnesses at Lang Park in Brisbane. Nonetheless, they told me that, as I had now become demonic, my association with the rest of the congregation was to be limited. I was on public reproof. They added, to my horror, that I should consider myself lucky as, if it was still legal, that they would have had me stoned to death as a witch, in accordance with numerous quoted bible verses. So much for Christian love, forgiveness and compassion. I was rather put out to say the least by this unfair treatment. I now know that it is abusive and a typical cult isolation technique designed to force conformity. At the time, I did not understand this; I just felt unfairly judged. After all, I had not asked to become "demonic." I pointed out that unusual things had occurred around many sainted biblical characters at an early age, but this only upset them further, as a female is not supposed to talk back to the congregational elders. The upside was that I had never thought of myself as a witch before, so I began to research witchcraft. Some of the first spells I ever tried were from Kerry Kulkens, whom I had the privilege of meeting.

Psychic Explosion

After the elders prayed over me things temporarily stopped happening. For a while, my bedroom went cold, but then it got hotter than before. There was a feeling of something building up. Then some very strange things happened. A couple of the books that I had seen my mother burn just reappeared in my bedroom. One was "Gift of Unknown Things" by Lyle Watson. It is the true story of abilities awakening in another young girl and her struggle with a religious leader who thought her evil even though she did no harm. My mother found these on my dressing table and accused me of bringing them back into the house unobserved even though she knew she had torn them up and burnt them herself. Still, I was thrashed for it. After that the knocking sounds in the house began again very loudly and they started to follow my mother around the house, from room to room driving her crazy.

Then something really big happened. My mother and father were fighting one night. I could hear them from my room. Mum's usual pattern when upset about something, anything, was to come into our rooms, drag us from our beds and thrash us simply because she was in a bad mood. That night I heard them fighting and I kept thinking over and over to myself; "Not again, not in here, not tonight, not ever again." Much to my surprise, she bypassed our rooms and stormed out of the house to sleep in the caravan we kept in the front yard. I then started to think of my poor father having to put up with her behaviour and that someone should teach her a lesson in manners she had obviously never learnt as a child. I began to doze off but was roused by the strangest sound. It was a long continuous yell growing louder and closer from far away. It sounded like a cartoon sound effect. Yet it was not a neighbour's television too loud, it was Mum running towards the front door. Still yelling without pause, she ran up the front path, through the front door, down the hallway and dived back into bed with Dad. When we went to see what was wrong with her, mum described the caravan being picked up and shaken around violently with her inside. Dad tried to dismiss it saying she was hallucinating because of her drugs but she insisted that was not the case. She just stared at me, so I went back to bed. Nevertheless, she never again came into my room at night to vent her anger on me. My first menarche began the next day and the poltergeist activity stopped as suddenly as it had started. I was really happy that it had stopped. I thought I could now get on with a relatively normal, non-demonic, Christian life.

Unfortunately, people's reaction to me did not go back to normal. The church members feared me. This made my social interaction with them hard even when my public reproof was lifted and I was allowed to speak with them again. Mum had nothing better to do than sit on the phone most of the day, so everyone came to know about my shame. She told the neighbours and they told their children to stay away from me. Mum dyed my long light coloured hair bright burgundy red "...as a warning to others..." she said.

Psychic At School

The other children at high school treated me the way they treated anything that is different or weird. I was mercilessly teased. I learnt to make a joke out of it or just ignore it. In one of those wonderful sweeps of universal bad timing, Stephen King's "Carrie" had just been released at the cinemas. So, guess what my nickname was at school. Because of this, I was too scared to go to any of the high school dances and my social circle shrank to non-existence. The upside at school was that I was also a novelty. They discovered that I could "find" things. Finding things, as demonstrated by my appearance on the T.V series "The One" by my finding the little boy, has remained a strong talent. Hiding things and having me find them became a great source of amusement for my classmates. I very quickly became tired of being treated like a circus freak. This "talent" was discovered by them whilst they were picking on someone else outside a classroom when we were waiting to go in. She was crying, saying "They have thrown away my bag, and I can't find it." A strange knowing came over me. I just knew exactly where it was. I excused myself to the teacher and had an irresistible urge to run straight to where they had hidden the bag and brought it back. Then I was suddenly exhausted and the teacher let me put my head down on the tabletop and sleep through class. The kids were confounded, but the teachers became very curious.

After that, the teachers would try their own little experiments with me, like: -

- Guess the playing card.
- What does my girlfriend look like?
- Can you foresee the outcome of a future event from these cards?

Their interest in my abilities and this testing gave me direction and taught me a lot about my abilities and their limitations. An English teacher had my IQ tested. He said it was high but did not tell me the result. He arranged for me to be shifted into higher grades of mathematics and science. My science teacher realized that electricity reacted differently around me and conducted a few class experiments on me.

That bit was fun but the fun ended abruptly one morning when our pastoral care teacher asked me if I had had any interesting dreams. I had a dream in which a boy was running on the school oval and fell face first and lay still. When his friends lifted him his head was flat and fell in half. Additionally Valkyries came and carried him away. I told the teacher I thought someone was going to die. The teacher laughed it off and said I was letting all of this go to my head, and that I should not try to panic people.

That day whilst playing football on the oval at Miami High School a senior student slipped under heavy earthmoving equipment and had his head crushed. I did not know the boy. Later that day the dead boy's girlfriend, whom I also had never met before, raced up to me whilst I was in a class activity in the school hall, and started shaking me, saying "... You should have warned him, you should have warned him ..."

I ran away from her. I felt guilty and confused. I did not go to school for several days after that. When I did return the teachers stopped asking me questions, preferring to ignore my talent altogether. They wanted it to go away and pretend it never happened. So did I. In addition, I was approached on school grounds by a person identifying himself as being from a nearby witch's coven telling me I had to join them. Because of my strict Christian upbringing the very thought of this terrified me. I panicked and ran. They may have been able to help me at this early stage but it did feel rather heavy. Not coping with any of this, I decided to stay away from school for about another week after that.

A Near Death Experience

I became terribly depressed and tried to kill myself. I was miserable. I could see no way of escaping the constant violence of my home life. On top of that, I felt cursed by my so-called gift. If this was what life was about I wanted out. I attempted suicide with a bottle of my mother's sleeping pills. This was not a half-hearted effort in order to gain attention as is often the case with young people, but a genuine attempt to bring to a close the pain and misery that I had for so long endured.

Later Mum and Dad told me they had found me next to the suicide note and empty pill bottle, and had realized what I had done. They decided not to take me to the hospital so I would not be exposed to the ridicule of being strapped to the bed in the suicide ward. Nor would it expose them to questions about their treatment of me. They gave me strong salty coffee to make me vomit the tablets. To this day I still cannot stand the smell of coffee. They said they could see the tablets in my vomit so they felt sure that I had not digested enough for it to be lethal. However, they made a mistake because, at one point, I stopped breathing and my body wastes came out. They said it took Dad about 20 minutes to revive me. Technically, I had died and yet they still did not take me to the hospital. In hindsight I now realise it was because there would have been questions about why they had not taken me in straight away. There were, it would appear, far more important considerations than my wellbeing.

The bad thing about being psychic is people cannot lie to you, especially those closest to you. You know their motivation, you want to believe the best of them, but you know. You start to doubt yourself because you want so much to believe them, but you know. I could see that their motivation for doing something like that was that they thought if it all went wrong they could put me back in bed and say they had not found me until it was too late. Anyway, my death would have solved a problem for them. Later I told them that I knew that this is what they were thinking. I told them what they did and what was going on in the room. They could see that I knew what they were thinking and what they were doing but they wanted to ignore it and forget about it. How very convenient.

During this near death experience, I had the classic sensation of looking down on the whole room from a great height. My mother was in her pink dressing gown, her hair set in rollers and pins for the evening. She was standing back toward the wall, looking down at the scene. She had no tears, and was shaking her head resentfully with her teeth clenched. I remember looking down on my limp body and seeing my father crying and holding me, asking, "Why does she want to die?" I remember trying to comfort him and telling him I had changed my mind and that I would not die. Then, whack! I was back in my body with all the pain of what I had done to myself. Their attempts to revive me were torturous. It felt like being in hell. I remember thinking, "What did I come back to all this pain for? I should have stayed where it was peaceful and pain free." However, it was too late. I could not go back. My parents were stunned upon hearing that I was aware of all of this. They have never tried to deny it and it has never again been discussed.

I never fully recovered from this. I had changed. I had damaged myself. Suicidal people never think "What happens to me if I botch this? What will my life be like in a wheelchair?"

I suffered a minor stroke. I could no longer control all the muscles in my face, and to this day my smile is crooked. I began to have corona migraines. These are severe gouging migraine headaches preceded by bright flashing lights that send me temporarily blind. I became dyslexic and could not read properly for the next five years or so. My grades plummeted. I went from being gifted to remedial. Yet, it was not only my brain and physical body that was damaged. Spiritually I had changed. I heard from my grandmother in spirit less and less but I did not come back alone. The best way I can describe it is there was a surging electrical presence with me that would sometimes immobilise me at night. It would really frighten me but I was never hurt.

I learnt my hard lesson and have never since felt suicidal. It was a turning point in my life. I realised that nothing is worth dying for; not love, nor relatives, nor religion, nor any other thing. You will never see me as a martyr. Dying is now against my religion!

Psychic Experimentation

A few weeks later when I returned to school everyone left me alone except for Lisa, a close friend of mine. She kept me sane through all of this by repeatedly reassuring me that she believed I wasn't evil or demonic, and that I just had a gift like an artist or a dancer. Like an artist's talent for art, I would one day be able to choose how to express my talent. She believed that my human spirit would find a way to use my gift for the good of others as well as myself. She has proven to be right.

Lisa eventually introduced me to a small group of people who had an interest in the paranormal. We all experimented psychically together. There was a core group of five of us: my friend Lisa, Mark, Robbie, Bruce, a weird but lovable and loyal Scottish guy, and me. We all had abilities to some extent. We would huddle together in the library courtyard, discuss things, and then research them in the school library. We would find exercises in books, practice them there or at home, and share the results with each other the next day. The exercises we played with then are now considered very advanced by most spiritual teachers. It was the best way to learn. We were just kids playing and having fun. There were no moralistic judgments, no fear of ridicule, and no one trying to make money out of us. Moreover, together we were advancing our skills and got some great results.

We practised: -

- Samadhi Techniques
- Mirror work
- Aura seeing techniques
- Aura manipulation techniques
- Remote Viewing
- Scrying and techniques to predict the future,
- Face altering and throwing a glamour – a magickal method of changing one's outward appearance using only the power of the mind.
- Influencing others' unconscious impulses, like twitching and scratching.
- Yoga postures. Bruce was not happy until he got both feet behind his neck and could walk around on his knees whilst in the full lotus position. But then Bruce danced to the beat of his own drum.
- Robbie made beams come out of his eyes. One day they bounced off the mirror and scared us all!
- Eventually this developed into more regimented disciplines like spells and solitary witchcraft. Yet, we never did a working nor cast a circle together.

Whilst most kids were experimenting with sex and drugs, we were experimenting with the esoteric and the occult. You name it and we probably tried it. Sadly as we grew older and one by one left school we all lost contact with each other. I would love to catch up with them again to find out what they have done with their abilities over the ensuing years.

The Higher Self

After leaving school, there was life. Mistakes. Marriage. Children. Divorce. More study. Career. There were many significant psychic experiences during these years. One of the most important for me was contacting my Higher Self, or what some call the Holy Guardian Angel. It got sick of waiting for me to make contact, and instead contacted me, thereupon giving me a shove in the right direction.

Since the suicide attempt I frequently experienced a sensation that occurs between waking and sleeping in which I would become fully conscious but unable to move my body. When this occurred it was accompanied by a sensation of electric energy rushing up and down the length of my body, and a sense that someone was trying to communicate with me. The religion I was raised in had me convinced that this was the devil trying to take possession of me. Therefore, each time it happened I would be very frightened and would fight it and resist. When I was eventually free of this religion, during one of these experiences, I had the courage to ask what it wanted. When I asked this question mentally I realised it was a higher part of myself that had become fractured from me. It was neither external not anything to be afraid of. After I formed the question in my mind I felt an enormous rushing-in of energy, accompanied with the knowledge of everything in the universe. For a moment or two I knew everything and was all-powerful, but my physical body could not contain either the energy or the knowledge, so it drained quickly away. I had the sensation of being taken somewhere, rather like going for a walk with a friend in the park who wishes to tell you something important and therefore wants all of your attention. Though I cannot consciously recall what was communicated to me, a knowing remained in my subconscious. These experiences I now know to be the result of "cosmic consciousness" that is detailed in many writings. I have had several moments of "cosmic consciousness" before and since. Yet, what was significant about this, was that afterwards a hawk would appear to me when I was doing a reading or in moment of deep personal inquiry or meditation and would bring me whatever it was that I needed, whether it was knowledge of a particular subject or person or an introduction to another spirit entity, or an opportunity. Upon further study, I have been able to identify this as my Higher Self or my Holy Guardian Angel. The ancient Egyptians used to call this the Ka and draw it as a small hawk, which is how I experience it. Since then, I have been able to do amazingly accurate readings.

A Bad Teacher

Not long after this, teachers began to present themselves to me. The saying goes: "When the student is ready…." I still had some tough and humbling lessons to learn and I received them in the form of a bad teacher and a good teacher.

"Who's Afraid Of The Big Bad Witch?" - by - Dr. S. D'Montford

The bad teacher's name I do not even want to mention. She deserves to disappear back into the obscurity from which she came. I used to work for her teaching courses on hospitality. She knew about my past and had esoteric leanings herself, though I have never seen a practical demonstration of her abilities. She told me she wanted to put together courses for us to teach on psychic self-development. She used to pick my brains about my experiences. By the time her courses were finally off the ground, I had moved on. I had already begun teaching in Newcastle through the Spiritualist Church, and had just established "Shambhallah Awareness Centre" as a foundation for the study and preservation of ancient wisdom. After the birth of my second child I returned to my hometown of the Gold Coast. She contacted me there unexpectedly, and asked to come and stay with me. She asked for my help in developing the courses, so we ran through some at her home. I loaned her my course materials and many reference books. She invited me to attend one of her courses in Brisbane to give her some feedback. The first one was benign, but I could not understand why she kept targeting me in front of the group. It was a continual and cowardly attack on me. I began to realise she was insecure when no credit was given to me for the research and development of these courses. I could see her motivation but I just did not want to believe it. I decided to leave her alone and withdraw my energies from her projects. About a month later she very excitedly contacted me, apologised for her behaviour and insisted that I attend another of her courses, saying that she had found "The Key" to it all. But she wanted me to pay $2000 to attend! I said I would not go as I could not afford it. Without my knowledge she contacted an old friend of mine and told him to pay for me because, she told him, it was something I really needed. He trustingly paid her because he loved me, had met her, and knew I had referred to her in the past as a friend. I had never said a bad word to him about her so he thought it must be something that would really benefit me and handed over to her the dollars without consulting me. When he rang me to tell me what he had done, I was horrified. She then rang me and said I could come free of charge. I knew this was a lie. I could not understand why she lied, and told her to refund his money. She said she could refund the money, and if I did not attend, I would be responsible for blowing his money. This was all so horribly manipulative but, silly me, I went. During the course, she starved, sleep-deprived, threatened, and intimidated everyone. She cut off all of my long hair, the symbol of a woman's power. She had become a psychic vampire of the worst kind. She drained everyone's power to try to strengthen her own. We were driven from place to place in a bus with blacked out windows. It was horrible. My boyfriend at the time took photos of me on the day of my return. I looked like a concentration camp victim. All the while my higher self was screaming at me to get out, but I thought "No! This is my friend. She won't hurt me." I was so terribly wrong.

The very valuable spiritual lesson I learned from her, as a bad teacher, was to leave if you get bad vibes. Listen to your higher self when it tries to protect you from abuse. I learned that even though *you* may function with pure intent, many people who profess spirituality do not. Never be afraid to tell an individual or a group to 'fuck off' if you feel they are trying to spiritually manipulate you. Sometimes strong language can be spiritually empowering. I decided then that I would never again allow myself to be abused.

The moral of the story is *No one needs a guru and no one needs to be a guru.* There are some people who claim to have what you need but will exploit that for money. Every specialist deserves fair remuneration, but sometimes they demand more than what is fair and want you to surrender your personal power to them. Be cautious. Always use your commonsense and do not give away your power to anyone. A spiritual teacher should strengthen you, not drain you. Do not ever let yourself be intimidated by someone trying to put you down to make themselves look like an all knowing guru that you can't question. Always remember that you are the world's expert on you. If someone tells you contrary to what you know to be true, do not go there. If they lie to you do not be afraid to tell them to their face that they are lying. If you ever feel you are being taken advantage of, even for a minute, leave. Cut and run. Remember, no one needs a guru and no one needs to be a guru.

A True Teacher

In stark contrast to the above, my good teacher was a tiny humble Tibetan woman of indeterminate age, with very dark skin and so many wrinkles that when I first met her I thought she looked for all the world like a cracked mud puddle drying in the sun. She called herself only Kushog, which I now know is merely a title of respect like Sir. Nevertheless, I like to think we were close. For one year I loved her like the mother I have never known. I did not seek her or choose her, she chose me.

Kushog did not give me a choice. She rang me up one day and in a very thick accent, that I could barely understand made an appointment to see me at my practice. Right on time she just appeared on my doorstep. She was on foot but I did not see her come up the road or up the stairs for that matter. It is usually very hard to sneak up on me. It was as though she just materialised. To top off my startled state, though we had never before met physically, I knew her face, as I had seen her in a series of dreams I had experienced since I was a little girl. I was stunned. I knew instantly that this was a private consultation to assist *me*, not her. From the moment she just appeared at my front door I knew she was there for me, and there was nothing I could do for this funny, confident, self-possessed little person.

I conducted my consultations around a kitchen table. My habit was to relax my clients by sitting them down at the kitchen table and making them a cup of herbal tea before we began. Kushog seemed to know this. She just marched right in and asked where her cup of tea was. She then chastised me for not making it correctly and asked me that if I could not make a good cup of tea, how could I expect to be able to help anyone? She was right. And there it began.

She healed the wounds left by my so-called friend, religion, and family. She bamboozled me and amazed me with her undeniable psychic skills. They all appeared to come so naturally. She demonstrated abilities such as knowing when the phone was going to ring and even knew who was calling, why they were calling, and how I should handle them. She appeared to already know all about everyone I discussed with her. She often changed the weather, the time, and her mind as well as creating the future. She could see things I initially could not with all of my talent and she showed me how to see and when not to look. Things moved, things appeared or vanished. She shone with mischievous life, just like a small child. She could find things lost, including pieces of a person's soul. Spirits obeyed her. All animals liked her, understood her, and obeyed her, although she never commanded anything.

She taught me how little I really knew, and that a wise person unlearns something each day. At that stage in my life I did not think I could find a teacher who could show me anything new. I was very disillusioned by the malevolence of my friend in her attempts to be a new-age spiritual guru. Though I knew I never wanted to be self-aggrandising like that, I was quietly very proud of all the paranormal things I had done. Yet, on the day I met her Kushog laughed at my fears and my abilities in her high pitched Asian style.

Her attitude had me off centre, but then, to top it off, she began to scold me for not coming to see her. This confused me at the time, but now I know I had received a call and ignored it, so she had to come to me. Whether she had come all the way from Tibet or was already resident in Australia was never clear to me. I have since been told that *Gomchenmas* or female Tibetan hermits who work wonders often will travel to impart instruction, and give a piece of their soul to a specially selected student before they die. I knew she was very old. I had no idea how old she was, and I never asked. It never seemed important when we were together. Kushog spoke of events four hundred years ago as if she had seen them herself. The most important thing was that she humbled me and I needed it. She began my instruction on that very first day by teaching me how to make a cup of tea. She was tough on me but loving and gentle. From that day forward my life has been much larger. There are so many funny and amazing stories I could tell you about her, but that is a tale for another time.

She taught me by example. By her just being around me. I never really knew when she would turn up, but she was always welcome. I always witnessed something astounding when in her presence and she would explain how it was natural and not so amazing and how I could begin to experience this aspect in my world. She would just wander in to my home as if she owned it. She made herself quite comfortable and, without being told, she knew where everything was located in the house. Sometimes she stayed only ten minutes to point me in the right direction about something of importance, then vanish as quickly as she had arrived. More often than not Kushog would stay for a couple of hours. Once, when I was sick, she stayed two days and nursed me. Then, without the slightest formality, when she was ready she would wander off. I can still see her waddling down the road if I close my eyes. I always watched her leave but never saw her coming. Even now I hope I will turn around one day and she will be there telling me to "watch how to..." do something correctly or to just talk to me as we share some chocolates and tea with gobs of butter in it. That was her favourite. Over time, she repaired much of the damage that had been done to me, and just when I began to feel really close to her, think of her as a mother and expect that she would always be there, she never came again. For a long while I felt I was once again isolated in the world by my gifts, so, for the next seven years, I retreated to the seclusion of a 160-acre rural property in Tallebudgera Valley, until I was tipped back into the world to reconvene my work.

Even though Kushog is no longer here in the flesh, after having known her and loved her, I know that I will never ever be entirely alone again.

The last time I saw Kushog was 1994/5. I knew something was wrong on her last visit, for two reasons. Firstly, because she was very affectionate towards me. She kept touching me and patting me and she told me things she had never said to me before, such as never again to cut my hair short, as strength resides in the hair and that only slaves and public servants have short hair. That the spirits had chosen me well and that I was "a good *naljopa*." which I thought meant student-practitioner at the time, and that I had "done good" and "learned well", which she had very rarely told me, unless I had done something exceptional. But that day she told me several times for no apparent reason.

As she was leaving I realised that she would never again return, because she looked back over her shoulder at me. It was the only time she ever looked back as she walked away. I waved; she nodded and smiled at me. The smile was the happiest you could imagine. It cracked her face into a million deep crevasses like a dried out mud puddle on a sunny day. It was her special smile. The one she saved for me when I did something very right. I felt so warm and loved at that moment. The love I have never experienced from a mother. I hope wherever she is, that she is proud of how I am using what she taught me. She taught me so many things. These too I will tell another time. I feel very privileged to have known her and I miss her so much. But I do carry a piece of her with me and when I most need some advice, if I breathe deeply and correctly, and listen with my inner ear to the sounds of my own heartbeat and breathing, I can hear her loving jibes as if she were still standing beside me.

That woman had so much real knowledge. Knowledge is a devolving path. Students rarely know as much as their teachers, and even more rarely do they surpass them. Something is always lost in the transmission. I could never surpass her. Her presence around me made me realise that we have strayed away from nature and real knowledge of the changeless to artificial knowledge based upon findings in a world of illusion, which is ever changing according to the laws of restrictive and controlling propaganda. We often forget that what we consider the scientific laws are just ignorant best guesses about a reality that is far too complex for us to begin to understand. New physics terrifies the sceptics. The recent rediscovery of dark energy and dark matter has vindicated the teachings of the alchemists from 2500 years ago. We must go back to the old traditions to find the similarities and commonalities with science, in order to see a bigger picture. That will be the beginning of true knowledge, which is more timeless and unchanging than the sun and the moon. Breathe out illusion and let it return to where it came from with every out-breath and breathe in inspired wisdom and knowledge with every in-breath.

Do not lose that childlike wonder. No matter what life throws at you, there is magick, there are miracles, and they are everywhere every day. We are all born psychics. When you lose the fear and know how to ask, everything in the universe will conspire to help you succeed and overcome anything. That is the magick of the human spirit. So, do not give up on it because I know it will not give up on you!

The Open Secret

How can you do this? It is a secret I am willing to share, a secret that I found during one of my darkest moments, in the writings of Vivekananda. It is a message from my soul to your soul: -

No one can be degraded forever. No one can really die. Life is but a playground, no matter how gross the play may be. Remember we create the games; we create the rules; we choose to participate. God's playing at being children. In the midst of agonizing tortures, no matter how the body rebels, no matter how much the mind rebels. In the midst of utmost darkness in utmost despair, repeat this once, twice, thrice, and evermore. Light will come slowly and gently but it surely comes.

"Who's Afraid Of The Big Bad Witch?" - by - Dr. S. D'Montford

I never had fear or doubt

Death never came to me

I never had a father or a mother

For I was never born

Where are my foes?

For I am all

I am it! I am It!

I am existence

Knowledge and

Bliss absolute.

I am it! I am It!

I have no fear of death;

I never hunger or thirst

I am it! I am It!

The whole of nature cannot crush me

It is my servant

I say to myself

Assert thy strength

Thou forgetful Lord of Lords

And God of Gods

Regain thy lost empire

Arise, walk, and stop not.

And you will rise up, reinvigorated, I do. Here I am living today! Thus, whenever darkness comes, assert the reality and everything adverse must vanish; for it is but the dream, the illusion, and say, "Only I am real." No matter how big or dark the problem seems, it is only 'Maya,' illusion, and you are the co-creator and willing participant in this. Many times, I have been in the jaws of death and life would seem to be ebbing away. I could not speak I could scarcely think but at last my mind reverted to this concept. Fear not and it is banished; Crush it and it vanishes; Stamp your foot on it, be stubborn and firm and it will die; Be fearless; Think not how many times you have failed; Never mind; Time is infinite. Go Forward! Above the illusions, the misconceptions, the dreams and the games, assert your real self again and again..

Adapted from the Vedas by Vivekananda- Adapted from Vivekananda by Dr. S. D'Montford based on her life experiences.

www.ingramcontent.com/pod-product-compliance
Lightning Source LLC
Chambersburg PA
CBHW080833010526
44112CB00015B/2500